# Sophocles and Oedipus

# Sophocles and Oedipus

A Study of *Oedipus Tyrannus*
with a New Translation

PHILIP VELLACOTT

Ann Arbor
The University of Michigan Press

Printed in Great Britain

# *Contents*

# Contents

# *Preface*

The purpose of this book is to provide students of world literature, and students of drama in particular, with the means of studying closely in an English version one of the great classic plays, *Oedipus Tyrannus* by Sophocles. Such students everywhere (especially in modern English-speaking universities) are now claiming, justly, that their knowledge and understanding of dramatic literature and its special character qualify them, even without a knowledge of Greek, to study and interpret the plays of ancient Athens, and above all to direct their production on the stage; but translations differ widely, and scholarly comment is largely confined to the Greek text. This book begins therefore with a new translation, which aims at combining the greatest possible fidelity to the text with clarity and immediate impact of meaning, in a style which does not forget that the work is both a play and a poem. It is printed on the right-hand pages; and opposite, on the left-hand pages, appears another version, as literal as possible (and with a few explanatory notes), so that the Greekless reader can look behind my verse translation, see how I arrived at it, and feel able to judge it.

In both the translations I have tried to avoid using any turn of phrase which might strike an adherent of the traditional view of the play as giving an unwarranted bias to the meaning. In a few cases where alternative renderings are possible I have explained the matter either in one of the chapters or in a note on the line (e.g. on line 1035). I believe that my verse translation will be found usable by a director who wants to stage the play in its traditional guise; where English usage takes liberties, meanings will be found undisguised in the literal version.

In preparing this second version I have borne in mind that literal translation from Greek verse to English is an impossibility. I have not attempted to be consistent, except in one aim, which

ix

is to help the student who reads the verse translation to have some idea of the extent to which he is dependent on the translator, and of some of the differences between Greek idiom and English. Here and there, where it seemed helpful, I have preserved the Greek word-order at the cost of making a tiresome English sentence (e.g. 118–19, 145–6). It is possible that occasionally the reader may find the literal translation more satisfying than the verse; it is when the translator becomes aware of this that he has the opportunity of progressing a little in his art.

I have tried to keep the number of notes down to the minimum needed by a student or general reader who goes straight through the book. There seems to be no point in repeating information which has been admirably provided in editions and in books about Greek drama. I had thought also of including some notes on matters which would involve using the Greek text; but the number of such points which I felt it necessary to deal with proved to be so small as not to justify introducing Greek type. I have therefore followed Knox's example and printed Greek words in Roman type. I offer a sincere apology for this to Greek-readers who study this book, for I dislike Greek words in Roman type as much as I dislike the names Hecuba and Hercules and anything else that is Greek dressed up as Roman. My reason for using this method is cogent: there are valuable points which cannot be explained to English readers in any other way. The study of Greek drama has been seriously handicapped by the fact that many good literary minds feel themselves excluded from this field by want of the obviously specialised knowledge required for reading the Attic dramatists in the original; and in so far as classical scholarship has tended (whether consciously or not, and with much clear reason) to put up a 'No Trespassers' board over Melpomene's garden gate, this book ventures to invite a certain boldness in those who are intelligently resolved to know what grows behind the notice. It is true that an important part of the experience of a Greek play lies in the poetic values of the language; just as a significant part of the experience of reading Thucydides' *History* lies in the appreciation of his style. None the less a non-Greek-reading historian, by studying translations and occasionally consulting a Greek scholar, can acquire an impressive knowledge of the mind of Thucydides; and a student of world drama should be able, by the same method, to develop a knowledge of Greek tragedy that will qualify him to hold and to challenge opinions on most aspects of that literature other than its purely poetic values.

In the expository chapters I have limited to a very few the books to which I have referred the reader. Jebb's edition (1883) is everywhere available. Frequent criticism of his remarks is inevitable after eighty-five years, but this does not cancel the obligation which every student of the play owes to him. From time to time I have referred to his notes, especially where they can be followed without knowledge of Greek; and I have used his text and line-numbering. I have also referred constantly to B. M. W. Knox's *Oedipus at Thebes* (1957);[1] though I have often disagreed with his conclusions, I regard his book as indispensable to the study of the play, for the thorough examination of key-words, themes and images which it provides – an admirable example of the serious study of a sophisticated text. H. D. F. Kitto's *Form and Meaning in Drama*[2] is another book to which, clearly, I owe a considerable debt; the fact that it contains, along with its studies of Aeschylus and Sophocles, a brilliant essay on *Hamlet*, illustrates both the breadth and the exactness of approach which I would humbly wish to be able to claim as my model in studying *Oedipus Tyrannus*.

There is, as far as I know, only one other Greek play which has been given a full-length study for English readers: I refer to *Euripides and Dionysus*, R. P. Winnington-Ingram's inspiring exposition of *The Bacchae*. This state of things is unfair to students of literature, whose numbers are steadily increasing; and it is unfair to the cause of Hellenic studies. It is only by making translation true enough, and exposition sufficiently compelling and relevant to living issues, that we can hope to win, by legitimate means independent of social or academic tradition, a stable and honoured place for the study of the Greek language and the Hellenic world in the culture of the next generation.

[1] Referred to as OAT hereafter.  [2] Referred to as FMD hereafter.

To suggest a new interpretation of a familiar and celebrated work of art is a bold enterprise liable to arouse some emotion. I have tried to avoid the spirit of mere controversy, even when attacking familiar positions which I believe to be false. The book is intended to offer a fuller and more exact study of the content of the play, of the actual lines, and of the events described, than has yet been made; and from this study some new meaning, some different interpretation, inevitably results. The important thing is that the study did not arise from any wish to attach a new meaning or to propound a new interpretation, but from certain clear challenges presented by the text itself. Some at least of these challenges have, I believe, not been accepted before; this book accepts them and pursues them to certain primary conclusions, but not further. These conclusions, if correct, probably have significance for our general view of Greek thought and of Sophocles' contribution to it; this, however, is a broader subject, which I leave for the attention of those better qualified to discuss it.

I thought at first of ending the book with a chapter devoted to meeting and answering some of the more obvious objections which the controversial nature of my thesis is bound to provoke. However, when I had finished writing the main chapters, I felt that all I wanted to say had already found a place in the course of my exposition, or in the notes to the literal translation; and I decided instead to add to my Preface an unpolemical paragraph offering to the most indignant of my critics a final thought. In beginning to address them I cannot help being reminded of the preface which Lewis Carroll wrote to his epic, *The Hunting of the Snark*; it begins as follows: 'If – and the thing is wildly possible – the charge of writing nonsense were ever to be brought against the author . . .' The likelihood of incurring such a charge is, however, the sole point of comparison I can claim with Lewis Carroll; my method of refuting it will, I trust, be found to be different. To those who exclaim like the sardonic Antonio in *The Tempest*, 'His word is more than the miraculous harp', my answer will always be, 'Not my word, but Sophocles' word'. For there are two ways of studying a text. One is to see the text only, and contemplate it as an eternal fact. But even if manuscripts are

clear and unanimous, though the text may be immutable it is
not eternal; there was a day when the page was blank, and the
author sat before it pen in hand, full of his imagined creation.
What he wrote had first to be thought and designed. The surface
of the finished work shows only a small portion of the thought
from which the design arose; a perceptive student can see a
larger portion, but cannot hope to discover the whole. The whole,
however, existed when the author wrote; and the second way of
studying the text, involving both greater risk of error and the
only hope of true perception, is to relate every discovery to that
original concept in so far as it can be apprehended, in the faith
that this method alone will relate each detail to the rest.

So, to those who are tempted to brandish the time-honoured
flails of a general censure – 'unwarranted speculation', 'ingenious
fantasy', and the like – I reply that generalised objection of this
kind is irrelevant to an argument based throughout on the study
of an established text. A quick reading of this book, without time
spent on looking up references, questioning the sources of
assumptions, and making a new and unbiased study of what
Sophocles wrote, cannot base a refutation. If my thesis is to be
refuted, it must be by demonstration that I have failed to see
what is there, or argued falsely from what I have seen. Even a
challenge may be offered without arrogance; and modesty may
claim both proper qualification and good faith.

I am grateful to a number of scholars who at different stages have
read my typescript either in whole or in part, and helped me with
encouragement or suggestions: Professor Raymond Wilson, Mr
Oliver Stallybrass, Professor G. Wilson Knight, Professor Donald
MacKinnon, Professor Cedric H. Whitman; and very particu-
larly to Professor W. K. C. Guthrie and Professor B. M. W. Knox,
for a most generous expenditure of time, thought and goodwill.
The usefulness of the book will owe much to the thoroughness
and perception with which Mr Stallybrass has compiled the
Indexes. Finally I would like to thank Messrs Macmillan and

*Preface*

Company, and Mr Rex Allen, for their act of faith in welcoming, at a very early stage, a book devoted to propounding so egregious a heresy.

# Oedipus Tyrannus

*Characters*

OEDIPUS, son of Laius and king of Thebes

PRIEST of Zeus

CREON, brother of Iocasta

TEIRESIAS, a blind prophet

IOCASTA, wife of Oedipus

A CORINTHIAN

A SHEPHERD of Thebes

A MESSENGER

CHORUS of Theban Elders

*Scene:* Before the royal palace in Thebes

The play was first produced in Athens, under the author's direction, probably between 430 and 415 B.C.

# *Oedipus Tyrannus*

## Literal Translation with Notes

*Oedipus.* Children, the recent brood of Cadmus of former times, what are these sessions which you hold before me, wreathed with suppliant boughs? And the city is full at once of incense-offerings and of cries-for-deliverance and of lamentations.
5    / I, thinking-it-right to hear about these things, children, not from the report of others, have come here myself, called Oedipus the renowned among all men.

Then tell me, old man, since you are naturally fitted to speak
10   on behalf of these, in what frame-of-mind you are placed here, / as-a-result-of-fear or of desire? For I would be willing to give any-kind-of help; for I would be unfeeling if I did not pity such a session-of-suppliants.

*Priest.* Well, Oedipus, ruler of my land, you see of what ages
15   we are who sit / at your altars, some not yet strong enough to fly far, some heavy with age; priests, such as I [the priest] of Zeus, and these chosen ones of our young men; and the rest of the population sit, wearing wreaths, in the market-places, and by the
20   twin temples of Pallas, / and by the prophetic cinders of Ismenus. For the city, as you see yourself, is now too much wave-tossed, and cannot any more lift its head up from the depths of the deadly
25   surge; wasting away in the fruit-filled buds of the earth, / wasting away in the grazing herds of cattle, and in the abortive labours of women. Besides this, the fire-bearing god, the malign plague, has swooped on the city and ravages it, and by him the house of

1. *Cadmus.* The leader of a Phoenician colony who founded Thebes. See 267–8; Agenor was a king of Phoenicia.
21. *Ismenus* and Dirce were the two rivers of Thebes; near the Ismenus was a temple of Apollo.
25–8. The Priest seems to distinguish the *blight* on fertility of all kinds from the *plague* which affected humans.

# Oedipus Tyrannus

*Verse Translation*

*Thebes, the forecourt of the royal palace. A number of men,
women and children sit in postures of supplication at altars or
statues of Zeus and of Apollo; the Priest of Zeus stands with them.
Oedipus enters from the palace.*

*Oedipus.*   My children, of old Cadmus' stock the newest growth,
   Why do you hold this session at my door, bearing
   These boughs adorned for supplication, while the smoke
   Of sacrifice, hymns to the healing god, and groans
   Of anguish fill our city's streets? Wishing to learn
   Direct, not by report from others, I have come
   Myself, whose name is famed on all lips, Oedipus.
   Then tell me, reverend Priest, whose place it is to speak
   For all these, what mind brings you? What fear, what desire?
   My will is to give all you ask. My heart would be
   Hard indeed, should I not respect such suppliants.
*Priest.*   Oedipus, ruler of my land of Thebes, you see
   How various in years we are, who sit to entreat
   Your altars: some who cannot yet fly far, and some
   Heavy with age; priests – I, of Zeus; and these young men,
   Our best. Elsewhere your other citizens all sit
   With suppliant boughs, in market-places, by the twin
   Temples of Pallas, and by Ismenus' mantic fire.
   For Thebes, as your own eyes can tell, is at this hour
   Labouring in seas beyond her strength, and can no more
   Lift up her head, or mount over the surge of death;
   Sick in the quickening bud where earth's fruits die unborn,
   Sick in the pastures where our cattle die, and in
   The barren birth-pangs of our wives; to crown all this,
   The burning god has swooped on us, this deadly plague,

3

Cadmus is being emptied; and black Hades becomes rich in
lamentations and groans.

It is not because I, or these children here, judge you to be
equalled with gods, that we come as suppliants to your hearth,
but [because we judge you to be] the first of men, both in the
experiences of life and in dealings with unseen-powers. For you,
when you came to the town of Cadmus, / delivered us from the
tribute which we paid to the cruel enchantress; and that though
you had no special knowledge or instruction from us, but by the
help of a god you are said and believed to have raised up our life.
Now again, Oedipus most powerful in all eyes, / we beg you, all
we suppliants here, to find for us some deliverance, whether you
know through hearing the utterance of some god, or perhaps you
have learnt something [*or* you know a way of deliverance
arising] from some man; since I see that, for men of experience,
it is actually the events-he-has-taken-part-in which are the most
living of counsels. /

Come, best of mortals, raise the city up again. Come, have a
care; since now this land calls you saviour because of your former
zeal; let us by no means remember your reign as a time when,
after being raised upright, we subsequently fell; / but raise up
this city with stability. For as with good omen you gave us that
past fortune, so now be equal [to what you were then]. For if you
are going to govern this land, as you rule it now, it is better to
rule it with its men, than empty; / since neither a fortress nor a
ship is anything when it is destitute of men and none live together in it.

*Oedipus.* O piteous children, known and not unknown to me
are the longings with which you came; for I know well that you
all are sick, and being sick, / there is not one of you whose sickness is equal to mine. For your pain comes to one alone by himself, and to no other; but my heart grieves for the city, and for

30

35

40

45

50

55

60

---

36. *enchantress.* The Sphinx — a name which means 'strangler'.
*tribute.* The only hint given by Sophocles as to the nature of this tribute
is the word 'deaths', 1201.

44–5. *the events-he-has-taken-part-in.* See Note at end of Chapter 2
(p. 147).

Harrying our city, emptying Cadmus' house of men,
While black Hades grows rich in mortal groans and tears.
   It is not as judging you equal with gods that I –
No, nor these children – sit here suppliant at your hearth;
But holding you the first of men, both in the common
Crises of life, and in visitations sent by gods.
You came to Thebes and saved us from the tax we paid
To the cruel enchantress; this you did, having from us
No special knowledge, no instruction; by God's help,
Fame says – and we believe it – you restored our life.
So now, Oedipus, in all our eyes hero and chief,
We all, your suppliants here, beg you to find some way
Of deliverance for us, whether some utterance of a god
Has given you knowledge, or a secret known to man.
For I observe that to a man who knows the world,
His life's encounters are his most live counsellors.
   Come, best of mortals, raise our city up once more!
Come, guard your good name: once you saved us, and today
Thebes calls you saviour. When in years to come your reign
Is spoken of, shall we recall deliverance
Followed again by ruin? No! Let deliverance
Be our assured possession. With good omens then
You brought us fortune: show yourself the same today.
If you are to rule Thebes, as you do now, be king
Of men; there is no glory in ruling empty streets.
A town stripped of her men, whose life was once her life,
Is like an unmanned ship, a useless hulk, nothing.
*Oedipus.*   Children, my heart grieves for you. Not unknown
    to me,
But too well known, is all your need. You all, I know,
Are sick; and being sick, there is not one of you
Whose sickness equals mine. For each of you his pain
Is single, touches him alone; but my heart bears
The city's anguish, mine, and yours, alike in one.

myself, and for you together. So that you are not rousing me as one sunk in sleep, / but know that many indeed are the tears I have shed, and many the paths I have trodden in the wanderings of anxious thought. And the one cure which my careful search discovered, this I put into effect. I sent Creon, son of Menoeceus, my brother-in-law, to the Pythian / house of Phoebus, to learn by what act or word I might save this city. And by this time the day, measured with the time [since his departure], makes me uneasy [to know] how he fares; for he is away beyond what is reasonable, longer than the fitting time. / But when he comes, then I shall be no honest man if I fail to do all that the god discloses.

*Priest.* You have spoken opportunely; these men are just telling me that Creon is approaching.

*Oedipus.* O lord Apollo, if only he may come bright / in some saving fortune, as [I would guess] by his look.

*Priest.* [He comes] with-good-news, as one may guess; otherwise he would not be coming with his head thus wreathed in berry-laden laurel.

*Oedipus.* We shall soon know, for he is within earshot. – Prince, my kinsman, son of Menoeceus! / What oracle of the god have you brought us?

*Creon.* A good one. I tell you that even things hard to bear, if they happen to work out rightly, will all reach a happy issue.

*Oedipus.* But what is the message? For I am neither bold nor fearful as a result of what you have just said. /

*Creon.* If you wish to hear while these people are near, I am ready to speak; or, on the other hand, to go indoors.

*Oedipus.* Speak before all. The grief which I bear is more for them even than for my own life.

70. *Pythian house of Phoebus.* This god is as often called Phoebus as Apollo; another name frequently used is Loxias, which means 'giver of ambiguous oracles' but is not derogatory (e.g. 410, 1102). His temple at Delphi is sometimes called Pytho (152) or the Pythian temple.

85. *within earshot.* Literally, 'equal-in-measurement (*symmetros*) so as to hear'.

You have not waked me as one fast in sleep; be sure
I have shed many tears, and paced long wanderings
Of anxious thought. And the one hope of cure my search
Showed me, I have acted on. I sent my brother-in-law
Creon, Menoeceus' son, to Apollo's Pythian temple
To ask what act or word of mine can help our city.
And I am uneasy to know how he fares; the day
Of his return is, by my reckoning, overdue;
But when he comes, as I am a true man, I will
Perform in full whatever the god bids me do.

*Priest.* Your words are timely; here are some who tell me
Creon
Is arriving at this moment.

*Oedipus.* O divine Apollo!
Grant that he comes with saving fortune, and brings news
Bright as his cheerful look!

*Priest.* Good news, I am sure; he is
wearing
A wreath of laurel thick with berries.

*Oedipus.* We'll soon know;
He's close enough to hear. — Son of Menoeceus! Prince!
Kinsman! What message do you bring us from the god?

*Enter Creon.*

*Creon.* Good news. Our grievous sufferings, if fortune guides
Events on the right path, will reach a happy issue.

*Oedipus.* But what is the oracle? That answer gives me ground
Neither for hope nor fear.

*Creon.* If you desire to listen
With all these people present, I am ready to speak;
Or else, to go indoors.

*Oedipus.* Speak before all. The grief
My people bear counts more with me than my own life.

7

95      *Creon.*   I will tell what I heard from the god. / Lord Phoebus commands us plainly to drive out a pollution of the land which he says has been harboured on our soil, and not to harbour it so that it cannot be healed.

     *Oedipus.*   By what sort of purification? What is the manner of our predicament?

     *Creon.*   By banishing a man, or by atoning-for bloodshed
100   with bloodshed in turn; / for it is this blood that brings-storm-upon the city.

     *Oedipus.*   And who is the man for whom he indicates this fate?

     *Creon.*   We formerly, my lord, had Laius as commander of this land, before you set-the-course-for our city.

105      *Oedipus.*   I know – by hearsay, for I never saw him. /

     *Creon.*   He was killed; and Apollo now clearly commands us to punish with [heavy] hand his murderers, whoever they may be.

     *Oedipus.*   But where in the world are they? Where will be found the track, hard to trace, of this ancient crime?

110      *Creon.*   In this land, he said. That which is sought / can be caught; that which is neglected escapes.

     *Oedipus.*   Was it in the palace, or in the surrounding country, or in another land, that Laius met this violent death?

     *Creon.*   He left Thebes to inquire, as he said, at the oracle;
115   and, once he had set out, never reached home again. /

     *Oedipus.*   And was there no one to bring word, no companion of his journey who saw [the murder], whose evidence someone could have listened to carefully and used?

     *Creon.*   [No,] for they died; except one man who, fleeing in fear, about what he had seen, except one thing, had no certain information to give.

     *Oedipus.*   What thing? One thing could discover many things
120   for us to learn, / if we could seize a small beginning for hope.

     99. *predicament.* The word here is again *xymphoras*, the word already used in 33 and 44; it occurs frequently throughout the play.

*Creon.*    Hear then our lord. Apollo's words. His clear command
  Is that we drive out from our midst an unclean thing
  Which has been harboured in this city. Harboured still,
  It will defy all cure; so we must banish it.
*Oedipus.*    What ritual clears us? Of what nature is this curse?
*Creon.*    A man must be driven out, or blood appeased with
      blood;
  For from this blood rages the storm that wrecks our city.
*Oedipus.*    And for whom does Apollo indicate this fate?
*Creon.*    We had a king, Sir, in years past – Laius, who ruled
  In Thebes before you came to set our country's course,
*Oedipus.*    I know; I never saw him, but I have heard his name.
*Creon.*    Laius was killed. Apollo now gives clear command
  To bring to punishment his unknown murderers.
*Oedipus.*    And they – where now in the wide earth are they?
      and where
  Shall the obscure track of this ancient crime be found?
*Creon.*    In Thebes, Apollo said. What is searched for can be
  Caught; only what is left unheeded gets away.
*Oedipus.*    Well, where did Laius meet his murderers? At home?
  Or in the country round? Or in some other land?
*Creon.*    Abroad. He was going, he told us, to consult the god;
  And, once set out, he never returned home again.
*Oedipus.*    But news was brought, surely? Did no one see the
      crime –
  Some man travelling with him, whose evidence could help?
*Creon.*    They were all killed, except one man who ran away;
  And he could give no firm account – but for one thing.
*Oedipus.*    And what was that? One thing might bring many
      to light,
  Could we but seize on some small starting-point for hope.

*Creon.* He said that bandits fell in with them and killed them, not with a single strength, but with a large number of hands.

*Oedipus.* Then how could the bandit – unless there was some business with money from here – have reached that degree of
125 daring? /

*Creon.* This was surmised; but Laius was dead, and no champion was forthcoming in our troubles.

*Oedipus.* And what trouble stood in your way to prevent a full inquiry, when royalty had thus fallen?

*Creon.* The riddling Sphinx induced us to look at what lay
130 before our feet, / neglecting mysteries.

*Oedipus.* Well, I will again, from the beginning, bring these things to light. For worthily did Phoebus, and worthily did you, exert this care on behalf of the dead man; so you shall find me
135 too an ally, / as is just, seeking vengeance for this land and for the god at the same time. For on behalf of no distant friend, but myself on my own behalf, I shall dispel this pollution. For whoever was the killer of Laius might wish to take vengeance on me
140 too with similar violence. / Therefore in championing Laius I help myself.

So rise, children, quickly from the altar-steps, picking up these suppliant boughs; and let someone else gather here the people of Cadmus, telling them that I will do everything. For either as
145 fortunate, / with the god's help, we shall be revealed, or as fallen.

*Priest.* Let us rise, children; for this was our reason for coming here, which the king now promises. And may Phoebus, who sent these oracles, also come to us as saviour and deliverer
150 from the plague. /

*Chorus.* O sweetly-speaking message of Zeus, of-what-nature have you come from Pytho rich-in-gold to glorious Thebes? I am racked, shaking my fearful heart with terror, O Delian Paean

138. *on my own behalf.* The genitive *hautou*, 'myself', is governed by the preposition *hyper*, 'on behalf of', in 137; but in this position it could equally well be a possessive genitive and mean 'I will dispel *my own* pollution'.

146. *we shall be revealed.* This is the same verb which Oedipus uses in the first line of this speech, 132, 'I will . . . bring . . . to light'.

153. *racked.* Literally, 'stretched out', i.e. 'tense'.

10

*Creon.* They were killed, he said, by bandits who fell in with
    them;
  Not one lone robber, but a large and powerful gang.
*Oedipus.* How could this robber dare do such a thing, unless
  Treachery and money organised it all from Thebes?
*Creon.* We thought as much; but – King Laius was dead, and
    Thebes,
  Crushed with calamity, had no man to rescue her.
*Oedipus.* But, with your king thus fallen, what calamity
  So crippled you as to prevent a thorough search?
*Creon.* The riddling Sphinx caused us to turn our eyes to what
  Lay at our feet, and to leave mysteries aside.
*Oedipus.* I will begin again from the beginning, and bring
  These things to light. Rightly has Phoebus, rightly too
  Have you, bestowed this care upon the dead king's cause.
  You shall find me no less your ally, as is due,
  To uphold at once the cause of Thebes and of the god.
  Not for some distant friend, but on my own behalf
  I shall dispel this guilt. The unknown man who killed
  Laius may choose to turn his violence against me;
  So, if I stand by him, I do myself a service.
    Then come, my children, get up quickly from these steps,
  Pick up your suppliant branches; and let someone summon
  The whole people of Cadmus here, and say that I
  Will go to all lengths; for the issue shall reveal,
  With the god's favour, our deliverance, or our fall.
*Priest.* Rise, children, let us go; the king has promised what
  We came to beg. And may Apollo, who has sent
  This oracle, come and save us all, and end the plague.
    *Oedipus goes into the palace. The Priest and the*
    *suppliants go to the city. The Chorus enter.*
*Chorus.* O welcome word from the mouth of Zeus! (Strophe 1
  With what purport have you come
  From the golden hoards of Pytho
  To glorious Thebes? I am tense with terror,
  My heart throbs fearfully, bowed in awe before you,
  God of the raptured cry, Healer of Delos,

11

worshipped-with-wild-cries; awestruck because of you, [not
155 knowing] what you will perform for me, either something new, /
or something [appearing] again with the circling seasons. Tell me,
O child of golden hope, immortal voice.

First I call on you, daughter of Zeus, immortal Athene, and on
160 the guardian of this land, your sister / Artemis, who sits on her
throne in the round market-place, and on far-shooting Phoebus.
O shine forth on me, my three rescuers-from-death; if ever in the
165 past, to prevent destruction advancing on the city, / you drove
beyond our borders the flame of disaster, come now again.

Alas! for numberless are the pains I bear; and the whole of my
170 people is sick, and they have no weapon devised by thought, /
with which a man can defend himself. The crops of the famous
earth do not grow; women cannot achieve birth to relieve their
175 shrieking labours; one person after another you may see, / like a
swift-winged bird, speeding faster than irresistible fire towards
the shore of the western god.

Numberless in these, our city is being destroyed; her offspring
180 lie unpitied on the ground, death-bearing, / and no mourning
rite is performed. Meanwhile young wives, and grey mothers
besides, at altar-steps, on this side and on that, entreating help
185 for their fearful sorrows, groan aloud. / The paean gleams forth,
and the voice of lamentations blended with it; for these things,
golden daughter of Zeus, send us bright-faced deliverance.

190 As for this fierce Ares, who now, with no bronze shields, /
but surrounded with cries as of battle, flames as he advances against
me, grant that he may turn his back and run in hasty retreat
from our land, going with a fair wind either to the vast chamber

178. *in these.* I.e. in those who are dying.
186. *The paean.* Paian was the name given to Apollo as Healer.
Thence it was also used to mean a solemn chant invoking Apollo as
Healer or Deliverer, or giving thanks for victory.
*gleams.* The Chorus use this metaphor again in 473.

12

Questioning what event you will accomplish for me –
Something unheard hitherto,
Or renewed with the revolving seasons:
Tell me, O daughter of golden Hope, immortal Voice!
Immortal Athene, first I call on you,        (Antistrophe 1
Daughter of Zeus, and on your sister Artemis,
Keeper of Thebes, who in our central market-ring
Sits on the throne of her fame;
And I call on Phoebus the far-shooter:
Hear our cry and appear, our threefold shield against death!
If ever in time past, when ruin swooped on our city,
You drove the flame of disaster beyond our borders,
Come to our help today!
Help us! Beyond number are the pains we suffer.   (Strophe 2
Plague sickens our whole people; anxious thought
Offers a man no weapon for defence.
The crops of this famous land will not grow;
Women die howling in fruitless labour;
Life after life you may see hurry away,
More rapid than raging fire,
To the shore of the western god.
Thus deaths innumerable overwhelm our city; (Antistrophe 2
Unheeded her children lie on the ground
Loaded with death, and no one mourns for them.
Among them are wives, grey-haired mothers at their side,
On this hand and on that, wailing by altar-steps,
Begging release from tears and anguish.
The prayer to the Healer gleams forth,
And blended with it the voice of groaning.
From these miseries, golden daughter of Zeus,
Send us the bright face of deliverance.
And grant that Ares, whose fierce attack,      (Strophe 3
With not a bronze shield in sight,
Blazes against me in massed cries of death,
May turn his back, run headlong out of Thebes,
And a fair wind carry him either
To the vast Atlantic chamber of Amphitrite,

13

195 of Amphitrite, / or to that inhospitable anchorage the Thracian wave; for if night neglects any [disaster], day follows to complete
200 it. O father Zeus, you who wield / the powers of fire-bearing lightnings, destroy this Ares beneath your thunderbolt.

Lycean king, I wish too that your arrows, from the twisted
205 gold string of your bent bow, may be showered forth invincible, / our champions and defenders; and the flashing torch-fires of Artemis, with which she speeds over the Lycian hills; and I call on the god of the golden head-dress, whose name this land
210 bears, / wine-red Bacchus to-whom-we-cry-EUOI, companion of maenads, to come near, blazing with his cheerful pine-torch, our
215 ally against the god unhonoured among gods. /

*Oedipus.* You pray; and in answer to your prayer, if you are willing to hear and receive my words and to minister to your own disease, you will be likely to get help and relief from troubles. And I will speak to you as one who is a stranger to this report, and
220 a stranger to the deed. For I could not have gone far / in searching alone, not having some clue. As it is, since I was enrolled a Theban among Thebans later [than the time of Laius' death], I make this proclamation to all you Cadmeans: whoever of you
225 knows by what man Laius son of Labdacus was killed, / I command him to declare everything to me; and if he is afraid, [I command him] to remove the charge himself [by informing] against himself; for he shall suffer nothing else unpleasant, but shall depart from Thebes unharmed. If, again, anyone knows

203. *Lycean king.* Apollo as the god of light. A statue of Apollo in this capacity was often placed before a doorway facing the eastern sun.
208. *Lycian hills.* Lycia is a district on the south-west coast of Asia Minor.
211. *Bacchus.* The son of Semele, daughter of Cadmus.
215. *the god unhonoured among gods.* Ares.

Or towards stormy Thrace
Where no seaman finds anchorage.
For what destruction night leaves undone
Day follows to accomplish.
Look upon the destroyer, you who wield
The fiery forces of lightning, Zeus our father,
And crush him under your thunderbolt.
Bright lord Apollo, bend your bow,          (Antistrophe 3
And from its string of twisted gold,
I pray, let your arrows fly forth invincible,
Our champions and defenders; and with them
Artemis' flaming torches, by whose light
She speeds over the Lycian mountains.
And I call on him whose hair is bound with gold,
Whose name our city bears,
Bacchus of the glowing face,
Adored with cries of rapture,
Companion of Maenads,
To come with the blaze of his festive torch,
Our ally against the god unhonoured among gods.
>*During this Antistrophe Oedipus has entered.*

*Oedipus.*   You are praying; and your prayer, if you will hear
    my words,
And by accepting them deal rightly with this plague,
May well bring help, and win relief from our distress.
And I must now speak to you all as one who has been
A stranger to this report, a stranger to the deed;
Not far could I have pressed in single search, having
No clue to guide me. As it stands, since I became
A Theban citizen only after these events,
I make this proclamation now to all Cadmeans.
If any man among you knows by whom Laius
The son of Labdacus was killed, him I command
To make all known to me. And if he is afraid,
I bid him lift the dread of accusation clear
From his own life by self-disclosure: he shall suffer
No other pain, but only leave this land, unharmed.

230 another man from another country / as the murderer, let him not be silent; for I will pay the reward, and due gratitude shall be his in addition.

But if you keep silence, if any man in fear rejects this command of mine either from a friend or from himself, you must
235 now hear from me what I will do in such a case. / That man, whoever he is — I forbid any citizen of this land, over which I exercise power and royalty, either to give him shelter or speak to him, or allow him to share in prayers to the gods or sacrifices, or
240 in purifying water; / I command all men to ban him from their homes, knowing that this man is our defilement, as the Pythian oracle of the god has now made clear to me.

I therefore am in this way an ally both to the god and to the
245 man who was killed. / And I pray that the man guilty of this deed, whether being one alone, or with others, he has escaped detection — that he may wear out his wretched life in a manner as evil as himself. And for myself I pray that should he with my
250 knowledge come to share my hearth in my house, / I may suffer the same things which I have just now invoked on these. And I lay it upon you to fulfil all these words, for my own sake, for the sake of the god, and of this land so barrenly and godlessly destroyed.

255 For even if this duty had not been laid on us by a god, / it was not right that you should leave guilt thus unpurged, when a very noble man, and your king, had perished; it was your duty to search out [the matter]. And now, since I hold the powers which he formerly held, possessing his bed and the wife in-whom-he-
260 too-planted-seed, / and since a mutual bond between us, consisting of children from a common mother, had not offspring in his case been unfortunate, would have been born (but, in fact, chance leapt upon his head) — because of these things I will undertake this fight in his behalf as if he had been my father, and will
265 go to all lengths / in seeking to lay hands on the man who shed that blood, for the sake of the son of Labdacus and of Polydorus and of Cadmus and of Agenor of ancient times.

And for those who do not obey me I pray the gods to send them
270 neither any harvest of the earth / nor children of their wives, but

16

Or if any knows some alien as the murderer,
Let him not keep silent; I will pay his due reward,
And thanks shall be his in addition. But if you
Keep silent – if any man in fear shields friend or self
From this command, hear my next measure: such a man,
Whoever he be, is outlawed; no one in this land,
Where I hold power and royalty, may shelter him,
Speak to him, welcome him to prayer or sacrifice,
Serve him with holy water; all must shut their doors
On him, since he is our pollution, as Apollo
Now clearly shows me through his Pythian oracle.
I thus am, in this sense, an ally both to the god
And to the dead man. And I pray that the murderer,
Whether his secret guilt is his alone, or shared,
May drag his wretched life out to an end as evil
As he is evil. And should he ever, with my consent,
Become an inmate of my house, I pray that I
May suffer the same curse I have now laid on others.
    I charge it on you Thebans to make all my words
Effectual, for my sake, and for the god's, and for
Our barren, god-abandoned, devastated Thebes.
For, even if this search were not enjoined by heaven,
It was not right that you should leave blood thus unpurged
When death had come to one so noble, and your king;
You should have probed the matter. So now, since I hold
The power he held, possess his bed, and since his wife
Has borne my children – so that, had not a hard fate
Robbed him of issue, he and I would now be bound
With close bonds through our children; but a leap of chance
Lighted upon his head – then for these reasons I
Will fight in his cause, as for my own father's right,
And try all means to find and take the man whose hand
Killed Laius son of Labdacus, son of Polydorus,
Of Cadmus, and Agenor of the ancient days.
    For those who disobey my words, I pray that heaven
May send them neither increase of the earth, nor child

that they may perish by the present fate or by one even worse. For all you other Cadmeans, however, who approve my words, may our ally, Justice, and all the gods, be with you in blessing
275 for ever. /

*Chorus.* As you have put me under oath, so, my lord, I will speak. I did not kill him, nor can I point to the killer. As for the inquiry – it was for Phoebus, who sent [the message], to tell this – who can have been the doer.

280 *Oedipus.* What you say is just; but to force the gods / to what is against their will – no man can do that.

*Chorus.* I would like to say what seems to me next best after this.

*Oedipus.* Even if you have a third suggestion, do not neglect to speak of it.

*Chorus.* I know that, for clearness of vision, the one most comparable to our lord Phoebus is our lord Teiresias. From him,
285 O king, / an inquirer into these things would get the clearest information.

*Oedipus.* This too I have not failed to attend to. On Creon's suggestion I have twice sent someone to bring him. I have for some time been wondering why he is not here.

*Chorus.* Indeed, other [sources of information] are obscure
290 and old. /

*Oedipus.* What reports are these? I am examining all evidence.

*Chorus.* He was said to have been killed by certain travellers.

*Oedipus.* I too heard this; but the man who saw it no one sees.

*Chorus.* Well, if he has any particle of fear in him, he will
295 not stay, when he hears these terrible curses of yours. /

*Oedipus.* A man who does not shrink from a deed is not frightened by a word.

---

295. *he will not stay.* Curiously ambiguous. Does it mean 'He will come forward and confess', or 'He will fly the land'? I see no answer to this; but the former seems more appropriate to the eye-witness, the latter to the murderer.

18

Of woman's womb, but that they be destroyed, whether
By the present plague, or by some fate more horrible.
But for you loyal Cadmeans who uphold my words,
May Justice, fighting in your cause, and all the gods
Be amongst you with their blessing, now and evermore.

*Chorus.*   You have bound me to my oath; therefore on oath, my lord,
I will speak. I did not kill Laius, nor can I
Point to his killer. As for this search, it was for Phoebus,
Who sent the order, to tell us who can have done this deed.

*Oedipus.*   You speak most justly; but, to compel the gods to do
What they would not do – this is beyond the power of man.

*Chorus.*   Then, failing that, I would suggest a second thought.

*Oedipus.*   Yes, or a third; speak of it, do not hesitate.

*Chorus.*   Next to lord Phoebus in prophetic vision stands
The lord Teiresias. He is the man, Sir, to provide
The clearest answer to inquiries on this matter.

*Oedipus.*   This too I have not neglected; for on Creon's advice
I have twice sent to bring him – strange that he is not here.

*Chorus.*   Apart from him, the accounts are vague and dim with time.

*Oedipus.*   What accounts are there? I must examine everything.

*Chorus.*   Laius was murdered by some travellers, it was said.

*Oedipus.*   So I have heard; but the man who saw it – no one sees.

*Chorus.*   Why, if the man has fear in him, he will not stay
Once he has heard the heavy curses you pronounced.

*Oedipus.*   The man who dared the deed won't tremble at a word.

*Chorus.* Well, there is one who will convict him. Here they come at last, bringing the divine prophet, in whom alone of men truth is innate.

300 *Oedipus.* O Teiresias, contemplating all things, spoken / and unspoken, heavenly and earth-walking: you understand, even though you have no sight, the nature of the plague by which Thebes is visited. You, my lord, are the one defender and deliverer from the plague that we find. Phoebus – if indeed you have

305 not heard this from the messengers / – in answer to our question sent a message that deliverance from this plague could come only if we discovered those who killed Laius, and either killed them or sent them out of the land to exile. Then do not grudge [help]

310 either from the voice of birds / or any other way of prophecy that you have, but rescue yourself and the city, rescue me, rescue every defilement arising from the dead man. We are in your hands; and a man's noblest labour is to give help, out of his

315 resources and power. /

*Teiresias.* Alas! What a terrible thing wisdom is where it brings no profit to the wise! I knew this well, but destroyed it; otherwise I would not have come here.

*Oedipus.* What is this? How dejected you have come in!

320 *Teiresias.* Let me go home. It will be easiest for you / to endure your burden, and me mine, if you do as I ask.

*Oedipus.* What you say is against usage, and against the interests of this city which nurtured you, if you refuse to give this answer.

*Teiresias.* [I must not speak,] for I see that your speaking too comes forth untimely for you; so [I take care] not to be in the

325 same position myself. /

*Oedipus.* In the name of the gods, if you have knowledge, do not turn away; for we all kneel here before you as suppliants.

*Teiresias.* Yes, for you are all without knowledge; but I will never reveal my griefs – not to say yours.

*Chorus.*   But there is one who will convict him. Look, at last
They are bringing here the inspired prophet, Teiresias.
If the truth lives in any man, it lives in him.

*Enter Teiresias, guided by a boy.*

*Oedipus.*   Teiresias, whose mind compasses all things, spoken
And unspoken, things earth-footed or heaven-hung –
Behold this city. Blind though you are, you understand
What fierce plague grips us; from which you alone, my lord,
Appear our shield and saviour. To my inquiry, Phoebus
Sent answer – you have heard doubtless from my messengers –
That from this plague deliverance could only come
If we discovered what men killed King Laius
And killed them, or else sent them into banishment.
Then do not grudge your help, whether from voice of birds,
Or other mode of divination that you have,
But save yourself, and Thebes, save me, save everything
That bears defilement issuing from the murdered man.
For we are in your hands. Man's noblest labour is
To use his skill and power to help his fellow-men.
*Teiresias.*   Alas! To have perception, where the perceiver draws
No profit, is a dreadful thing. I knew this well,
But killed the thought; else I would never have come here.
*Oedipus.*   Why, how is this? In what a grim mood you have
come!
*Teiresias.*   Let me go home; you will most easily endure
Your destiny, and I mine, if you do as I say.
*Oedipus.*   This is against all custom, an unfriendly act
To Thebes, who reared you, if you thus withold your word.
*Teiresias.*   You too, I see, have spoken untimely to your own
hurt;
Lest I fall into the same error, I am dumb.
*Oedipus.*   No, in God's name, if you have knowledge, do not
turn
Away. We are all your suppliants, we kneel to you.
*Teiresias.*   Yes, for you all are without knowledge. I will never,
Never disclose my griefs – I would not say, *your* griefs.

21

*Oedipus.* What do you say? You know something, and will
330 not speak, but intend / to fail us and destroy the city?

*Teiresias.* I will pain neither myself nor you. Why ask these
vain questions? You will not learn the answer from me.

*Oedipus.* What, most vicious of vicious men – for you would
335 anger the nature of a rock – will you never speak out, / but still
show yourself unsoftened and inconclusive?

*Teiresias.* You have blamed *my* temper; but your own, living
with you, you have not seen; no, you blame *me*.

*Oedipus.* Why, who would not be angry, hearing such words,
340 with which you now slight this city? /

*Teiresias.* The future will come of itself, even if I cover it in
silence.

*Oedipus.* Then, since it will come, all the more reason why
you should tell me.

*Teiresias.* I will not speak further; so now, if you will, rage
with the wildest anger possible.

*Oedipus.* Yes indeed, and I will pass over nothing – so angry
345 am I – / of what I perceive. Know that in my opinion you actually
helped to plot the deed, and carried it out, short of killing with
your hands; if you had sight, I would have said that even the
doing of it was yours alone.

350 *Teiresias.* Is it true? I bid you abide by the proclamation /
which you have made, and from today to speak neither to these
nor to me, as being yourself the unholy polluter of this land.

337. *your own, living with you.* The word for 'temper', *orgë*, is
feminine; so that 'your own', and the participle 'living', are also both
feminine, and thus can mean, 'the woman living with you, who is your
own [mother]'. Cf. 990.

338. *you have not seen.* The tense used is the aorist, which may refer,
like the perfect, to something that has just happened; but its commoner
use is as a past tense, which would be appropriate to the second meaning
in 337; cf. 1484, 'neither seeing anything'.

*Oedipus.*   What? Then you know the truth, and will not
   speak, but mean
Both to betray me and to ruin the whole state?
*Teiresias.*   I will not bring pain either on myself or you.
   Questions are useless. From me you will learn nothing.
*Oedipus.*   Black-hearted criminal! Why, you would rouse a
   stone
To anger. Can you never speak out clear? How long
Will you keep up this stubborn, crass, evasive pose?
*Teiresias.*   You find fault with *my* temper; but you have not
   seen
Your own, that lives beside you. You blame me instead.
*Oedipus.*   Who would not? – words like yours, words of
   contempt, which shame
This city; what man could hear you, and contain his rage?
*Teiresias.*   The future will come, though my silence covers it.
*Oedipus.*   Why, then, if it will come, you are bound to tell it
   me.
*Teiresias.*   I'll speak not one word further. Therefore, if you
   will,
Fume, give free flow to your ungovernable rage.
*Oedipus.*   I will! My rage is such, that I will leave out nothing
Of all that I now understand. It is my belief
That you were an accomplice; indeed, short of striking
The very blow, you did the murder! Were you not blind,
I'd say the actual killing was your work alone.
*Teiresias.*   You say so? – I command you, abide by the decree
Your own mouth uttered, and from this day forward speak
No word either to these your citizens or to me.
You are the unholy desecrator of this land.

*Oedipus.* Do you so shamelessly start up this accusation? And
355 where do you think to escape [the punishment due for] this? /

*Teiresias.* I have escaped. The truth, in its own strength,
lives in me.

*Oedipus.* By whom were you taught? Certainly not by your
skill in divination.

*Teiresias.* By you. You impelled me to speak against my
will.

*Oedipus.* To speak what? Speak again, so that I may understand better.

*Teiresias.* Didn't you understand before? Or are you tempt-
360 ing me by saying this? /

*Oedipus.* Not so that I could call it known. Say it again.

*Teiresias.* I say that you are in fact the killer of the man
whose killer you are seeking.

*Oedipus.* You will regret that you have twice spoken so
calamitously.

*Teiresias.* Shall I now tell you more, so that you may be
more angry?

*Oedipus.* As much as you wish; all you say will be meaning-
365 less. /

*Teiresias.* I say that you are living, unaware, in the most
shameful intercourse with your nearest kin, and do not see what
a disastrous situation you are in.

*Oedipus.* Do you think you can always speak these things and
not suffer for it?

*Teiresias.* Yes, if there is such a thing as the strength of
truth.

*Oedipus.* Oh, there is, except for you; in your case this is not
370 so, since / you are blind in ears and mind as well as in eyes.

354. It is noticeable that throughout this scene Oedipus never says
'I did not kill Laius'; nor does he call Teiresias a liar. The only line
where he makes anything like a specific denial is 576, 'I shall not be
convicted as the murderer'. See the note on that line. (For 219–20, 'a
stranger to this report', see note on p. 153).

*Oedipus.*   Was ever man so shameless? Where have you
   started up
 That tale from? How do you hope to escape punishment?

*Teiresias.*   I have escaped. The truth lives in me, full of power.

*Oedipus.*   Who put you up to this? Your prophet's art? Oh, no!

*Teiresias.*   You did: it was you who made me speak against
   my will.

*Oedipus.*   Speak what? Speak it again, so I can take it in.

*Teiresias.*   Did you not understand? Are you trying to lead me
   on?

*Oedipus.*   I am not sure I grasped it fully. Say it again.

*Teiresias.*   I say you killed the man whose killer you are
   seeking.

*Oedipus.*   Twice over! You shall suffer for this infamy.

*Teiresias.*   Shall I say more, to make you even angrier?

*Oedipus.*   Say what you please; your words will all be meaningless.

*Teiresias.*   I say that, unaware, blind to the dreadful fact,
 You live in shameful union with your nearest kin.

*Oedipus.*   Do you think you can persist so, and not smart for
   it?

*Teiresias.*   I do, if any strength resides in truth.

*Oedipus.*                                         It does –
 Except for you. That strength cannot be yours; you're blind,
 Not only in sight, but blind in hearing, blind in brain.

*Teiresias.*   Yes, and you are a pitiable wretch, to utter taunts which soon every single man here will cast at you.

*Oedipus.*   Your life is passed in one unbroken night; *I* would
375   never hurt you, nor would any other man who sees the light. /

*Teiresias.*   No, [you would never hurt me,] for it is not my destiny to fall by your hand; since Apollo is sufficient, whose concern it is to bring these things to fulfilment.

*Oedipus.*   Are they Creon's, or yours – these fabrications?

*Teiresias.*   Oh, Creon is no plague to you; you are your own.

*Oedipus.*   O wealth, and regal power, and skill surpassing
380   skill / in this life so-full-of-emulation, how great is the envy which always attaches to you, if for the sake of *this* power, which the city put into my hands as a gift, not asked for – for the sake
385   of this, Creon the reliable, my friend from the first, / creeping on me by stealth desires to throw me out, suborning a scheming fortune-teller such as this, a slippery impostor, who has an eye only for profit, but in his art is blind. Why, come, tell me, in
390   what respect are you a proven prophet? / How was it, that when the riddle-chanting dog was here, you spoke no word that might set free these citizens? And that riddle was not for any chance comer to solve, but there was need of a prophet's art; and it was
395   evident that *you* did not have this, / either from birds, or as knowledge derived from some god. But I came, I, know-nothing Oedipus, and stopped her, finding the answer by intelligence, not learning it from birds. And I am the one you are trying to get rid
400   of, thinking that you will stand close to Creon's throne. / I think that both you and the plotter of all this will be sorry that you tried to drive out defilement. If you did not appear to be an old man, you should learn by suffering what your attitude is.

393. *that riddle.* A hexameter version of the Sphinx's riddle is translated as follows: 'There is on earth a thing two-footed and four-footed and three-footed, which has one voice . . . but when it goes on most feet, then its speed is feeblest.' The word for 'two-footed' is *dipous* – which may have offered *Oidipous* a clue.

397. *know-nothing.* See pp. 133, 170.

403. *attitude.* I.e. 'that your attitude to me is treason'.

*Teiresias.*   And you are pitiable, to cast at me such taunts
  As all men's tongues shall soon cast in contempt at you.
*Oedipus.*   You live in total darkness; I would not lay a finger
  On you, neither would any man who sees the light.
*Teiresias.*   My destiny is not to fall by you. Apollo
  Has power; it is his care to see these matters through.
*Oedipus.*   Creon! These fabrications – are they his? or yours?
*Teiresias.*   Creon is no enemy to you. You are your own.
*Oedipus.*   O wealth, and kingly state, and skill outmatching skill
  In this competitive world! What boundless jealousy
  Grapples upon you! For the sake of this power, which
  The city put into my hands as a free gift,
  Unasked – for this, Creon the trusty, who from the first
  Was close to me, goes furtively to work, longing
  To throw me out; and sends a hired trickster like this,
  A fortune-teller, a slippery charlatan, who has eyes
  Only for money-making, and in his art is blind.
  Come on, then, tell me, when have you proved yourself a
    prophet?
  When the spell-binding Sphinx was here, why had you then
  No word to save our citizens from their distress?
  Her riddle was not for every passer-by to solve;
  A prophet's word was needed; and it was evident
  You had no word to give, either from bird-lore or
  From any god's instruction. And then I arrived,
  Know-nothing Oedipus, and I put a stop to her,
  Finding the answer by my wit, not taught by birds.
  Now I'm the one you try to push out, making sure
  *Your* place will be at the right hand of Creon's throne.
  You and your fellow-schemer will regret the day
  You tried to purge Thebes. But that you seem old, you should
    learn
  From punishment the true name for such men as you.

*Chorus.* In our judgement both this man's words and yours,
405 Oedipus, seem to have been spoken in anger. / Our need is not
for such words, but to consider this – how we may best carry out
the oracular-commands of the god.

*Teiresias.* King though you are, at least the right of speaking
at equal length in reply must be regarded as equal [for us both];
for I too possess this. I do not live as slave to you at all, but to
410 Loxias; / so I shall not be enrolled under Creon as patron. And I
tell you – since you have actually reproached me with my blindness: you have sight, and yet do not see in what a depth of
disaster you are, nor where you are living, nor with whom. Do
you know from what parents you were born? And you have been,
415 unaware, an enemy / to your own kin, below, and on the earth
above. And as for you, your mother's and your own father's
curse, with double lash, with dread [pursuing] foot, will eventually drive you out of this land – you who now see well, but then
[you will see] darkness.

420 And for your shrieking what place shall not be harbour, / what
part of Cithaeron shall not resound with it soon, when you perceive the truth about that marriage, the haven into which, after
a fair voyage, you sailed, which proved no haven for your house?
And you are unaware of a multitude of other evils which shall
425 level you with yourself and with your own children. / So in view
of this, revile both Creon and my words; for there is no one among
mortals who shall ever be more miserably crushed than you.

*Oedipus.* Is it to be endured that I should listen to this from
430 him? To hell with you! Will you not go more quickly? Go back, /
turn away, away from this house!

*Teiresias.* I would not have come, had it not been you who
called me.

*Oedipus.* I had no idea that you were going to speak folly, or
I would have been slow to summon you to my house.

408. Or, 'I must claim equality, at least in regard to the right of
speaking at equal length in reply'.
430. *To hell with you.* A common vituperation, literally, 'Will you
not [go] to destruction?'

28

*Chorus.*   Oedipus, to our thinking both his words and yours
   Were spoken in anger. This is not what we need, but rather
   To seek how we may best discharge the god's commands.
*Teiresias.*   King though you are, you must allow me equal
    right
   To answer at equal length; this right is in my power.
   I do not live in bond to you, but to Apollo;
   I shall not, then, be enrolled in Creon's patronage.
   But, since you have taunted me as blind, I tell you this:
   You have sight, yet do not see your own dreadful state,
   Nor where you are living, nor with whom you share your
    home.
   Do you know who were your parents? Unaware, you have
    been
   An enemy to your own kin, living and in the grave;
   And soon your mother's – yes, and your true father's curse,
   With twofold lash, in dread pursuit shall harry you
   Hence; and your eyes, that now see clear, shall then be dark.
   Then, to your cries what place shall not give harbouring,
   What rock in all Cithaeron not re-echo them,
   When you shall comprehend this marriage into which
   You sailed from your successful voyaging, and achieved
   Shipwreck for your whole house? Aye, and a multitude
   Of other horrors you have yet to learn, which shall
   Level you with yourself and with your own offspring.
   Now pour abuse on Creon and on my words; no man
   Lives who shall be more miserably crushed than you.
*Oedipus.*   Must I listen to this from him? Intolerable!
   To hell with you! Get out, this instant! Turn your back
   And go! Away, out of this palace, away, away!
*Teiresias.*   I had no wish to come here; but you sent for me.

*He turns and goes to edge of stage.*

*Oedipus.*   How could I know what folly you would talk? If I
    had,
   You would have waited long for a summons to my house.

29

435      *Teiresias.* As to the kind of man I am – to you I seem / a fool, but to the parents who begot you, sane.

     *Oedipus.* What parents? Stay here. Who of men is my father?

     *Teiresias.* This day shall beget and shall destroy you.

     *Oedipus.* Everything you say is too enigmatic and obscure.

     *Teiresias.* Why, are not you the man most able to discover
440      these things? /

     *Oedipus.* [Go on,] reproach me with those things in which you will find me great.

     *Teiresias.* Yet it was in fact this fortune that undid you.

     *Oedipus.* Well, if I saved this city, I don't care.

     *Teiresias.* Then I will go; and you, boy, take me.

     *Oedipus.* Yes, let him take you. While you are here you are
445      in my way / and trouble me; once you are gone you will not distress me any more.

     *Teiresias.* I will go when I have said what I came for, not fearing your [threatening] face; for you have no chance of destroying me. And I tell you: this man, whom you have long been seeking, with your threatening proclamation about the
450      murder / of Laius – this man is here, known as a resident alien, but soon he shall be shown to be a native Theban, and he will not be pleased at this chance; for, blind after seeing and a beggar
455      instead of rich, he shall journey to a strange land, / feeling the ground before him with a stick. And he shall be revealed as being at once brother and father to his own children with whom he lives, and son and husband of the woman from whom he was born, and of his father both successor and killer. So, go in / and
460      think this out; and if you find me wrong, then say that I have no understanding in prophecy.

440. *these things.* I.e. enigmas; cf. 393.

*Teiresias* (*turning to Oedipus*).   Folly? In your opinion, then, I
   am a fool.

   Your true parents would say I had perception.

*Oedipus.*                                   What?

   What parents? Come back here. Who was my father, then?

*Teiresias.*   This day shall father you, and shall destroy your life.

*Oedipus.*   You speak always in riddles, never a plain word.

*Teiresias.*   And is not solving riddles your great accomplish-
   ment?

*Oedipus.*   Cast in my teeth that in which you shall find me
   great.

*Teiresias.*   Yet it was that same chance that proved your
   undoing.

*Oedipus.*   I care nothing for that, if I delivered Thebes.

*Teiresias.*   Then I will go. Come here, boy, lead me.

*Oedipus.*                             Yes, let him

   Lead you away. I find your presence troublesome.

   If you would only go, you would stop tormenting me.

*Teiresias.*   I am going, when I have said that which I came to
   say.

   I do not fear your anger; you have no power at all

   Over me. And I tell you: the man whom all this while

   You have searched for, with your threats, and proclamation
   about

   The murder of King Laius – that man is here,

   Known as a resident alien; but he shall soon

   Be shown a native Theban, and will not be glad

   To meet his fortune. Blind, who once had eyes; a beggar,

   Once rich; feeling the ground before him with a stick,

   He shall set forth to a foreign land. And he shall be shown

   At once brother and father of his own children

   With whom he lives; at once both son and husband to

   The woman who bore him; partner in his father's bed,

   Shedder of his father's blood. Go in and think of this.

   And if you find my utterance is at fault, then say

   I have no understanding in the prophetic art.

*Chorus.* Who is the man of whom the divine voice from the Delphian rock spoke, as having performed with bloody hands the 465 [most] unspeakable of unspeakable crimes? / It is time for him to ply in flight a foot stronger than storm-swift horses; for the son of 470 Zeus, armed with fire and lightnings, is leaping upon him, / and with him follow the dread, unerring Fates.

For the word has flashed forth, newly revealed from snowy 475 Parnassus, to trace by every means the unknown man. / For he is wandering under cover of the wild wood, among caves and rocks, like a bull, living pitiful in solitude with pitiful foot, keeping far 480 from him the oracles / given at the earth's navel; but they still living hover about him.

Dreadfully, it is true, dreadfully does the skilled augurer disturb me, while I neither approve nor deny. I am at a loss what 485 I should say. / I am fluttered with forebodings, seeing neither here nor after. For what quarrel existed either for the descend-ants of Labdacus or for the son of Polybus [one against the other] 490 I never heard, either in the past / or recently, which I might use as a proof [to justify me] in attacking the public reputation of Oedipus, [and appearing as] a champion of the house of Lab-495 dacus / in the matter of an obscure murder.

Well, Zeus and Apollo certainly are intelligent, and cognisant of mortal affairs; but, that any prophet who is a man achieves 500 more than I, / there is no clear decision; though a man may

---

463. Jebb's note on 463–512 illustrates how far a scholar can un-wittingly go in evasion of the problem before him.

475. *unknown.* The word is the same (*adēlos*) as that rendered 'obscure' in 495. See p. 172.

480. *keeping.* I.e. 'trying to keep'. The present tense and participle, and the imperfect tense, sometimes have this force; cf. 805, 'were for driving', where the simple imperfect tense is used.

493. *proof.* The literal meaning is 'touchstone'; the same word is rendered 'test' in 510.

500. *achieves.* The verb means 'win [a prize]'. Cf. 863.

*Exit Teiresias to the city,*
*Oedipus to the palace.*

*Chorus.*   Who is the man?                          (Strophe 1
   The prophetic rock of Delphi spoke of one who committed
   The unspeakable of unspeakable crimes,
   His hands red with blood.
   Now, if ever, let him run
   With a stride stronger than hurricane horses.
   The son of Zeus, full-armed in fiery lightnings,
   Bounds on his trail;
   And with him follow the dread Fates unerring.
   Newly revealed,                               (Antistrophe 1
   From snowy Parnassus the word flashed forth, commanding
   To track out by every means the unknown man.
   Under the wild wood's covert, among caves and rocks,
   He is roaming fierce as a bull,
   Wretched, forlorn on his joyless path,
   Resolved to keep at bay the prophetic word
   Uttered at the earth's navel;
   But about him still hovers the word undying.
   It is true, the sage prophet has said             (Strophe 2
   Things disturbing, deeply disturbing;
   I cannot accept, neither can I refute them.
   I do not know what I should say;
   I am disquieted with forebodings;
   Nothing, either present or to come, can I see clearly.
   I never heard, either then or recently,
   Of any standing feud between
   The house of Labdacus and the son of Polybus,
   Which would provide a test to justify me
   In attacking the public fame of Oedipus,
   To rescue the cause of Laius
   So mysteriously murdered.
   Well, it is true, Zeus and Apollo               (Antistrophe 2
   Have understanding, and know the affairs of men;
   But, that any mortal prophet
   Wins more success than I, admits no clear proof,

33

surpass skill with skill. However, never would I, before seeing a
505 convincing statement, / assent when they accuse [Oedipus]. What
is clear is, that the winged maiden long ago came against him,
and he was seen to be skilled, and by the test pleasing-to-the-
510 city. / Therefore, so far as concerns my feelings, he shall never
be held guilty of crime.

*Creon.* Men of this city, having been told of the terrible
words which King Oedipus is speaking in accusation against me,
515 I am here indignant. For if in the present troubles / he thinks
that he has suffered anything from me, by words or deeds, that
tends to harm, I certainly have no wish to live a long life, bearing
this charge. For the damage of this statement touches me not in
520 a single point, / but in the greatest degree, if I am going to be
called traitor in the city, traitor too by you and my friends.

*Chorus.* But this slander came, perhaps, under stress of anger
rather than with the judgement of the heart.

*Creon.* Was the statement made openly, that the prophet
525 was induced by my advice / to utter his falsehoods?

*Chorus.* This indeed was said, but I do not know with what
purpose.

*Creon.* But was it from steady eyes, and out of a sound mind,
that this charge was laid against me?

530 *Chorus.* I do not know; I do not see what those in power do. /
But now here he comes himself out of the house.

*Oedipus.* You, there! How is it you have come here? Or have
you such a face of boldness that you have come to my house,
being evidently the assassin of myself and the palpable robber of
535 my kingship? / Come, tell me, in the god's name, was it some
cowardice or folly that you saw in me, [that led you] to plot this
action? Did you think that I would not be aware of this operation
of yours treacherously creeping up on me, or that on discovering

526. *his falsehoods.* 'His' translates the definite article, which should
imply that Creon knew what these falsehoods were. That in 574 he
should deny such knowledge is fully in character.

528. *from steady eyes.* The same phrase is used in 1385.

34

Though in wisdom one man may surpass another.
So I will never, till I see a convincing statement,
Agree with anyone who accuses Oedipus.
It was plain enough long ago, when the winged maid came
    against him,
That he had wisdom; he became, by test,
The hero of Thebes; therefore in my judgement
He shall never be found guilty of wickedness.

*Enter Creon.*

*Creon.*   Thebans, I am told that Oedipus the king has laid
  Grave charges against me. I am indignant. If he thinks
  That in the present troubles he has received from me,
  By word or action, any potential injury,
  I assure you, under such imputation, I've no wish
  For long life. Such a charge touches me not merely
  In one point, but in all, if I am to be called traitor
  In Thebes, traitor by you no less, and all my friends.
*Chorus.*   But this slander was uttered, surely, under stress
  Of anger, rather than from his considered thought.
*Creon.*   But was this statement plainly made, that it was I
  Prompted the prophet to pronounce his falsehoods here?
*Chorus.*   This was indeed said; with what purpose, I don't
  know.
*Creon.*   But did his eyes look clear, and was he in his right
  mind,
  When he framed such an accusation against me?
*Chorus.*   I can't tell; I see nothing that my masters do.
  But look – he himself is coming from the palace now.

*Enter Oedipus.*

*Oedipus.*   So, you've come, have you? You have the effrontery
  To show your face in my house? Yes, you – clearly proved
  My murderer, in broad daylight stealing my throne?
  Just tell me: was it cowardice, or stupidity
  You saw in me, that inspired you to this act? Perhaps
  You thought I would not see your treachery creeping up,
  Or if I saw it, that I'd fail to defend myself?

35

it I would not defend myself? Is not this a foolish undertaking of
540 yours, / without a large following, or friends, to hunt for a
throne – a thing which is captured by numbers and money?

*Creon.*   Do you know what you should do? Give equal
hearing to my reply to your words, and when you have heard for
yourself, then judge.

545   *Oedipus.*   You are a clever speaker, and I am a bad learner /
from you; for I have found you an enemy, and a malignant one.

*Creon.*   That is the very point I will speak of first; now listen.

*Oedipus.*   That is the very point I forbid you to explain – that
you are no traitor.

*Creon.*   If you think that stubbornness without intelligence is
550 something to be prized, you are out of your mind. /

*Oedipus.*   If you think that you can wrong your kinsman and
not be subject to the penalty, you are out of your mind.

*Creon.*   I endorse what you say as just; but tell me what
injury you claim to have received.

*Oedipus.*   Did you, or did you not, persuade me that I ought
555 to send for that pretentious prophet? /

*Creon.*   And now I am still of the same mind.

*Oedipus.*   And how long ago is it now since Laius——

*Creon.*   Did what deed? I don't understand.

*Oedipus.*   ——vanished from sight by an act of deadly
560 violence? /

*Creon.*   Long and ancient would be the times measured.

*Oedipus.*   Well, was this prophet then in his trade?

*Creon.*   Yes, skilled as now, and equally honoured.

*Oedipus.*   Well, did he mention me at all at that time?

565   *Creon.*   Certainly not when I was standing anywhere near. /

*Oedipus.*   Did you not hold an inquiry into the murder?

*Creon.*   We held one, naturally; and we did not hear.

*Oedipus.*   Well, how was it that this learned man did not say
this then?

What a fool's enterprise! – without troops, or influence,
To go hunting kingdoms! You need men for that, and money.
*Creon.*   Listen to me now. You have had your say; allow
Me to have mine, and when you have learnt the facts, then
judge.
*Oedipus.*   You'll state them cleverly, no doubt; but since I
have found
You my sworn enemy, I shall be slow to learn from you.
*Creon.*   Now, first of all give me a hearing on one point——
*Oedipus.*   One point, that you're no traitor? Don't dare tell me
that.
*Creon.*   If you consider stubbornness divorced from all
Reason is something to be proud of, you're mistaken.
*Oedipus.*   If you imagine you can lay plots against your own
Family and not be punished for it, you're mistaken.
*Creon.*   I agree, that is a just statement; but what is
This injury you say you have suffered? Tell me plainly.
*Oedipus.*   Did you, or did you not, say that I ought to summon
That pompous prophet?
*Creon.*                         I did. I would say the same again.
*Oedipus.*   How many years have gone by since King Laius——
*Creon.*   Since Laius did what? I don't follow you.
*Oedipus.*                                      Since he
Vanished from sight, the victim of a murderous crime?
*Creon.*   To reckon that, you'd have to go back many years.
*Oedipus.*   And at that period, was this prophet in his trade?
*Creon.*   As learned then as now, and held in no less honour.
*Oedipus.*   And did he ever at that time mention my name?
*Creon.*   No; not, at least, when I was standing anywhere near.
*Oedipus.*   You held an inquiry into the murder, did you not?
*Creon.*   We did, of course; and we received no information.
*Oedipus.*   How was it that this sage did not say all this then?

*Creon.* I don't know. In matters that I don't understand I prefer to say nothing.

*Oedipus.* This much at least you know, and could say with
570   perfect understanding—— /

*Creon.* What do you mean? If I know, I will not deny it.

*Oedipus.* That, if he had not conferred with you, he would never have spoken of *my* murder of Laius.

*Creon.* If he says this, you yourself know. But I claim to
575   question you in the same way as you questioned me just now. /

*Oedipus.* Ask fully. I shall not be convicted as the murderer.

*Creon.* Well, then: you have married my sister?

*Oedipus.* There is no denial of what you ask.

*Creon.* And you rule the land in the same degree as she, with equal power?

580   *Oedipus.* Everything she wishes she obtains from me. /

*Creon.* And am not I, as third, equal to you two?

*Oedipus.* Yes; it is just there that you appear as a false friend.

*Creon.* Not so, if you would reason with yourself as I do [with myself]. First examine this point, whether you think that anyone would choose to be a ruler [living] among terrors, rather
585   than / one sleeping tranquilly – granted that he is to have the same powers. I, for one, have no innate desire to be a king rather than to act as a king, nor has any other man who knows how to keep a sober mind. For now I gain all [my requests] from
590   you without fear; / but if I were ruler myself, I would be doing many things even against my will. How, then, could royalty be sweeter for me to have than unworried rule and power? I am not yet so deceived as to desire honours other than those which come
595   with profit. / Now I am on friendly terms with all, now everyone greets me. Now those who desire something from you call out me, since there lies all the achievement of their wish. Why indeed should I take that and renounce this? No man would

576. *I shall not be convicted* . . . Who is on trial at the moment – Oedipus as a murderer, or Creon as a traitor? See p. 179.

38

*Creon.* I don't know; when I'm in the dark, I choose silence.

*Oedipus.* You know this much – and you could tell me
   clearly enough –

*Creon.* What could I tell? If I know, I will not deny it.

*Oedipus.* You know that, if the prophet had not conferred
   with you,
He'd never have said the death of Laius was my doing.

*Creon.* If he says that – you best know. But it is now my turn
  To ask you a few questions such as you asked me.

*Oedipus.* Ask anything. I shall not be proved the murderer.

*Creon.* Well, then: you have my sister as your wedded wife?

*Oedipus.* There's no denying what you ask me; it is true.

*Creon.* And you and she share equal authority in Thebes?

*Oedipus.* She receives from me everything that she desires.

*Creon.* And I as third partner rank equal with you both?

*Oedipus.* This makes your falsehood the more glaring – a
   false friend.

*Creon.* Not if you reason with your own heart, as I with mine.
  Consider this first: do you think a man would choose
  To rule amidst fears, rather than with a quiet mind
  And sound sleep, his power being the same in either case?
  I, for one, have no inborn preference for the name
  Of king over the kingly power; and any man
  In his right mind will say the same. As things are now,
  I gain from you every request, and have no fear;
  Were I king, I would be doing much against my will.
  To me, how could a throne seem more desirable
  Than rule and influence freed from their attendant cares?
  I am not yet so misguided as to crave honours
  Other than those which bring advantage. As things are,
  I enjoy good wishes and warm greetings from all men;
  Those who desire something from you speak first to me,
  As their best hope of getting it. Then why should I
  Throw this away, for that? No sane man turns traitor.

600 turn traitor while in his right mind. / I neither am a lover of
such policy, nor could I ever tolerate [partnership] with one who
acted so. In proof of this, first, go to Pytho, and ask about the
605 oracle, if I reported it to you truly; next, if you find that I / have
laid any scheme in partnership with the augurer, take and kill
me, not by one vote but two, mine as well as yours. But do not
find me guilty apart, on an unproved opinion. As it is not just to
assume foolishly that bad men are good, so [it is not just] to think
610 the good bad. / To cast off a true friend is, I say, equivalent to
casting away the life which is within oneself, the dearest thing a
man has. Well, in time you will learn these things with certainty,
since it is time alone that shows the just man; but an evil man
615 you could discern even in a single day. /

*Chorus.*   He has spoken well, king, for [the instruction of]
one who takes care not to fall; in judging, the quick are not sure.

*Oedipus.*   When the man plotting against me is quick, moving
stealthily, I too must be quick in counter-plotting. If I keep quiet
620 and wait for him, his ends / will have been gained and mine
missed.

*Creon.*   What in fact do you want? To banish me from the
land?

*Oedipus.*   Not at all; your death, not your banishment, I want,
so that you may [be an example to] show what sort of thing
envy is.

*Creon.*   Do you speak as one who will not yield, will not
625 believe? /

[*Oedipus.*   You do not convince me that I ought to believe
you.]

*Creon.*   No, for I see that you are not sane.

*Oedipus.*   Sane at least in my own interest.

*Creon.*   You should be equally concerned for mine.

*Oedipus.*   You are a traitor.

608. *apart.* I.e. in a hole-and-corner fashion.
626. Oedipus' line here is missing in the MSS; the line given is a
conjecture.

I am no lover of such policy, nor could I
Bear to consort with such a man. For proof of this,
First, go to Pytho, and ask there if my report
Of the oracle was true; then, if you find that I
Laid any scheme with Teiresias, you have my voice
Added to yours, to take and kill me; but without
Evidence, on your sole opinion, you shall not
Accuse me. To call good men bad is as unjust
As it is foolish to take wicked men for saints.
The man who casts off a true friend does nothing else,
I hold, than throw away his own most precious life.
In time you will learn this, and know it. Time alone
Shows the just man; the bad, a single day reveals.

*Chorus.*   King, he has spoken well, to one who is on his guard
Against a fall. The quick in counsel are unsure.

*Oedipus.*   When stealthy treason makes quick moves against
me, I
Must move quickly to counter it. If I stay quiet
And wait for him, his ends will be achieved, while mine
Will miss the mark.

*Creon.*                   Why, what's your wish? To banish me?

*Oedipus.*   Oh, no. I want you dead, not banished; an example
To show the soul of envy.

*Creon.*                   This is your last word?
Unyielding, unbelieving?

*Oedipus.*                   Why should I believe you?

*Creon.*   You are not in your right mind.

*Oedipus.*                                   I can defend myself.

*Creon.*   You should defend me equally.

*Oedipus.*                                   You are a traitor.

41

*Creon.* But if you understand nothing?

*Oedipus.* In any case I must rule.

*Creon.* Not if you rule badly.

*Oedipus.* O city, city!

630 *Creon.* The city is partly mine too, not only yours. /

*Chorus.* Stop, lords. At a timely moment for you, I see Iocasta coming here out of the house. With her help you must compose well the quarrel which has just arisen.

*Iocasta.* Why, unhappy men, have you raised this ill-considered strife of tongues? Are you not ashamed, when the

635 land / is so sick, to stir up private troubles? Oedipus, go into the house, and you, Creon, go home; and both of you – do not magnify a trifling grievance.

*Creon.* Sister, your husband Oedipus treats me outrageously; he thinks it right to inflict on me one of two evils, at his own

640 choice: / either to thrust me out of my native land, or take and kill me.

*Oedipus.* That is so; for I have caught him, my wife, engaged in evil practices, by evil arts, against my person.

*Creon.* Now may I not prosper, but perish accursed, if I have

645 done anything of what you accuse me of doing! /

*Iocasta.* In the name of the gods believe this, Oedipus, chiefly out of respect for this oath sworn to the gods, but next out of respect for me and for these men who are present before you.

*Chorus.* Do so, king, I beg; consent, reflect.

*Oedipus.* Then what concession do you want me to make for

650 you? /

*Chorus.* A man who formerly was no fool, who now is strong in his oath, you should respect.

*Oedipus.* Then do you know what it is you desire?

*Chorus.* I know.

655 *Oedipus.* Then explain what you mean. /

*Chorus.* When a friend is liable to a curse, you should never, on unproved report, lay a dishonouring charge against him.

642. *That is so.* Literally, 'I agree', 'say the same'.

42

*Creon.* What if you are utterly mistaken?
*Oedipus.*                                        Yet I must rule.
*Creon.* Not if your rule is wicked.
*Oedipus.*                              Hear him, city of Thebes!
*Creon.* I too am a citizen of Thebes, not you alone.
*Chorus.* My lords, no more! Here comes Iocasta, in good time.
Come — with her help, compose this quarrel sensibly.

*Enter Iocasta.*

*Iocasta.* Misguided men! What is this foolish war of words
You have raised? With Thebes so stricken, do you feel no
shame
In airing private grievances? Come, come indoors,
Oedipus; and you, Creon, go to your own house.
Why build up trifling matters into serious wrongs?
*Creon.* Sister, your husband Oedipus has gone too far.
He takes to himself the right either to banish me
From my own native country, or kill me out of hand.
*Oedipus.* That is so, Iocasta; I have caught him in the act
Of treason wickedly devised against my person.
*Creon.* May I never thrive again, but die under a curse,
If I am guilty of anything you accuse me of!
*Iocasta.* Oh, Oedipus, believe him, in the name of the gods!
Chiefly, respect his solemn oath; next, for my sake
Believe him, and for these Elders, who are witnesses.
*Chorus.* Do so, King Oedipus, we beg;
Consent, use reason!
*Oedipus.* Then what concession would you have me make?
*Chorus.* In the past a man not to be despised,
At this moment strong in his oath —
You should respect him.
*Oedipus.* You know what you ask?
*Chorus.* I know.
*Oedipus.* Say clearly what you mean.
*Chorus.* When a friend has bound himself with a curse
You should not, on unproved report,
Lay a disgraceful charge against him.

*Oedipus.* Then know well that, when you seek this, you seek my destruction or exile from this land.

660 *Chorus.* No, by the god who is first of all gods, / the sun; for may I perish utterly, god-forsaken, friendless, if I have this
665 thought. But the wasting of the land wears out / my unhappy heart, and again [I suffer] if to our former ills you are going to add those [which arise] from you two.

*Oedipus.* Then let him go, even if I must altogether die, or
670 be forcibly thrust away dishonoured from this land. / It is your mouth, not his, that I take pity on, [finding it] pitiable. But he, wherever he be, shall be hated.

*Creon.* You are seen to be as sullen in yielding as you are malignant when excessive in anger. Such natures are, as is just,
675 most painful to themselves to bear. /

*Oedipus.* Then will you not leave me alone and get out?

*Creon.* I will be on my way; having found you undiscerning, but being, in these men's judgement, upright.

*Chorus.* Lady, why do you delay to take this man into the house?

680 *Iocasta.* [I will do so] when I have learnt what happened. /

*Chorus.* A supposition, resting on words, not knowledge, arose; also, injustice stings.

*Iocasta.* From them both?

*Chorus.* Yes, indeed.

*Iocasta.* Well, what was said?

*Chorus.* It is enough, in my opinion, when the land is al-
685 ready troubled, / enough that the matter should remain where it has stopped.

665. *the wasting of the land.* This is the last reference to the blight and the plague.
671. Here Oedipus says he has more respect for the Chorus than for Creon: in 700 he says he respects Iocasta more than the Chorus: a subtle indication of his emotional instability at this point in the scene.

*Oedipus.*   When you ask this, be sure that what you are
   seeking
Is my death, or my banishment from Thebes.
*Chorus.*   No, by the Sun-god, of all gods the first!
May gods and friends reject me,
Death utterly destroy me,
If I hold such a thought!
But I am heartbroken, first
By the suffering of our country,
Next, that new sorrow rising from your quarrel
Should crown the sorrow we already had.
*Oedipus.*   Then let him go, even if his acquittal means my
   death,
Or my rejection in dishonour from this land.
(*To the Chorus-Leader*) It is your plea, not his, that moves
   me to relent.
Creon, wherever he may be, shall have my hate.
*Creon.*   Your hate in yielding matches the malignancy
You show when anger breaks its bounds. Natures like yours
Are, as is just, most painful for themselves to bear.
*Oedipus.*   Will you not leave me alone now, and get out?
*Creon.*                                                    I'll go.
I find you an ill judge; these know I am innocent.


*Exit Creon.*


*Chorus.*   Madam, why do you not take him
At once into the palace?
*Iocasta.*   I will, when I have learnt what happened here.
*Chorus.*   Ill-judged suspicion – words, no more;
Injustice rankling on the other side.
*Iocasta.*   The quarrel rose from both?
*Chorus.*   Indeed.
*Iocasta.*             Well, what was said?
*Chorus.*   Enough, my lady! Thebes is troubled already.
In my opinion it is enough
To let the matter rest where it has stopped.

*Oedipus.*   You see what you have come to, honest man as you are, in trying to slacken and blunt my purpose.

690
695
*Chorus.*   King, I have said it not only once: know that I would be evidently mad, / useless for counsel, if I were trying-to-get-rid-of you, who gave a straight course to my dear country in troubles, / and who now may well prove our helpful guide.

*Iocasta.*   In the gods' name tell me too, king, on what account you fixedly hold such strong resentment.

700
*Oedipus.*   I will tell you, for I respect you, wife, more than these men. / It is on account of Creon – such plots he has laid against me.

*Iocasta.*   Speak, if you will make a clear statement in imputing the quarrel.

*Oedipus.*   He says that I stand as the killer of Laius.

*Iocasta.*   As on his own knowledge? or having learnt it from someone else?

705
*Oedipus.*   Oh, no; he sent in a criminal prophet, since / so far as concerns himself he keeps his lips entirely free.

710
715
*Iocasta.*   Then absolve yourself from the matters you speak of, and listen to me and learn that there is nothing mortal, you may be sure, that has any share in prophetic art. And I will show you precise evidence of this. / An oracle once came to Laius – I will not say from Phoebus himself, but from his servants – that the destiny should come upon him to be killed by the son who should be born from me and him. Now Laius – so at least the story said – was murdered one day / by foreign bandits at a junction of three highways; while as for the child, its birth was not three days past when Laius fastened together its ankles and cast it out, by the hands of others, on the trackless mountain.

687–8. Oedipus means: I was resolved to put Creon to death: you, in your zeal to oppose me, have reached the point of saying (684) that I am as much to blame as Creon.

691. *if I were trying* . . ' They refer to 658–9.

711. *I will not say* . . . This is the literal translation. But in English this phrase *limits* the application of the example Iocasta is about to give; what is logically needed is a phrase to *point* the application; and this is done by the equally valid rendering, 'not, mark you . . .'.

*Oedipus.* See where it leads you, honest man as you are –
    Trying to soften me, turn the edge of my anger!
*Chorus.* King, I have said once and again,
    I should have been plainly out of my mind,
    Incapable of sound advice,
    If my intent in defending Creon
    Had been to exile you –
    You who, when our beloved land
    Was lost in disasters, came like a fair wind
    And set us on course;
    To whom we still look for prosperous guidance.
*Iocasta.* In God's name tell me too, my lord, what is the
    cause
    That fills you with this fixed resentment.
*Oedipus.*                              Yes, I will.
    I respect you, my wife, more than these men. Creon
    Has laid vile plots against me.
*Iocasta.*                       But be more precise;
    Creon, you say, began this quarrel – how?
*Oedipus.*                         He says
    That it was I who killed King Laius.
*Iocasta.*                     Does he say
    He knows this, or that he heard it from some other man?
*Oedipus.* No, he sends in this crooked prophet to tell his lie,
    Taking good care to keep his own lips innocent.
*Iocasta.* Then, Oedipus, absolve yourself on this account.
    Listen to me: no mortal agency has part
    Nor lot in the prophetic art. Here's precise proof.
    An oracle once came to Laius – not, mark you,
    Spoken by Phoebus himself, but by his servants – saying
    That he was fated to be killed by his own son
    Whom I should bear him. Now, Laius was killed – or so
    Report has it – by foreign bandits at a place
    Where three roads meet; as for the child, it was not three
    Days old, when Laius fastened its two feet together
    And had it thrown out on the pathless mountainside.

So in that case Apollo did not bring it about either that the
720     child / should become his father's murderer or that Laius should
be killed by his son – which was the dreadful thing he feared.
Thus did prophetic utterances plot out the future; of them you
should take no heed at all. Whatever a god needs and searches
725     for, he himself will easily bring to light. /

*Oedipus.*    While I have been listening just now, my wife,
what a wandering of heart and disturbance of mind holds me!

*Iocasta.*    What anxiety has startled you, that you say this?

*Oedipus.*    I thought I heard you say that Laius was slaught-
730     ered at a junction of three highways. /

*Iocasta.*    Yes, that is what was said; and it has not ceased yet.

*Oedipus.*    And where is this place at which this happened?

*Iocasta.*    The country is called Phocis, and a split road leads to
the same spot from Delphi and from Daulia.

735     *Oedipus.*    And what time has elapsed since these events? /

*Iocasta.*    It was shortly before you appeared holding rule over
this land, that this news was brought to the city.

*Oedipus.*    O Zeus, what have you planned to do to me?

*Iocasta.*    But why, Oedipus, is this heavy on your heart?

*Oedipus.*    Do not ask me yet; but tell me about Laius – of
740     what build / was he, what maturity of youth had he reached?

*Iocasta.*    He was tall, his head touched with a recent bloom of
white hair, and in appearance he was not very different from
you.

*Oedipus.*    Alas, what misery! It seems that just now, without
745     knowing it, I was involving myself in dreadful curses. /

*Iocasta.*    What are you saying? I tremble as I look at you, my
lord.

*Oedipus.*    I am horribly afraid that the prophet can see. But
you will show more clearly, if you tell one further thing.

*Iocasta.*    Indeed, though I am trembling, I will answer what
you ask, when I hear it.

750     *Oedipus.*    Was he travelling with a small party, or with many/
armed men, as a ruler would?

48

So, in this case, Phoebus did not fulfil his word:
The son was not his father's killer, nor did Laius
Meet with the fate he dreaded, death at his son's hands.
Thus did prophetic utterance map out the event!
Give such things not a moment's thought; whatever God
Desires and seeks, he will with ease himself reveal.

*Oedipus.* My wife, some words you spoke just now have sent my mind
Wandering, and made my heart pound with a nameless dread.

*Iocasta.* What do you mean? What fearful thought so startles you?

*Oedipus.* I thought I heard you say Laius was murdered where
Three roads meet?

*Iocasta.* That was the report then, and is still.

*Oedipus.* This place you have described, where he was killed –
where is it?

*Iocasta.* The region is called Phocis; at that spot two roads
Join at an angle, from Delphi and from Daulia.

*Oedipus.* How long is it since this took place?

*Iocasta.* The news reached us
Shortly before you were proclaimed as king of Thebes.

*Oedipus.* O Zeus, what is this doom you have designed for me?

*Iocasta.* But, Oedipus, what is it so weighs on your heart?

*Oedipus.* Don't ask me yet. Tell me about Laius. What did he
Look like? How old? Had he the vigour of his years?

*Iocasta.* A tall man; his dark hair recently flecked with grey;
In figure – his was then not much unlike your own.

*Oedipus.* Heaven help me! I think that just now, without knowing it,
I was invoking a dire curse on my own head.

*Iocasta.* What are you saying? I tremble as I look at you,
My lord.

*Oedipus.* I am appalled to think perhaps the seer
Can see. To make all clearer, tell me one thing more.

*Iocasta.* What thing? I dread it, but I'll answer all you ask.

*Oedipus.* Was Laius travelling with a small escort, or with
The strong armed force that usually attends a king?

49

*Iocasta.* They were five in all, and among them was a herald; and one coach carried Laius.

*Oedipus.* Alas, these things are now transparent. Who was
755  the man who gave you [*plural*] this account, lady? /

*Iocasta.* A servant, the only survivor who came back.

*Oedipus.* Is he in fact here in the palace now?

*Iocasta.* No indeed; for when he came thence and saw that you held the royal power, and that Laius was dead, he earnestly
760  begged me, with his hand on mine, / to send him into the country, to the sheep-pastures, so that he might be as far as possible from sight of this city. And I sent him; for he deserved, as a [faithful] slave, to be granted an even greater request than that.

765  *Oedipus.* How could we get him back here quickly? /

*Iocasta.* It is easy; but with what in mind do you desire this?

*Oedipus.* I fear that I myself have spoken too many words; and it is because of them that I want to see him.

*Iocasta.* Well, he shall come. But I too, surely, deserve to be
770  told what lies heavy on your heart, my lord. /

*Oedipus.* Indeed it shall not be kept from you, now that I have gone so far in foreboding. For who means more to me than you, to whom I should speak when passing through such a [crisis of] chance?

My father was Polybus of Corinth, my mother Merope, a
775  Dorian. I was regarded as a man / pre-eminent among the Corinthians, until such a chance befell me, certainly worthy of wonder, but not worthy of the deep concern that I showed. At a banquet, a man over-filled with drinking shouted in his wine that
780  I was not my father's son. / And I, deeply offended, restrained myself with difficulty for that day, and on the next I went to my mother and father and questioned them; and they were indignant with the man who had let the word slip, for the slander [he
785  had uttered]. I was pleased at their attitude, but all the same / this worried me continually; for the rumour was spreading widely. So, unknown to my mother and father, I went to

*Iocasta.*   There were five men in all; and that included one
   Herald; there was one carriage, in which Laius rode.
*Oedipus.*   All clear; all too, too clear! My wife, who was the
      man
   Who brought this news to Thebes?
*Iocasta.*                                    A servant, the only man
   To escape.
*Oedipus.*      And is he still by chance here in the palace?
*Iocasta.*   No. After he returned, and saw you on the throne,
   And Laius dead, he came, and with his hand on mine
   Begged me to send him into the country to tend sheep,
   To live as far as possible out of sight of Thebes.
   I let him go. He was a well-deserving slave,
   And this seemed the least kindness I could do for him.
*Oedipus.*   I want him back, quickly. Can he come here at once?
*Iocasta.*   He can. But why do you want this?
*Oedipus.*                                    Oh, dear wife, I
      fear
   Myself; I have said too much. That's why I must see him.
*Iocasta.*   Well, he shall come. But surely I too have a claim,
   My lord, to know what lies so heavy on your heart.
*Oedipus.*   You have; and I will not deny you, since my own
   Forebodings threaten so. To whom, indeed, should I
   Speak rather than to you, in such a critical
   Hour of my life? My father was Polybus of Corinth;
   My mother a Dorian, Merope. And in Corinth I
   Had some pre-eminence, till a chance event occurred,
   Perhaps worth comment, but not worth the importance I
   Attached to it. At dinner once a man got drunk
   And shouted at me that I was not my father's son.
   That angered me. For the moment I with difficulty
   Restrained myself. Next day I went to both my parents
   And questioned them; and they were angry with the man
   Who had let out the word, for uttering such an insult.
   Well, I was pleased with what they said; but none the less
   The thought gnawed at me; for this rumour was wide-
      spread.

Pytho; and Phoebus sent me away disappointed of the knowledge for which I came, but in his answer revealed other things,
790     miserable and terrible and calamitous: / that I was fated to have
intercourse with my mother, and to show to men a progeny they
could not bear to see; and that I should be the killer of my father
who begot me.

When I heard this I fled, thenceforth measuring the distance
795     of the land of Corinth by the stars / – [fled towards any place]
where I might never see fulfilled the shames of my evil oracles.
And in my journey I reach these regions in which you say this
800     king perished. And to you, lady, I will tell the full truth. / When
as I went along I was near this junction of three roads, there I
was met by a herald, and a man riding in a horse-drawn coach,
such as you describe; and both the leader and the old man him-
805     self were for driving me forcibly from the road. / I angrily struck
the man who was pushing me aside, the driver of the carriage;
and when the old man saw this, he watched from the carriage till
I was going past, and came down full on my head with his
810     double goad. I tell you, he more than paid for it. In an instant, /
hit by the staff in this hand of mine, he immediately rolls out of the
middle of the carriage on his back; and I kill every man of them.

But if there is any blood-relationship between this stranger and
815     Laius, who is now more wretched than myself? / What man
could prove more hated by the gods? whom none, either stranger
or citizen, may lawfully receive in his house, whom no one may
speak to, whom all must repel from their homes? And these
things – these curses – I am the man who laid them on myself,
820     I and no one else. / And I stain the bed of the dead man with my
hands, by which he died. Am I by nature evil? Am I not altogether impure? since I must be banished, and in banishment I
cannot see my own family, nor even tread my native soil, or I am

805. *were for driving*. See note on 480.
814. *this stranger*. The word may imply either Laius, as Oedipus
intends, or Oedipus himself (see 452).

So, without word to mother or father, I set off
For Delphi; and there Phoebus sent me away denied
The answer I had come for, but disclosed to me
Other things, horrible and frightful; that I was fated
To sleep with my own mother, show before men's eyes
A progeny intolerable; and that I should
Become the murderer of the man who gave me life.

When I heard this, I fled away from Corinth, resolved
Thenceforth to know that country only by the stars,
And made for − any place where I might never see
The loathed fulfilment of this dreadful oracle.
And on my way I came to this same spot in which
You tell me this king perished. Now, my wife, this is
The exact truth. When in my journey I was close
To where those roads join, there a herald, and a man
Riding in a horse-drawn carriage, just as you described,
Met me; and both the herald and the old man himself
Wanted to force me off the path. The driver pushed me,
And in a rage I hit him. When the old man saw that,
He watched me from the carriage as I went past, and brought
The pronged goad down full on my head. He paid for it,
And more; in a moment, with a blow from the stick in my
     hand,
He was rolling right out of the carriage, and on his back;
And I killed every man of them.
                                             But, if this stranger
Has any bond in blood with Laius, what man now
Can be more miserable than myself? Could any man
Meet with a more malignant fate? It is forbidden
That any, foreigner or Theban, receive me in his house;
I must not be spoken to, but driven from every door.
And this fate − no one else but I − I am the man
Who laid this curse on my own life! And I defile
The dead man's bed, for these hands killed him. Was I born
Evil? Am I not utterly unclean? Since I
Must go into exile, and in exile may not see
My own parents, nor set foot on my native earth,

825 doomed to marry / my mother, and to kill my father Polybus
who begot me and brought me up. Would not a man be speaking
the truth, who judged that these things came upon me from a
830 cruel divinity? Never, never, O pure holiness of gods, / may I see
that day, but depart out of sight of men, before I see such a stain
of disaster settled upon me!

*Chorus.* To us certainly, O king, these things are full of fear;
but until you learn fully from the man who was present, have
835 hope. /

*Oedipus.* Yes, I have indeed thus much hope, to wait for the
shepherd – only that.

*Iocasta.* And when he appears, what do you want from him?

*Oedipus.* I will explain to you. If it be found that he says the
840 same as you, I shall have escaped this danger. /

*Iocasta.* And what special word did you hear from me?

*Oedipus.* You were saying that he told you that bandits
killed Laius. So, if he still says the same number, I was not the
845 killer; for one cannot be equal to many. / But if he speaks of one
lone traveller, then plainly [the guilt of] this deed inclines
towards me.

*Iocasta.* But be assured that this is how the report was first
put forth; this at least he cannot now reject, for the city heard it,
850 not only I. / And even if he were to deviate somewhat from his
earlier account, he will certainly never show, my lord, that the
murder of Laius was justly straight; who Loxias plainly said was
to die by the hand of my child. And, you see, it was never my
855 poor child who / killed him; he himself [the child] perished first.
So that, for all that prophecy is worth, I would not in future look
either this way or that.

*Oedipus.* You judge well. All the same, send someone to
860 fetch that labourer; do not neglect this. /

*Iocasta.* I will make haste and send. But let us go into the
house; for I will do nothing that is not pleasing to you.

853. *justly straight.* A curiously confused phrase, which evidently
must mean 'carried out according to the prophecy'.

Or I am doomed to wed my mother, and to kill
The father who begot and reared me, Polybus.
Are not the powers above guilty of cruelty?
What other word fits such a fate? You holy gods!
Let me not see that day, no, never, never! Let me
Vanish from sight of men, before I see such guilt
Stain my unhappy life!

Chorus.                 Your words, my lord, fill us
With dread; yet, till you learn from this eye-witness all
He has to tell, hold fast to hope.

Oedipus.                 Yes, I still have
This shred of hope, to await the shepherd; only this.

Iocasta.   And when he comes, what do you want to learn from
   him?

Oedipus.   I'll tell you. If his story should be found to tally
With what you said, then I am cleared.

Iocasta.                 What word of mine
Do you especially mean?

Oedipus.                 You said his story was
That Laius was killed by robbers; so, if he still says
There were a number, I was not the killer. One
Can't be the same as many. But if he now speaks
Of one lone traveller, clearly this guilt falls on me.

Iocasta.   I assure you, that is how the story was first told;
The man cannot now take it back – not only I
But all Thebes heard it. Even if he should diverge
In some point from his first account – at least, my lord,
He cannot ever show that Laius' death conformed
To prophecy; for Loxias said he should be killed
By my son. That poor child, so far from killing Laius,
Perished himself. In future, then, for prophecy
Or prophets I would not turn my head this way or that.

Oedipus.   You take the right view. None the less, dispatch
   someone
To bring that shepherd here; don't let the matter slip.

Iocasta.   I'll send at once. But come now, let us go indoors;
Be sure I will do nothing but what you approve.

55

*Chorus.* May my portion still and always be to win that [prize, namely] reverent purity from all words and deeds con-
865 cerning which laws are established for us, / [laws] lofty-footed, begotten in the heavenly regions of the sky, whose father is Olympus alone, nor did any mortal nature of men engender
870 them, nor shall oblivion ever lay them to sleep; / divinity is great in them, and does not grow old.

Arrogance begets the tyrant. Arrogance, if it be surfeited to no
875 good end with many things neither proper nor profitable, / after climbing the topmost ramparts plunges to the most miserable straits, where no service of the foot can serve. But that struggle
880 which is advantageous for the city, I pray the god never to end. / The god I will not cease to hold as our defender.

But if a man walks haughtily in deed or in word, with no fear
885 of judgement, and not / reverencing statues of gods, may an evil portion destroy him, because of his ill-fated self-indulgence, if he will not gain his profit justly and keep himself from impious
890 acts, / or if he will in his folly touch things untouchable. What man in such circumstances can ever again boast that he repels from his life the arrows of the gods? For if actions of this kind are
895 held in honour, / why should I dance?

No more will I go as a worshipper to the inviolate navel of
900 the earth, nor to the temple at Abae, nor to Olympia, / if these things shall not fit so that all men point at them with the hand.

874. *to no good end.* This is the adverb *matān*, which can also mean 'in vain' or 'foolishly'. See 891 below, where the participle *matázōn* is used, 'acting foolishly'.

885. *judgement.* Or, 'justice' – the word is *dikē*. See note on 1214.

886. *statues.* The word is *hedē*, plural of *hedos*, 'seat' or 'abode'; but when used in connection with gods it seems usually to mean 'statue' rather than 'temple'.

898. *navel.* There was in the sanctuary of Delphi a stone known as the *omphalos*, or navel, supposedly marking the centre of the earth.

899. *Abae.* A wealthy temple of Apollo, about seventy miles east of Delphi.

*Oedipus and Iocasta go into the palace.*

*Chorus.* May my life's destiny still find me      (Strophe 1
  Winning the purity of a pious life;
  Keep me unsullied from all words and deeds
  Against which are established those laws of lofty range,
  Begotten in the clear regions of the sky,
  Whose father is Olympus alone;
  No mortal human nature gave these laws birth,
  Nor shall oblivion ever lay them to sleep;
  Divinity is powerful in them and never grows old.

  Arrogance begets the tyrant;      (Antistrophe 1
  Arrogance, if in its folly it be surfeited
  With improper and unprofitable possessions,
  First climbs to the topmost ramparts,
  Then plunges miserably to its helpless fate,
  Where no firm foothold is to be found.
  Yet, such emulation as benefits the city
  I pray heaven may never bring to an end.
  Heaven I shall always hold as our protector.

  But if a man treads a proud path in deed or word, (Strophe 2
  Shows no fear of Justice,
  No reverence for shrines of the gods,
  May an evil destiny destroy him
  For his perverse self-indulgence,
  If he will not gain his advantage justly,
  Nor keep himself from impious deeds,
  But in his folly will touch the untouchable.
  In such a case, who can boast any more
  Of keeping his life safe from arrows of the gods?
  If acts like these are held in honour,
  Why worship the gods with a Chorus?

  No more will I go as worshipper      (Antistrophe 2
  To the inviolate navel of the earth,
  Nor to the Abaean temple, nor to Olympia,
  If these prophecies shall not fit together
  So that all men point at them.

Therefore, O almighty (if you are rightly so called) Zeus, ruling all things, let not these things be hidden from you and your ever-

905 undying rule! / For the old prophecies of Laius are fading, and people now exclude them [from consideration], and nowhere is Apollo conspicuous by honours [paid to him]; but worship of the

910 gods is vanishing. /

*Iocasta.* Lords of Thebes, the thought has occurred to me to visit [as a suppliant] the temples of the gods, taking in my hands these garlands and incense-offerings; for Oedipus excites his spirit too high with distresses of all kinds, and does not, like a

915 rational / man, judge new things by old, but is swayed by the speaker, if he speaks of fears. So, since by admonishing him I get no further, I have come as a suppliant first to you, Lycean

920 Apollo, for you are nearest, with these prayers, / that you may find for us some purifying release. For now we are all afraid, seeing him terror-struck, as helmsman of the ship.

*Corinthian.* May I learn from you, strangers, where the

925 house of King Oedipus is? / Or better still, tell me where he himself is, if you know.

*Chorus.* This is his house, and he himself is indoors, stranger; and this lady is the mother of his children.

*Corinthian.* Then may she always be happy, and with happy

930 ones, since she is the fulfilled wife of the great Oedipus. /

*Iocasta.* May you too [be happy] in the same way, stranger; you deserve it for your kind greeting. But tell me why you have come — what request you have to make, or what news to tell.

*Corinthian.* Good news, lady, both for your house and for your husband.

*Iocasta.* What good news is this? From whom have you

935 come? /

919. *Lycean.* See note on 203.
930. *fulfilled.* I.e. by bearing children.

Therefore, Zeus Almighty, if you are truly named,
Universal King, let this not pass unnoticed
By you and your ever-immortal power.
The prophecies given long ago to Laius
Are now set aside as obsolete;
Nowhere is Apollo glorified with worship;
Religion is vanishing from sight.

*Enter Iocasta.*

*Iocasta.* Princes of our country, the thought has occurred to me
To bring garlands and incense-offerings, and pray
Before the altars of the gods. For Oedipus
Excites his spirit past reason with anxieties
Of every kind, and does not, like a rational man,
Judge new events by old; swayed by each speaker, if
He speaks of fears. So, since my advice carried no weight
With him, I have come first to you, Lycean Apollo
(For you are nearest), with these prayers; entreating you
To keep pollution from us, and bring us release.
For now we are all in terror, seeing Oedipus
Unnerved, to whom we look as helmsman of our ship.

*Enter a Corinthian Shepherd.*

*Corinthian.* Would you please tell me, gentlemen, where I
    may find
The palace of King Oedipus – or, better still,
The king himself, if you know where he is?

*Chorus.*                                        Indeed,
This is his palace, stranger, and he is at home.
This lady here is mother to the king's children.

*Corinthian.* May she be always happy in a happy home,
Since heaven has blessed her marriage with so great a king.

*Iocasta.* Happiness to you too, stranger, as your courteous
    greeting
Merits. But tell me, why have you come to Thebes? Is there
Something you seek, or have you a message to deliver?

*Corinthian.* I have good news for this house, and for your
    husband, lady.

*Iocasta.* What is your news? And who sent you?

59

*Corinthian.* From Corinth. As for the message which I will give you in a moment, you will be pleased at it – who wouldn't? but you may perhaps be upset.

*Iocasta.* What is the message? What sort of double force is this which it has?

*Corinthian.* The people of the Isthmian country are going to
940 make him king, as it was being said there. /

*Iocasta.* But what is this? Is old Polybus no longer in power?

*Corinthian.* No, indeed; for death holds him in the grave.

*Iocasta.* What do you say? Is Polybus dead, old man?

*Corinthian.* If I don't speak the truth, I am ready to die.

*Iocasta.* Servant, go as fast as you can and tell your master
945 this. / O oracles of the gods, where are you? This is the man whom Oedipus long feared and avoided, lest he should kill him. And now he has died in the course of chance, and not by Oedipus' hand.

950 *Oedipus.* O my dearest wife Iocasta, / why have you sent for me out of the house?

*Iocasta.* Listen to this man, and as you listen observe what they have come to – those solemn oracles of the god.

*Oedipus.* Who is he, and what has he to say to me?

955 *Iocasta.* He comes from Corinth, to tell us / that your father Polybus is no longer alive, but dead.

*Oedipus.* What do you say, stranger? Give me the message yourself.

*Corinthian.* If this is what I must make clear first, be assured that Polybus has gone the way of all mortals.

960 *Oedipus.* Was it by treachery, or by visitation of disease? /

*Corinthian.* A light tip of the scale lays old bodies to their rest.

*Oedipus.* By sickness, apparently, the poor old man died.

*Corinthian.* Yes, and the long length of time that he had measured.

960, 962. The form of these two sentences shows a singular absence of excitement. 962 seems to be addressed to Iocasta.

*Corinthian.*                                    I come from
    Corinth.
    The news I have to tell will cause you some pleasure,
    I think – in fact, I am sure; but some pain too, perhaps.
*Iocasta.*   What news is it that has this twofold character?
*Corinthian.*   The people of the Isthmus will make Oedipus
    Their king – so it was being said when I left home.
*Iocasta.*   Their king? Is not old Polybus, then, still in power?
*Corinthian.*   Indeed, no. Death has taken him; he is in his
    grave.
*Iocasta.*   What are you saying, old man? Polybus is dead?
*Corinthian.*   If I am not speaking the truth, then may I die.
*Iocasta* (*to an attendant*).   Here, girl! Run quickly to the king
    and tell him this.
    Oracles of the gods, what has become of you?
    This is the man Oedipus fled from all these years,
    In dread that he might kill him. Now the man has died,
    And in the natural course, not killed by Oedipus!
               *Enter Oedipus.*
*Oedipus.*   Iocasta, dearest wife, why have you sent for me?
*Iocasta.*   Listen to this man's message, and as you listen judge
    What has become now of the god's dread oracles.
*Oedipus.*   Who is this man, then? What has he to say to me?
*Iocasta.*   He has just come from Corinth; and his message is
    That Polybus your father lives no more; he is dead.
*Oedipus.*   What's this, man? Let me have the message in your
    own words.
*Corinthian.*   Well, since I had better make one thing clear at
    a time,
    I do assure you, Polybus is dead and gone.
*Oedipus.*   Was it by treachery? or did sickness take him off?
*Corinthian.*   A trifle tips the scale, to lay an old man to rest.
*Oedipus.*   I take it, then, he died from sickness. Poor old man.
*Corinthian.*   Well, yes; and he had counted a long sum of
    years.

*Oedipus.* Well, well; why indeed, my wife, should one look
965 to the hearth of the Pythian prophet, or to birds / that screech
above us, according to whose indications I was destined to kill my
father? But he is dead and lies below the earth; while here am I,
who have not touched a spear — unless to some extent he wasted
away through longing for me, and in this sense he would have
970 died through me. / But in any case, the oracles as they stand
Polybus has packed-up-and-taken to where he lies in Hades;
they are worth nothing.

*Iocasta.* So, did I not tell you this long ago?

*Oedipus.* You told me; but I was misled by my fear.

975 *Iocasta.* Then do not take any such thing to heart in future./

*Oedipus.* But surely I must fear my mother's bed?

*Iocasta.* Why, what should a mortal fear, for whom chance
reigns supreme, and who has clear foresight of nothing? At
random is the best way to live, as one can. And you — have no
980 fear in regard to marriage with your mother. / Many a man
before now, in dreams too, has gone to bed with his mother. But
the man to whom these things count for nothing bears his life
most easily.

*Oedipus.* All these bold words of yours would have been well
985 spoken, if my mother were not alive; but since / she is, it is very
necessary — however right you may be — to fear.

*Iocasta.* But the burial of your father is a great light of hope.

*Oedipus.* Great, I am aware; but there is fear of her who lives.

*Corinthian.* And what woman is it who moves you to such
fear?

990 *Oedipus.* Merope, old man, whom Polybus lived with. /

*Corinthian.* And what is it in her that you find alarming?

*Oedipus.* A god-sent prophecy — a dreadful one, stranger.

*Corinthian.* May it be told? Or is it not lawful for another to
know?

*Oedipus.* Why, certainly. Loxias once said that I was fated
995 to have intercourse with my own mother, and to / shed my
father's blood with my own hands. It is for this reason that
Corinth has been all this time kept at a distance by me; with

62

*Oedipus.*    Indeed, Iocasta, why should anyone take note
   Of the prophetic shrine of Pytho, or of birds
   That scream above us – on whose showing I was doomed
   To kill my father? Now he's dead, safe out of sight
   Below the ground; and here am I – I have not put hand
   To weapon; unless grief at my absence wore him out,
   And so his death was due to me. Those prophecies
   In their plain meaning – Polybus has packed them up,
   And there they lie with him in Hades, worth nothing.
*Iocasta.*    See now, is this not what I told you long ago?
*Oedipus.*    You did say so; but I was misled by my fears.
*Iocasta.*    Then let your mind rest free from such anxieties.
*Oedipus.*    But how can I? I must still fear my mother's bed.
*Iocasta.*    Why, what should any mortal fear? Our mortal life
   Is ruled by Chance; there's no such thing as foreknowledge.
   To live at hazard, as one can, is the best way.
   As for your mother's bed – have no fears on that score;
   Many a man has dreamt he found himself in bed
   With his mother. Once let fears like that upset you, life
   Is intolerable. Forget them.
*Oedipus.*                                   I would agree with you
   Fully, if my mother were not still living; since she is,
   Though all you have said is true, I must be on my guard.
*Iocasta.*    At least your father's death is a great comfort to us.
*Oedipus.*    It is, I know; still I must shrink from her who lives.
*Corinthian.*    But, Sir, who is this woman you both fear so
      much?
*Oedipus.*    Merope, my friend, who was wife to King Polybus.
*Corinthian.*    What is there about Merope to cause you fear?
*Oedipus.*    A dreadful oracle, of divine authority.
*Corinthian.*    May I hear it? or is it something you should not
      disclose?
*Oedipus.*    You may hear it. Apollo once told me that I
   Was destined to be married to my own mother, and with
   My own hands shed my father's blood. This is the reason
   Why all these years I have lived so far from Corinth. I've
      had

63

happy result indeed, but all the same it is very pleasant to see the face of parents.

   *Corinthian.*   Was it really in fear of this that you lived as an exile from Corinth? /

   *Oedipus.*   And because I did not wish to be my father's killer, old man.

   *Corinthian.*   Then why have I not freed you from this fear, my lord, since I came with good will?

   *Oedipus.*   Indeed you shall have a fitting reward from me.

   *Corinthian.*   Indeed my chief reason for coming was to / gain some advancement once you returned home.

   *Oedipus.*   No, I will never go near my parents.

   *Corinthian.*   My son, it's beautifully plain that you don't know what you're doing——

   *Oedipus.*   How is that, old man? In the gods' name explain to me.

   *Corinthian.*   ——if it's because of them that you avoid coming home. /

   *Oedipus.*   Of course – I am afraid of finding Phoebus prove a true prophet.

   *Corinthian.*   You mean, so as not to incur guilt through your parents?

   *Oedipus.*   It is this, old man, this very thing that always frightens me.

   *Corinthian.*   Do you indeed know that your fears are quite groundless?

   *Oedipus.*   How so, if I was their child and they my parents? /

   *Corinthian.*   Because Polybus was nothing to you in blood.

   *Oedipus.*   What did you say? It was not Polybus who begot me?

   *Corinthian.*   No more than I myself, but equally.

   *Oedipus.*   And how can he who begot me count equally with him who is nothing to me?

A good life; but to see one's parents is good too.

*Corinthian.* Fear of this marriage, then, kept you exiled from
    Corinth?

*Oedipus.* That, and the wish to avoid causing my father's
    death.

*Corinthian.* Well, then, since I came here out of good will to
    you,

My lord, why have I not released you from this fear?

*Oedipus.* Indeed, if you did that, I would reward you well.

*Corinthian.* Indeed, I had chiefly that in mind when I came
    here;

I thought your homecoming might bring some good to me.

*Oedipus.* I never will go near my parents.

*Corinthian.*                         Why, my son,

It's clear you're under some delusion——

*Oedipus.*                      What do you mean?

Explain.

*Corinthian.* ——if they are the reason why you won't come
    home.

*Oedipus.* Of course; I don't want Phoebus' oracle to prove
    true.

*Corinthian.* You don't want to incur guilt through contact
    with your parents?

*Oedipus.* That is my fear, old friend, my constant dread.

*Corinthian.*                       Do

you know

That all your fears are groundless?

*Oedipus.*                 How can they be groundless,

If I am my parents' child?

*Corinthian.*               Why, because Polybus

Was no relation to you.

*Oedipus.*             What? Polybus was not

My father?

*Corinthian.* No, no more than I am.

*Oedipus.*                 But how can

My father be no more than you, who are nothing to me?

1020     *Corinthian.*   Why, neither did Polybus beget you, nor did I./

    *Oedipus.*   Then for what reason did he name me his son?

    *Corinthian.*   You were a gift, you must know, that he once received from my hands.

    *Oedipus.*   And, in spite of receiving me from someone else, he loved me so much?

    *Corinthian.*   Yes, his former childlessness persuaded him.

    *Oedipus.*   When you gave me to him, had you bought me, or
1025   found me? /

    *Corinthian.*   Found you in the winding glens of Cithaeron.

    *Oedipus.*   For what purpose were you travelling in these regions?

    *Corinthian.*   I was there in charge of mountain flocks.

    *Oedipus.*   Oh, you were a shepherd and wandered about finding work?

1030     *Corinthian.*   And, my son, your preserver at that time. /

    *Oedipus.*   What pain had I when you took me in your arms?

    *Corinthian.*   The joints of your feet could witness.

    *Oedipus.*   Alas, why do you mention that ancient deformity?

    *Corinthian.*   It was I who freed you when you had your ankles pierced.

    *Oedipus.*   Yes, that was the bitter disgrace that I received by
1035   way of birth-tokens. /

    *Corinthian.*   With the result that you received from this chance the name which you bear now.

    *Oedipus.*   In the gods' name, [did I receive this injury] from my mother or from my father?

1023. A line hard to fit into any interpretation. Is it ironical?

1035. *birth-tokens.* There are two possible translations of this line; see Jebb's note. He takes the genitive *sparganōn* as depending on the verb *aneilomēn*, 'I received from my cradle'; and he seems to understand 'from' as referring to *time*, whereas in such a construction it could only refer to *place*. The line is better sense and better Greek if *sparganōn* is a 'defining genitive' dependent on *oneidos*, 'a disgrace of a birth-token', i.e. a birth-token which, so far from bringing me honour, brought me dishonour. See pp. 132, 221.

66

*Corinthian.*   I certainly was not your father; nor was he.

*Oedipus.*   What caused him, then, to have me known as his own son?

*Corinthian.*   I gave you to him; he received you from my hands.

*Oedipus.*   And yet he loved me, though I came to him as a gift?

*Corinthian.*   He had no child of his own; that made the difference.

*Oedipus.*   Then – had you bought me from a merchant, or just found me?

*Corinthian.*   I found you in the wooded valleys of Cithaeron.

*Oedipus.*   Cithaeron is some way from Corinth; why were you there?

*Corinthian.*   I worked there; I was looking after mountain sheep.

*Oedipus.*   You were a shepherd, wandering about in search of work?

*Corinthian.*   And I was your preserver on that day, my son.

*Oedipus.*   And what pain had I when you took me in your arms?

*Corinthian.*   Why, your own feet will provide evidence of that.

*Oedipus.*   For pity's sake, why speak of that old injury?

*Corinthian.*   I found you with your feet pierced through, and set you free.

*Oedipus.*   That mark of shame was what I got for birth-tokens!

*Corinthian.*   Yes, you are Oedipus; it was this gave you your name.

*Oedipus.*   Who did it, for God's sake? My mother, or my father?

*Corinthian.* I don't know. The man who gave [you to me] understands these things better than I.

*Oedipus.* What? You received me from someone else, you didn't find me yourself?

1040 *Corinthian.* No, another shepherd handed you over to me. /

*Oedipus.* Who was he? Do you know, so as to tell me?

*Corinthian.* He was said, I believe, to be one of Laius' men.

*Oedipus.* You mean the one who was king of this land long ago?

*Corinthian.* Yes; this man was one of his shepherds.

1045 *Oedipus.* Is this man still alive, so that I could see him? /

*Corinthian.* You men who are native here would know that best.

*Oedipus.* Is there any of you standing near, who knows the shepherd he speaks of, having seen him either in the country or

1050 here? Speak, for it is time that these things should be discovered. /

*Chorus.* I think he is no other than that man from the country whom earlier you were anxious to see; but Iocasta here could best speak of this.

*Oedipus.* Lady, you know that man whom just now we sent

1055 for to come here – is he the man this shepherd means? /

*Iocasta.* Why ask whom he spoke of? Give it no attention. Please do not waste a thought on what he said.

*Oedipus.* This is impossible, that having such clues I should not bring my birth to light.

1060 *Iocasta.* In the gods' name, if you have any care for / your own life, do not pursue this. My suffering is enough.

*Oedipus.* Take comfort; *you* will not be proved low-born, even if it be shown that my mother was a slave of the third generation – that I am three times a slave.

*Iocasta.* None the less, listen to me, I beg you; do not do this.

*Oedipus.* I will not listen, before I unravel this whole

1065 matter. /

*Corinthian.*   I don't know; the man who gave you to me
could tell more.

*Oedipus.*   You had me from someone else, then? Didn't *you*
find me
Yourself?

*Corinthian.*   No; another shepherd handed you on to me.

*Oedipus.*   And who was he? Do you know him? Can you name
the man?

*Corinthian.*   Why, yes; he was known, I think, as one of Laius'
men.

*Oedipus.*   Laius – you mean the former king of Thebes?

*Corinthian.*                                         That's right;
This man was one of his shepherds.

*Oedipus.*                              I must see him, then.
Is he still alive?

*Corinthian* (*to the Elders*).   You who live here would best
know that.

*Oedipus.*   Is there any of you standing here who knows the
shepherd
He speaks of – who has seen him in the country, or here?
If so, speak out; it's time this mystery was solved.

*Chorus.*   I think this is no other than that countryman
Whom you already wished to see. But on this matter
No doubt Iocasta here could best enlighten you.

*Oedipus.*   Iocasta, you recall this man whom we just now
Sent for to come here – is he the one this stranger means?

*Iocasta.*   Why ask what man he means? Pay him no heed,
forget
Whatever he said; it's meaningless.

*Oedipus.*                              Impossible!
With clues like these – I must and will trace out my birth.

*Iocasta.*   In the gods' name, if you have any care for your life,
Do not search further! What I suffer is enough.

*Oedipus.*   Have courage! *You* will not be found unroyal, even if
Three slave-mothers in line brand *me* three times a slave.

*Iocasta.*   Yet do not do this; I implore you, listen to me.

*Oedipus.*   I will not listen. I must discover the whole truth.

*Iocasta.* I speak out of love, I am saying what is best for you.

*Oedipus.* I have long been sick of this 'best for you'.

*Iocasta.* Unhappy man, may you never learn who you are!

*Oedipus.* Will someone go and bring me that shepherd here?

1070 Leave the queen to glory in her royal descent. /

*Iocasta.* Alas, alas, miserable man! That is the only word I can say to you, and no other word ever after this.

*Chorus.* Why has the lady gone rushing away, Oedipus, in a frenzy of distress? I fear that from this reticence troubles will

1075 break forth. /

*Oedipus.* Break forth what will! But I, even if my race be humble, will resolve to see it. She, perhaps – for she has all a woman's pride – is ashamed of my humble birth; but I, holding

1080 myself the child of Fortune, / the giver of good, will not be dishonoured. *She* is the mother from whom I was born; and the months who were born with me have marked me out [now] humble and [now] great. Being such a man by descent, henceforth I can never prove to be of another kind, so as to cease from

1085 probing the secret of my birth. /

*Chorus.* If I am a prophet and skilled in judgement, I swear by Olympus that you, Cithaeron, shall not be unaware at to-

1090 morrow's full moon / that it is you Oedipus honours as belonging to his fatherland, as his nurse, and as his mother; and [you shall know] that you are celebrated in our dance and song / as the

1095 bringer of blessing to my king. O Phoebus to whom we cry, may these things be pleasing to you!

Who then was it, son, which of the long-lived ones, who lay

1087. *in judgement.* The word is *gnōmē*, which was the quality Oedipus was famous for – see 398, 'by intelligence', *et al.*

*Iocasta.* I tell you, I speak in love, I advise you for the best.
*Oedipus.* And I tell you, your 'best' has galled me long
    enough.
*Iocasta.* Ill-fated man, may you never learn who you are!
*Oedipus.* Where is that shepherd? Go, someone, fetch him
    here at once;
  And leave the queen to glory in her princely blood.
*Iocasta.* Oh, miserable, miserable! That is the only word
  I can speak to you, and no other word ever again!
       *Iocasta rushes away into the palace.*
*Chorus.* Why has the queen gone, Oedipus, in a frenzy of wild
  Anguish? I fear that from this reticence disaster
  Will burst forth.
*Oedipus.*        Let burst forth what will! *My* will shall
    stand
  To find and face my origin, however humble.
  The queen, perhaps, with pride beyond a woman's place,
  Blushes at my mean lineage; but I hold myself
  The child of Chance, who bestows blessing, and I shall
  Not be dishonoured. Chance is my mother, I her son;
  My brother months have marked my path, once low, now
    high.
  Such being my origin, henceforth I can never prove
  Other than I am, or shrink from searching out my birth.
      *During the Ode Oedipus remains on stage.*
*Chorus.* If I am a true prophet           (Strophe
  Or have any skill in judgement,
  I swear by holy Olympus
  That you, Cithaeron, at tomorrow's full moon
  Shall know beyond doubt that it is you Oedipus honours
  As native to his father's city,
  As his nurse, and his mother;
  That it is you we worship in dance
  As bringer of blessing to our royal house.
  Phoebus, Healer, may this be pleasing to you!
  Who was it, son,           (Antistrophe
  Which of the long-lived nymphs, then, was it

1100    with mountain-roaming Pan / and bore you to him? Or did
some bedfellow of Loxias [bear you to a father worthy of you]?
For to him all the wild pastures are dear. Or did the ruler of
1105    Cyllene, or the Bacchic god / who lives on the mountain-tops,
receive you as an unexpected-find from one of the nymphs of
Helicon, with whom he most often plays?

     *Oedipus.*   If I too may guess, who have never before met
1110    him, / I think I see the shepherd whom we have long been in
search of. For in his advanced age he is comparable with this man
and tallies with him; and besides, I recognise those who bring
1115    him as servants of mine. But in knowledge you perhaps / have
the advantage of me, having seen the shepherd before.

     *Chorus.*   Yes, I know him, be sure. He was Laius' man – only
a shepherd, but as reliable as any.

     *Oedipus.*   Now, my Corinthian friend, I ask you first: is this
the man you mean?

1120    *Corinthian.*   Yes, this man whom you see. /

     *Oedipus.*   Now you, old man, look this way and answer my
questions. You were once a servant of Laius?

     *Shepherd.*   I was; not a bought slave, but one raised in his
house.

     *Oedipus.*   What sort of occupation did you follow, what kind
of life?

1125    *Shepherd.*   For most of my life I tended flocks. /

     *Oedipus.*   In what regions did you chiefly spend your time?

     *Shepherd.*   Sometimes it was Cithaeron, sometimes the neigh-
bouring country.

     1101. *to a father worthy of you.* This is an attempt to represent the
untranslatable emphasis given to the pronoun 'you', *se g'*, at the beginning of its clause.

     1113. *comparable.* Again the word *symmetros*; cf. 85.

     1118. *only a shepherd, but* . . . Literally, 'trustworthy if any other
[was], as being a shepherd'. Iocasta makes a similar estimate of the
same man in 763, literally, 'worthy . . . as being a slave'.

That lay with Pan as he roamed the mountain
And made him your father?
Or were you, Oedipus,
Son of a bride of Loxias?
For all mountain pastures are dear to him.
Or perhaps Hermes, lord of Cyllene,
Or the Bacchic god who haunts the high peaks,
Was given you, as a charming surprise,
By one of the nymphs of Helicon
With whom he often sports.

*The old Servant of Laius approaches.*

*Oedipus.*  Elders, if it is my turn to guess – though I have never
Met him before – I think I see this shepherd whom
We have long been seeking. His advanced age matches the years
Of our friend here; besides, I recognise the men
Who bring him as my own servants. But you, perhaps,
Have seen the man before, and so have surer knowledge.
*Chorus.*  Yes, certainly I know him; he was one of Laius'
Servants – only a shepherd, but most trustworthy.
*Oedipus.*  First, then – you, friend from Corinth, answer me: is this
The man you mean?
*Corinthian.*          That's him, the man you're looking at.
*Oedipus.*  Now you, old man – just turn your eyes this way and answer
My questions. Were you once a slave of Laius?
*Shepherd.*  I was – not from the market, but reared in his house.
*Oedipus.*  And what work did you do? How did you spend your time?
*Shepherd.*  I spent the best part of my life in tending sheep.
*Oedipus.*  And where? What part of the country did you most frequent?
*Shepherd.*  Sometimes Cithaeron, or other places thereabouts.

*Oedipus.* Now, this man here – are you aware of having noticed him hereabouts?

*Shepherd.* Doing what thing? What man is this you're talking of?

*Oedipus.* This man in front of you. Did you ever meet him 1130 before? /

*Shepherd.* Not so as to say quickly from memory.

*Corinthian.* And no wonder, master; but since he does not know me, I will remind him clearly. I know well that he knows [of the time] when, in the neighbourhood of Cithaeron, I was 1135 near to this man for three whole six-month seasons, / from spring to Arcturus, he with two flocks and I with one; then for the winter I would drive my sheep to the fold, and he would take his 1140 to Laius' farmstead. Is what I am saying fact, or is it not? /

*Shepherd.* What you say is true, though it's a long time ago.

*Corinthian.* Come now, tell me, you know that you gave me then a certain child, for me to bring up as my own?

*Shepherd.* What about it? Why are you asking me this question?

*Corinthian.* Here is the man, my friend, who was then that 1145 child. /

*Shepherd.* Death take you! Be silent once for all!

*Oedipus.* Here now, don't rebuke him, old man, for your words call for rebuke more than his.

*Shepherd.* Best of masters, in what do I offend?

1150 *Oedipus.* In not telling of the child he asks about. /

*Shepherd.* He speaks with no knowledge, he is taking trouble for nothing.

*Oedipus.* Though you won't speak willingly, you will speak when you are hurt.

*Shepherd.* For the gods' sake – I'm an old man – don't ill-treat me.

---

1137. *Arcturus.* I.e. September.
1146. *Death take you.* The immediacy of the shepherd's reaction compared with, for example, the slowness of 1000–15, confirms the clear implication of 758–62; see p. 187.

74

*Oedipus.*   This man here – do you remember seeing him in
   those parts?

*Shepherd.*   What would he be doing? What man do you mean?

*Oedipus.*                                        This man
   In front of you. Do you remember ever meeting him?

*Shepherd.*   Not so as to tell you all at once – I can't recall.

*Corinthian.*   And that's no wonder, master. But if he doesn't
   know me
   I'll jog his memory. I'm sure he remembers well
   The times we were next neighbours on Cithaeron there,
   Three full half-years, from spring to autumn; he had two
   Flocks, I had one; and in the winter I'd drive mine
   Back to the home farm, he'd take his to Laius' folds.
   Now, is there any truth in what I've said, or not?

*Shepherd.*   Why, yes, that's true enough; though it's a long
   way back.

*Corinthian.*   Then tell me, do you remember one day giving
   me
   A baby boy, for me to bring up as my own?

*Shepherd.*   What of it? What are you after? Why bring that
   up now?

*Corinthian.*   Why, here he is, my friend! This was your baby
   boy.

   *Shepherd.*   Plague take you! Can't you keep your mouth
   shut?

*Oedipus.*   Come now, don't
   Blame *him*, old man. Your words deserve more blame than
   his.

*Shepherd.*   But, noble master, tell me what I have done wrong.

*Oedipus.*   You're unwilling to speak of this child he asks about.

*Shepherd.*   He doesn't know what he's saying; all this is
   meaningless.

*Oedipus.*   If you won't speak to help *me*, you'll speak to save
   your skin.

*Shepherd.*   No, don't, Sir – for the gods' sake, don't hurt an
   old man!

*Oedipus.*  Quick, someone, twist his arms back.

1155  *Shepherd.*  Alas, for what? What more do you want to know? /

*Oedipus.*  You gave this man that child he's asking about?

*Shepherd.*  I did. I wish I had died that day.

*Oedipus.*  You will come to that if you don't give me a straight answer.

*Shepherd.*  And if I speak, I am undone much more.

1160  *Oedipus.*  This man apparently is bent on delays. /

*Shepherd.*  No, no; I said before that I gave it to him.

*Oedipus.*  Where did you get it from? Was it your own, or did you get it from someone else?

*Shepherd.*  It was not mine; I had received it from someone.

*Oedipus.*  From which of these citizens? From what house?

*Shepherd.*  Don't, for the gods' sake, master, don't ask any

1165  more. /

*Oedipus.*  You die if I have to ask you this again.

*Shepherd.*  Then – it was a child of the household of Laius.

*Oedipus.*  A slave? Or a legitimate son of his?

*Shepherd.*  Alas, I am on the dreadful brink of speaking.

1170  *Oedipus.*  And I of hearing; none the less I must hear. /

*Shepherd.*  Indeed, then, the child was said to be Laius'; but your wife indoors could best tell the truth of the matter.

*Oedipus.*  What? Did my wife give it to you?

*Shepherd.*  Yes, my lord.

*Oedipus.*  For what purpose?

*Shepherd.*  That I should destroy it.

*Oedipus.*  She, its mother, had the heart?

1175  *Shepherd.*  She was afraid of evil oracles. /

1173. There is no need to take this line ('Did my wife give it to you?' – 'Yes, my lord') as contradicting Iocasta's statement in 718–19; to mention at this point the long-forgotten Laius would make the whole narative remote, whereas Iocasta was present a few minutes ago. The discrepancy is of no importance, except as an illustration of the dramatist's unerring technique.

*Oedipus.* One of you, quick there – twist his arms behind his
 back.

*Shepherd.* For pity's sake, what for? What else do you want to
 know?

*Oedipus.* Did you give him this child he's asking you about?

*Shepherd.* I did – and how I wish I had died that very day!

*Oedipus.* You'll come to that now, if you won't speak the
 plain truth.

*Shepherd.* And if I speak, it's death no less – and even worse.

*Oedipus.* This man evidently is bent on more delays.

*Shepherd.* No, no! I told you already I gave him the child.

*Oedipus.* Where did you get it? Was it yours, or another
 man's?

*Shepherd.* It wasn't my child; I had it from someone else.

*Oedipus.* From whom, then? From some Theban citizen?
 From what house?

*Shepherd.* Don't master, don't, in God's name, ask me any
 more!

*Oedipus.* You are a dead man, if I have to ask you again.

*Shepherd.* Well, then, it was a child born in King Laius'
 house.

*Oedipus.* Was it a slave, or child of the blood royal?

*Shepherd.*              Alas!
I am on the very brink of horror, and I must speak.

*Oedipus.* I am there too, for hearing; and yet I must hear.

*Shepherd.* Laius' own child it was said to be; the queen,
Your wife, could best inform you of the exact truth.

*Oedipus.* The queen – why, did *she* give it you?

*Shepherd.*            She did, my
 lord.

*Oedipus.* And for what purpose?

*Shepherd.*          I was to destroy the child.

*Oedipus.* And she, its mother, had the heart to——

*Shepherd.*            Yes, in
 fear
Of a dreadful prophecy.

*Oedipus.* What oracles?

*Shepherd.* It was said that the child would kill its father.

*Oedipus.* Then how came you to give the child up to this old man?

*Shepherd.* I was sorry for it, master, and I thought he would take it away to another country, where he came from; but he
1180 saved it for the most dreadful destiny. For if you are the man / he says you are, know that you were born to misery.

*Oedipus.* Alas, alas! All fulfilled, all true! O light, let me now look on you for the last time, I who have been revealed as born from whom I ought not [to have been born], associating with
1185 whom I ought not, and having killed whom I should not. /

*Chorus.* O generations of men, how I number you as living
1190 a life equal to nothing. For who, who wins more of happiness / than so much as to seem, and having seemed, to decline away? Indeed, having as an example this your, this your fate, yours, O
1195 unhappy Oedipus, I call happy / nothing of mortal creatures.

For he, having aimed his bow superlatively, achieved a prosperity happy in all respects, O Zeus, having destroyed the crook-
1200 clawed maiden-enchantress, and rose up / as a defence for my country against deaths; and from that time you are called my

1183. *O light . . . last time.* The Elders would naturally take this as expressing an intention to kill himself.

1193–4. *this your, this your . . .* The threefold repetition of *ton son* is not easy to relate to any emphasis natural in English.

78

*Oedipus.*          What prophecy?

*Shepherd.*                 It was said
   The child would kill its father.

*Oedipus.*          Why then did you hand
   The child over to this old man?

*Shepherd.*         I was soft-hearted,
   Master. I thought he'd take it far away to the place
   He came from; but he saved its life, for the worst fate
   Of all. If you are truly the man he says you are,
   I tell you, you were born to live under a curse.

*Oedipus.*    All true, all plain, fulfilled to the last word! O light
   Of day, now let me look on you for the last time!
   I am exposed – a blasphemy in being born,
   Guilty in her I married, cursed in him I killed!

           *Exit Oedipus to the palace.*

*Chorus.*    O men who live to perish,        (Strophe 1
   You dying generations!
   I count your sum of living,
   And the total equals nothing.
   For who – for what man ever
   Wins more of happiness than
   So much as builds illusion,
   Till illusion falls to pieces?
   Your life displays the pattern,
   Yours, yours I take for token,
   Oedipus, man of terror;
   Your fate I see – and nothing
   Mortal can I call happy.

   Oedipus, aiming his arrow        (Antistrophe 1
   With superb mastery, achieved
   All fame, joy and prosperity –
   Be witness, Zeus! – by defeating
   The hook-clawed maiden-enchantress;
   Rising as a tower of defence
   He delivered Thebes from the toll of deaths;
   And from that time, Oedipus,
   You have been named our king

king, and you were given the highest honour, ruling in great
Thebes.

But now, whose story is more miserable to hear? Who [is more
miserable] as living amid sufferings, / now that his life is reversed? O famous Oedipus, for whom the same large harbour
sufficed as child, and as father when you fell thereon a bride-
groom / – how ever could your father's furrows, unhappy man,
how ever could they bear you in silence for so long?

Time that sees all things has found you out, though-this-was-
not-your-intention. [Time] judges the marriage which-is-no-
marriage, which for so long has been both begetting and begotten. / Ah, child of Laius, if only – if only I had never seen
you! For I mourn as one who pours from his lips a dirge-for-the-
dead. To speak truly, / because of you I both received new life
and have [now] laid my eyes to sleep.

*Messenger.* O men always most highly honoured of this
land, what deeds you shall hear of, what sights you shall see, and
what sorrow you shall take upon you, if as true-born Thebans you
still / care for the house of Labdacus! For I think that neither
Ister nor Phasis could wash this house clean, so many things it
hides, while other disasters will soon come out into the light,

1214. *judges. dikazei* here perhaps recalls 885, *dikās aphobētos*, 'with
no fear of judgement'.

1221–2. This recalls the Priest's words in 49–50.

1223. *always most highly honoured.* These words show the speaker,
in despair, looking for something permanent in Thebes.

1228. *clean.* Literally, 'with purification', the word used in 99.

And held in supreme honour,
Ruling in Thebes the renowned.
But now, what man is more pitiable       (Strophe 2
For the pathos of his story,
For the cruel demon that pursued him,
For the pain that shares his home,
For his whole life overturned?
Alas, far-famed Oedipus!
The same ample harbour
Gave room to your resting childhood,
Bore the weight of your creating manhood.
How could it be, how was it possible
That the furrow your own father ploughed
Endured so long in silence
You, its miserable burden?
Time, that sees everything,       (Antistrophe 2
Has discovered you unaware;
Brings to judgement the nameless, truthless marriage
Which for so long has been
At once begetting and begotten.
Alas, son of Laius! If only,
If only I had never seen you!
I mourn as a man whose lips
Pour out a dirge for the departed.
This is the strange truth:
From you once I received new life;
Through you my eyes now close in death.

*Enter from the palace a Messenger.*

*Messenger.* Elders, whose honour stands unshaken still in
    Thebes,
What doings you shall hear of, what sights you will see,
What grief shall load your hearts, if like true men you still
Have care and feeling for the house of Labdacus!
Surely not all the water of Ister nor of Phasis
Could wash this house clean from the horrors it conceals,
The horrors it will soon expose to light, things done

1230    deeds performed deliberately, not involuntarily. Of all griefs, / those which are revealed as self-chosen hurt most.

      *Chorus.*   Indeed, those that we knew before do not fall short of calling for grievous lamentation; what do you say in addition to them?

      *Messenger.*   Of what I have to tell, this is the soonest said and
1235    heard: our royal lady Iocasta is dead. /

      *Chorus.*   O unhappy woman! From what cause could it be?

      *Messenger.*   By her own hand. Of the things that have been done, the most painful are not for you, for you cannot see them. All the same, so far as my own memory serves, you shall learn
1240    the sad end of that unhappy woman. /

      When, in a state of frenzy, she had gone inside the palace porch, she rushed straight to her marriage-bed, tearing her hair with the fingers of both hands. After entering she slammed the
1245    doors to, and there she called on Laius, long since a corpse, / calling to mind that son long ago begotten, by whom Laius had been killed, leaving the mother to an infamous breeding of children from the son of his own body. And she mourned over the bed where, wretched woman, she had borne a double off-
1250    spring, a husband by her husband, children by her child. /

      And how, after this, she died I do not know; for with a roar Oedipus burst in, and made it impossible to watch her agony to the end; but our eyes were on him as he rushed around. For he
1255    was going to and fro asking us to give him a sword, / asking where he should find the wife who was no wife, but the maternal soil where both he and his children had been sown. And as he raged about, some god showed him; for it was none of us men who stood
1260    near. With a terrible cry, as if someone were guiding him, / he leapt at the double doors; and from their sockets he forced the bending bolts, and stumbled into the room.

     1257. *where he should find.* The verb used here for 'find', *kinchano*, is one very often used in the sense of a weapon finding its mark, i.e. in the sense of 'conquer' or 'kill'.

With purpose, not unwitting. Of all miseries
Those that we see were our own choice torture us most.
*Chorus.*   Indeed, what we already knew fell nothing short
In tears and anguish. What more have you now to tell?
*Messenger.*   Of all I have to say, this is the soonest told,
For teller and hearer: Queen Iocasta is no more.
*Chorus.*   O doomed, unhappy woman! But what caused her
death?
*Messenger.*   She died by her own hand. Of all this, the worst
pain
Is spared you, for the sight of it cannot be yours.
Yet, in so far as my poor memory may serve,
You shall learn all the agony of her last hour.
When she had entered, wild with passion, through the
porch,
She flew straight to her marriage-chamber, her hair
clutched
In the fingers of both hands; went in, and slammed the
doors
After her, and there called on Laius, long since dead,
With memory of that seed sown in old days, the son
Under whose hand he died, and left his son's mother
To be a tainted breeder of offspring to his own.
And she bewailed the bed where she had borne sorrows
Twofold, husband from husband, children from her child.
What happened next, or how she perished, I do not know;
For with a clamour Oedipus burst in – a sight
To drag our eyes away from the queen's last despair,
And fix them on him, as he went this way and that,
Coming up to us, begging us to give him a sword,
Asking where he should find the wife who was no wife,
But the twice-fertile soil from which both he and his
Had sprung. And in his frenzy some invisible power
Guided him; it was none of us men standing by.
Then with a terrifying shout, as if someone
Were leading him, he hurled his weight at the twin doors,
Bending the bolts, forcing them from their sockets, and

There we saw the woman hanging, twisted fast in a swinging woven cord. When he saw her, the unhappy man gave a terrible
1265 roar, / and undid the noose by which she hung. And when the poor woman was lying on the ground, what happened next was terrible to see. For he pulled from her dress the golden brooches with which she was equipped, and lifted them up, and struck his
1270 own eyeballs, / saying things such as this, that they should not behold either that wickedness he suffered or what he performed, but that in darkness thenceforth they should see those they had no right to see, since they had failed to recognise those whom he longed for. Chanting words like these, not once but many times
1275 / raising [his hand] he violently struck at his eyes; and at each blow the eyeballs wetted his beard, and sent forth, not oozing drops of gore, but all at once a dark shower of bloody hail flowed.

Thus from the two of them evils have burst forth not upon one
1280 alone, / but mingled [disaster] for man and wife. Their old-established prosperity was once truly called prosperity; but now today, groaning, ruin, death, shame, whatever names there are
1285 of all evils – not one is missing. /

*Chorus.* And is the unhappy man now in some respite from anguish?

*Messenger.* He is shouting for someone to unbar the doors and show to all the Cadmeans his father's killer, his mother's – uttering unholy words that I dare not speak, as though resolved
1290 to cast himself out of the land and remain / no longer to curse the house with the curse which he uttered. However, he lacks strength and someone to lead him; for his suffering is more than can be borne. And he will show this to you too: look, the barred
1295 doors are opening, and you shall soon see a sight / such as you must pity, though you abhor it.

*Chorus.* O suffering dreadful for men to see, O most dreadful

---

1280. *have burst forth.* The same verb as in 1076.

Stumbled into the room; and then we saw her there,
Hanging, her neck noosed in a swinging cord. And he,
Seeing her, gave a terrible, heart-rending roar,
And loosed the rope she hung by. And as her poor body
Lay on the ground, then came a fearful spectacle.
He tore off the gold brooches that adorned her dress,
And lifted them, and struck straight into his own eyes,
Shouting that they should never more behold what crimes
He suffered and committed. 'Long enough,' he cried,
'You have looked on those you never should have seen, been
    blind
To those I yearned for sight of; henceforth, then, be dark!'
Uttering this dreadful chant, with upraised hand, not once
But many times he stabbed his eyes; and with each stab
His bleeding eyeballs drenched his beard, not with slow drops
Of gore, but one dark flood poured down like crimson hail.
    Thus, from the deeds of both, these horrors have burst
      forth,
Joining in one calamity man and wife together.
The happiness of their ancestral house was once
Truly called happiness; now in one day have come
Groaning, disaster, death and shame. Of all the ills
That can be named, not one is missing; all are here.
*Chorus.*   Is there now some abatement in his sufferings?
*Messenger.*   He shouts for someone to unbar the doors and
    show
To all Cadmeans his father's murderer, his mother's –
I dare not speak his profane word; he is resolved
To cast himself out of this land, and stay no longer
Making the house curse-ridden with the curse he spoke.
Yet he lacks strength, and one to guide him; for his pain
Is more than man can bear. You too shall see this – look,
The doors are opening. He will show you such a sight
That, though you shrink aghast, yet you will pity him.
        *Enter Oedipus blinded.*
*Chorus.*   What a dreadful vision of suffering
For men to witness! The most dreadful

of all that I have yet met with! What madness came over you,
1300 wretched man? What supernatural power leapt / upon your ill-
fated life with a leap beyond the longest? Alas, alas, unhappy
man! I cannot even look at you, though I wish to ask many
1305 questions, to find out many things, to gaze and gaze again; / such
suffering do you cause me.

*Oedipus.* Alas, alas, unhappy that I am! To what place of
earth am I borne in my misery? Where is my voice scattered aloft
1310 on the air? / O my destiny, to what a point you have leapt!

*Chorus.* To a point of terror, unfit either for hearing or for
seeing.

*Oedipus.* O my cloud of darkness, repellent, coming upon me
1315 unspeakable, invincible, fatally favourable! / Alas! Alas yet
again! How forcibly the sting of these goads has entered into me,
together with the memory of my misfortunes!

*Chorus.* Indeed it is no wonder that amid so many griefs you
1320 have twofold sufferings to lament, twofold to endure. /

*Oedipus.* Ah, friend! you are still my steadfast attendant; you
are still patient in caring for the blind man. Alas, alas! You are
not unknown to me, but although I am in darkness none the less
1325 I recognise you clearly / by your voice.

*Chorus.* O you who have done terrible things, how could you
bear to quench your eyes in this way? Which of the gods urged
you?

*Oedipus.* It was Apollo, friends, Apollo who brought about
1330 these evil, evil things that have happened to me. / But the one

1329. *It was Apollo* . . . What does Oedipus mean here? (1) He may
mean, 'Apollo, by foretelling my actions, compelled them' – see p. 150;
or (2) he may mean 'Apollo has brought my hidden crimes to light' –
see pp. 112–13; or (3) he may not mean what he says at all, but be
primarily concerned to conceal the truth of his own complete knowledge,
and therefore to give to the Elders' question the answer they would
expect – see p. 243.

Of all that I ever met with.
O wretched man, what madness
Came on you? What unearthly power,
With a range outreaching the farthest,
Leapt to destroy your ill-starred life?
Alas, miserable Oedipus!
I cannot even look at you,
Though there is much that I want to ask,
Much to know, much to gaze at;
You fill me with such shuddering!

*Oedipus.*   O agony, O misery, O cruelty!
Where are my pitiable steps taking me?
Where does my voice float on the winged air?
O my destiny, what a leap you have made!

*Chorus.*   A leap into terror too fierce
For hearing or for sight.

*Oedipus.*   O my dark, my enfolding horror,
Advancing on me indescribable,
Invincible, set fair for abomination!
O pain, pain, pain, pain!
How I am pierced at once
With the maddening stab of these daggers
And with memories intolerable!

*Chorus.*   No wonder, that amidst these countless griefs your
part
Is twofold lamentation, twofold suffering.

*Oedipus.*   O my friend, my unfailing helper,
You still are with me, still you patiently
Care for me in my blindness. Oh, for pity!
No, I am not deceived; darkened though I may be,
Still I can clearly recognise your voice.

*Chorus.*   What harsh resolve so drove you that you could
destroy
Your own sight? What was this demonic ecstasy?

*Oedipus.*   It was Apollo, friends, it was Apollo
Who brought to fulfilment
These fearful, fearful sufferings of mine;

who struck my eyes with his own hand was no other but my wretched self. What need had I to see, to whom seeing could
1335    show nothing lovely? /

    *Chorus.*    The case was just as you say yourself.

    *Oedipus.*    What indeed is there any more that I could look at, or love? What greeting can I hear with pleasure, friends? Take me
1340    away from here as quickly as possible, / take me away, friends, a
1345    man utterly destroyed, utterly accursed, and of all mortals / the most hateful to the gods.

    *Chorus.*    Miserable equally in your resolve and in your misfortune, how I wish that I had never even known you!

    *Oedipus.*    May the man perish, whoever he was, who freed me in the pasture from the cruel fetter on my feet and rescued
1350    me / from death, and preserved my life, doing me a thankless service! For then I would have died, and would not have been so
1355    great a grief to my friends or to myself. /

    *Chorus.*    That would have agreed with my wishes too.

    *Oedipus.*    Then I would not have come [to Thebes] my father's killer, nor been known among men as the husband of her from whom I was born. But as it is I am god-forsaken, the son of
1360    a defiled mother, / and a partner-in-begetting of the man from whom my wretched life began; and if there be still one evil surpassing another evil, / this Oedipus has received-as-his-portion.
1365

    *Chorus.*    I do not know how I can say that you have made a right decision; for you would be better dead than living and blind.

    *Oedipus.*    Do not try to explain to me that what I have done

---

1331. *with his own hand.* The word *autocheir* is nominative, in agreement with *outis*, 'no one'. Here it must mean 'the one who *with his own hand* struck my eyes'; and *nin*, 'them', must mean 'my eyes', in answer to the Chorus's question. But the word *autocheir* was used twice earlier in the play (231, 266), in Oedipus' proclamation, meaning 'the actual killer'.

1358. *I would not have come* [*to Thebes*]. See Jebb's note, which establishes a few clear instances where a verb usually meaning 'come' is used for 'come to be', (e.g. 'become' 1519). There is no reason why *ēlthon* should bear that meaning here; its more usual, simple meaning is also the more forceful.

But the self hand that struck
Was no other than my own miserable hand.
What right had I to see,
When no sight could bring me pleasure in seeing?
*Chorus.*   This was so; you have spoken the plain truth.
*Oedipus.*   Indeed I have. What is there now
I could enjoy seeing, or loving?
What kind greeting now can warm my heart?
Take me away – at once, quickly!
Take me away, friends, out of sight and hearing!
I am utterly destroyed,
Of all men the most accursed,
The most hateful even to the gods.
*Chorus.*   Pitiable equally for your understanding as
For what you suffer, I wish I had never even known you.
*Oedipus.*   Death take that man, whoever he was,
Who found me abandoned, and freed me
From the cruel fetters on my feet,
Saved me from death, restored me to life;
It was no kindness that he did me!
If I had died then,
I would not have been so heavy a grief
Either to my friends or to myself.
*Chorus.*   I too wish that it had been so.
*Oedipus.*   Then I would not have come here
Stained with my father's blood,
Nor have been called the husband
Of the woman from whom I was born.
Now I am cast off by gods,
Son of a polluted mother, successor
To his bed from whom my wretched life began.
If there is any horror deeper than other horrors,
This Oedipus has inherited.
*Chorus.*   To say you chose a wise course is impossible;
Better that you were with the dead than living and blind.
*Oedipus.*   Read me no reasons now to show that what I did

was not the best thing to do, and do not give me any more

1370 advice. / For I do not know with what eyes, if I had sight, I could ever have looked upon my father, when I came to the house of Hades, nor yet my unhappy mother, against both of whom crimes have been committed by me greater than strangling

1375 [could punish]. Or will you say that the sight of children, born / as they were born, was lovely for me to look at? Never, indeed, to my eyes; no, nor was this town, nor its towered walls, nor the sacred statues of the gods; of which things I, utterly wretched,

1380 the noblest man native to Thebes, / have deprived myself, when I myself commanded that all should repel the impious one, the man revealed by the gods as unholy – and of the race of Laius! After I had disclosed such a stain upon myself, was I going to

1385 look with straight eyes upon these men? / Certainly not; indeed, had it been possible further to stop up the fount of hearing through the ears, I would not have refrained from shutting off my miserable body, so that I should be both blind and hearing nothing; since it seems desirable that our thought should live out

1390 of reach of suffering. /

Ah, Cithaeron, why did you give me shelter? Why did you not take and kill me at once, so that I should never have shown to men whence I was born? O Polybus, and Corinth, and the ancient

1395 home that I called my ancestors', what beauty / festering with hideousness was I, when you fostered me! Yes, now I am found to be evil and of evil origin.

O you three paths, and hidden glen, little wood, and narrow pass where three roads meet, which drank my blood, my father's

1400 blood, from my own hands, / do you at all remember me, what things I did in your sight, and what further things I went on to do, when I came here?

O marriage, marriage, you engendered me, and having brought

1369. The change from lyric to iambic metre may well mark the point where Oedipus, having hitherto assumed sympathy in the Elders, realises his error from their last remark, 1368.

1371. *with what eyes.* Cf. 528, 1385.

1403. *marriage, marriage.* The word *gamoi* has the widest possible range embracing the formal, legal, personal and physical aspects of the sex-relationship. Here it seems to mean, very generally, the 'ritual of sex'.

Was not the best to do; give me no more advice.
When I come to the land of death – if I could see,
I do not know with what eyes I should face my father
Or my unhappy mother, since against them both
I am guilty of sins too black for strangling to atone.
Or could you think my children were a sight my eyes
Must long to look at – born as they were born? Never!
Not to these eyes of mine! No, nor the town of Thebes,
Her towered walls, nor her sacred images of gods;
Since I, the crown of misery – I, the noblest man
Of true-born Thebans – have pronounced my banishment,
Commanded all to expel the impious man, whom heaven
Has shown unclean, born of the blood of Laius.
This was the stain which my own evidence revealed
Upon me: how could I look my people in the face?
Never! Had it been possible, I would not have spared
To stop the source of hearing too, to immure my wretched
Body alike from sight and sound; then thought at least
Could live exempt from misery – that is some comfort.
Alas, Cithaeron! Why did you give me shelter? Why
Not kill me as soon as you received me, so that I
Might never have shown to men the source whence I was
    born?
O Polybus! O Corinth, once – in name – my old
Ancestral home! Who was in truth that handsome child
You reared and fostered, festering with filthiness?
I am revealed, myself foul, born of one defiled.
O you three roads, and overshadowed glen, and copse
Where the path narrows by the cross-ways, you who drank
My blood, my father's blood, shed by my hands! Do you
Perchance recall what act of mine you witnessed then,
And what I did thereafter when I came to Thebes?
   O marriage, marriage! You begot me; and having given

1405 me forth, again you produced seed from my same self, and
displayed / fathers, brothers, sons, an incestuous kinship, brides,
wives and mothers, all the most shameful deeds that are done
among mankind. But, since it is wrong to voice what is wrong to
do, hide me away, in the gods' name, as soon as possible some-
1410 where / outside [the city], or kill me, or throw me into the sea,
where you shall never look on me again. Come, deign to touch a
miserable man. Do what I ask, don't be afraid; for my evils no
1415 mortal man except myself is able to bear. /

*Chorus.* Well, for your requests, here is Creon, in good time
to act or give advice, since he alone is left in your place as guardian of the land.

*Oedipus.* Alas, what word indeed shall I say to Creon? What
1420 just claim-to-a-hearing can be shown for me? for / in the past I
have been found altogether wicked to him.

*Creon.* Not as a mocker, Oedipus, have I come, nor to reproach you with any past fault. – But if you [*plural*] no longer
respect the race of mortals, at least reverence the all-nurturing
1425 flame / of our lord the sun, and do not thus display such pollution
uncovered, such that neither earth nor holy rain nor light will
receive. Take him as quickly as possible into the house; only
1430 those in the family should see / and hear the family's troubles –
that is the most pious course.

*Oedipus.* For the gods' sake, since you have plucked me away
from my expectation, coming with so noble a heart to me, a man
most wicked – do something that I ask; for I will speak in your
interest, not my own.

*Creon.* And what is the need for which you thus importune
1435 me? /

*Oedipus.* Cast me as soon as possible out of this land, to a
place where no mortal shall greet me on sight.

*Creon.* Be sure I would have done this, but that I wished
first to learn exactly from the god what ought to be done.

1440 *Oedipus.* But the god's injunction was made plain in full, / to
destroy the father-killer, the impious man, me.

1424. *But if you* . . . See Note at end of Chapter 7, p. 245.

92

Me life, in turn raised the self-seed of your own sowing,
Displayed to view a blood-kinship of fathers, sons,
Brothers, brides, wives and mothers – every shape of shame
That flesh knows! – No more; evil acts make evil speech.
Therefore, in God's name, lose no time. Get rid of me,
Cover me, kill me, throw me into the sea, where you
May never more set eyes on me! Come, do not shrink,
Wretched though I am, from touching me. Do what I ask,
Touch me! What should you fear? The evil that is mine
No living soul can bear the weight of, but myself.

*Enter Creon.*

*Chorus.*   Well, in good time to deal with your requests, either
   By act or counsel, here is Creon; he alone
   Is left to take your place as guardian of this land.
*Oedipus.*   Alas! What can I say to Creon? What indeed?
   What will convince him of my good faith? In the past,
   As is too clear now, I betrayed and slandered him.
*Creon.*   I have come, Oedipus, neither to exult over you
   Nor utter any reproach for faults that are now past.
   – You Elders, even if you no longer respect the race
   Of men, at least show reverence for the all-nurturing
   Flame of the Sun-god; do not thus nakedly display
   Pollution such as neither earth, nor holy rain,
   Nor light of day can welcome. (*To Attendants*) Quickly, take
      him in.
   It is only for kinsmen to witness and to hear
   A kinsman's miseries; thus much piety demands.
*Oedipus.*   In the gods' name, since you have plucked me back
      from fear,
   Bringing a heart so noble to front my wickedness,
   Grant me one thing; I ask for your sake, not my own.
*Creon.*   What is it you so earnestly beg me to grant?
*Oedipus.*   Expel me from this land with all possible speed, to
      where
   I never shall be greeted by a human voice.
*Creon.*   Be sure I would have done this, but that I wished first
   To have the god's instruction what is best to do.
*Oedipus.*   But surely Apollo's ruling was set forth in full.
   As parricide, as polluted, I must be destroyed.

*Creon.* Such was the message; all the same, in our present predicament, it is better to learn exactly what is to be done.

*Oedipus.* Then you will seek an answer on behalf of a man so wretched as I am?

*Creon.* Yes; for even you will now, no doubt, render belief

1445 to the god. /

*Oedipus.* Yes, and on you I lay this duty, and I beg of you: for her who is in the house perform such burial as you yourself wish; she is your [sister], and you will fulfil what is right for her. But as for me – never let this my father's city be condemned to

1450 have me as an inhabitant during my lifetime, / but let me live in the mountains, where this Cithaeron is named as mine, the place which my mother and my father, while they lived, appointed as my proper tomb; so that I may receive my death from them, who wanted to destroy me.

1455 And yet I know this much, that neither sickness / nor any other thing can ever destroy me. For I would never have been saved when I was dying, except for some terrible evil.

However, let my own destiny go whither it will go. But for my children – do not trouble yourself, Creon, about my sons; being

1460 men they will never / lack the means of life, wherever they are. But my two unhappy, pitiable girls – the table at which I fed never stood separate from them, they were never without me,

1465 but always shared everything that I touched; / look after them for me; and above all allow me to touch them with my hands and to weep for my sorrow to the full. Come, my lord; come, you who are noble by birth. If I touched them with my hands I could

1470 think I still had them, as when I had sight. / What am I saying? Why, by the gods, surely I hear my two dear ones crying? Creon has taken pity on me and sent me these dearest of children. Am I

1475 right? /

1446. *Yes, and on you* . . . 'Yes' here represents the particle *ge*, which carries a less emphatic assent than 'yes' usually implies.

1466. *above all.* The word *malista* as used here means 'this is the request I would wish granted if possible' – implying 'if you will not grant it, I have a lesser alternative to ask'.

*Creon.*　Those were his words; yet in this grave predicament
　It is better to inquire exactly what we should do.
*Oedipus.*　You will consult the god about – this miserable man?
*Creon.*　Yes; this time, surely, you too will respect his word.
*Oedipus.*　I will. And from you, Creon, I claim this – I beg
　this:
　She who is indoors – let her burial be your concern.
　You will ensure due rites are paid; she is your own.
　As for me – this place is my father's city: never
　Let Thebes be punished with my presence while I live!
　Let my home be the mountains, where Cithaeron's name
　And mine are linked for ever – the place my mother and
　My father, while they lived, appointed as my grave;
　So that on their injunction I may die, since they
　Were set to kill me. – And yet I know this: neither can
　Sickness nor any other thing destroy me. Never
　Would I have been saved from death, but in reserve for some
　Appalling fate. Enough; let my own destiny
　Lead where it will; but for my children – do not, Creon,
　Take on yourself anxiety for my sons; they are men,
　And will not want for a living, wherever they may be.
　But the two girls, my poor, unhappy daughters, who
　Took never a meal but at my table, shared with me
　Everything that I tasted – Creon, care for them.
　And – this above all – let me touch them with my hands
　And ease my heart in weeping . . . Come, O King!
　Come, true and noble heart! If I could touch them once,
　I should feel that they were with me, as when I had sight.

*Attendants lead in Antigone and Ismene.*

　What am I saying? . . . O you gods!
　My two dear children – yes, I hear them! And they weep!
　Creon has taken pity and has brought them here –
　My darling daughters! . . . Am I not right?

*Creon.*   You are. It was I who provided this, knowing this present joy, which possessed you in the past.

*Oedipus.*   Oh, may you be fortunate! and in return for your sending them, may heaven prove to you a kinder guardian than
1480  it has to me! – Children, where are you? Come here, come / to these hands of mine – your brother's hands, which have performed this service, that the once bright eyes of your begetting father should see thus. For I, children, neither seeing anything nor making any inquiry, became your father by her from whom
1485  I was begotten. / I weep for you too (for I have no power to see you) when I think of the bitterness of life that remains for you, which people will make you both undergo. What gatherings of
1490  citizens will you go to, what festival, from which you will not / return home weeping, instead of seeing the show? When you come to the age for marriage, who shall be the man – who will risk taking upon himself such reproaches as will be ruinous to my
1495  offspring and equally to yours? / For what evil thing is wanting? Your father killed his father, begot children of the mother of whom he himself was begotten, and begot you from the same source whence he himself was born. Thus you will be reproached;
1500  and then who will marry you? / There is not a man, my children; but it is clear that you must waste away barren and unmarried.

O son of Menoeceus, listen – since you are left as the only father to these two, for we their parents are both destroyed: do
1505  not stand-by-and-see / your kinswomen wandering as beggars and unmarried, nor make them level with my miseries; but pity them, when you see them, so young, thus destitute of everything except the help you may give them. Signify your consent, noble
1510  man, by touching me with your hand. /

1483. *have performed this service.* The verb used here is *proxenein,* which means 'to perform services on behalf of a stranger'. Cf. 452 and other references to Oedipus as a 'stranger'.

1484. *nor making any inquiry.* The verb *historein* regularly means 'inquire', occasionally 'know'. Jebb's note is strangely obtuse.

1497–9. In these three lines three words are used for 'to beget': *aroun,* literally 'to plough', *speirein,* literally 'to scatter seed', and *ktasthai,* 'to acquire, get'.

*Creon.*  You are. They come by my provision; for I knew
The joy you always found in them, as you do now.
*Oepidus.*  Ah, blessings on you, Creon! For this kind act may
heaven
Be to you a kinder guardian than it has to me!
O children, where – where are you? Come here, come to me,
Come to these arms, your brother's arms, and still my arms!
Come, touch these hands whose friendly offices have caused
Your father's once bright eyes to look so darkly forth.
For I saw nothing, asked no question then, when I
Fathered you from the field where I myself was sown.
My eyes weep for you (though they cannot rest on you)
When I think what awaits you, how you will be made
To feel the bitterness of your life. What gatherings,
What Theban festivals will you attend, from which
You will not come home in tears, and miss the sight-seeing?
Then, when your years are ripe for marriage – then what
man
Will risk bearing the burden of disgrace which must
Attach not only to my children but to yours?
Who will accept that hazard? What article of shame
Is wanting? Your father killed his father, and sowed seed
In the very womb where he was sown, and begot you
At the same source whence he himself came forth. Such
gibes
Will be aimed at you; and who then will marry you?
No one will – no one, children! It is clear that you
Are doomed to wither away in barren spinsterhood.
  I beg you, son of Menoeceus, since you alone are left
As father to these girls – for we their parents both
Are now destroyed – you are their kinsman; let them not
Wander in poverty and unmarried, levelled with
The depth of my misfortunes. See how young they are,
And pity them; they are entirely destitute, except
For your protection. Noble Creon, touch my hand

97

To you, my children, if you now had understanding, I would have given much advice; but as it is, this is what I would have you pray: that you may live where occasion permits, and that you may find your life a happier one than your father's who begot you.

*Creon.* You have indulged your tears far enough; now go

1515   into the house. /

*Oedipus.* I must obey, though all is bitter.

*Creon.* True; for all things are good in their proper season.

*Oedipus.* Do you know, then, on what conditions I will go?

*Creon.* You shall tell me; and then, when I hear, I shall know.

*Oedipus.* See that you send me to live outside outside this land.

*Creon.* What you ask is the god's gift.

*Oedipus.* But I have become most hateful to the gods.

*Creon.* Why, then, you shall receive what you ask soon.

*Oedipus.* Then you agree to this?

*Creon.* For I do not care to say to no purpose what I do not

1520   mean. /

*Oedipus.* Then lead me away now.

*Creon.* Come, then; and let your children go.

*Oedipus.* No, no, do not take *them* away from me.

*Creon.* Do not wish to exercise power in everything; for the power which you won did not follow you through your life.

*Chorus.* O inhabitants of our native Thebes, look, this is Oedipus, who knew the famous riddle and was a most powerful

1525   man, / on whose fortunes which of the citizens did not look with envy? – see into what a storm of fearful trouble he has come. Therefore, with eyes alert to see that final day, we should call happy no one who is mortal, until he crosses the boundary of his life having suffered nothing painful.

---

1520. *For I do not care....* ' The conjunction 'for' would usually imply 'yes', but (see Jebb's note) could also imply 'no'. Creon is equivocating and will not commit himself. Oedipus takes his words, apparently, as a promise. The question of consistency with *Oedipus Coloneus*, 765 ff., seems irrelevant.

To show me that you promise! – Children, I would have said
Much for your guidance, were your minds mature; but now
I bid you pray – to live where circumstance permits
And find your life's lot happier than your father's was.

*Creon.*  Come, your tears have had full measure. Now withdraw into the house.

*Oedipus.*  Though unwilling, I must obey you.

*Creon.*                                    There is a time
for everything.

*Oedipus.*  I will go on one condition. Do you know it?

*Creon.*                                    Tell me, then.

*Oedipus.*  That you expel me from this city.

*Creon.*                                    The god must
grant that; I cannot.

*Oedipus.*  To the gods I have become most hateful.

*Creon.*                                    Then you
soon shall have your wish.

*Oedipus.*  You consent?

*Creon.*                    It is not my practice to speak words I
do not mean.

*Oedipus.*  Lead me away, then; I am ready.

*Creon.*                                    Come, now, let
your children go.

*Oedipus.*  No! Don't take the children from me!

*Creon.*                                    Do not try to
give commands
In all matters. You have outlived your one-time authority.

> *Creon leads Oedipus into the palace;*
> *Attendants follow them with the children.*

*Chorus.*  See, you people of our native Thebes – see! This was
Oedipus,
He who solved the famous riddle. Great and powerful was
his name;
His high fortune drew the gaze and envy of all citizens.
See him, overwhelmed now in the vortex of calamity!
Therefore we, with eyes fixed on the final day of life, must
learn
To call no man happy who is of mortal flesh, until the hour
When he steps, untouched by anguish, past the boundary of life.

# 1

## The Play and Its Author

*Oedipus Tyrannus* is among the half-dozen most celebrated plays ever written. It has not only been performed, read, praised and explained (with long intervals of neglect) for nearly twenty-four centuries; but on its first appearance it attained such renown that both it and its author seem to have suffered a kind of canonisation. The most often quoted personal stories about Sophocles are: that when he was fifteen he was among the youths chosen to dance in the procession of thanksgiving after the victory of Salamis; and that when he was ninety he made his actors appear dressed in mourning for the death of Euripides. The canonising effect of these anecdotes is nicely balanced by Plato's reference to him (was it, perhaps, put in to jolt the canonisers?) in Book I of *The Republic*, where the aged Cephalus tells of the jocular reply he received when he asked, 'Sophocles, how is your sex-life? Can you still make love to a woman?' There is also the anecdote recorded by Ion of Chios in his *Epidemiae*, of amorous jests at a wine-party.[1] But it is the first two stories rather than the last two which have settled Sophocles' image in the minds of most of his twentieth-century readers. For the enjoyment and study of his extant writings it does not much matter whether we picture him personally as a prophet or as a hedonist; but any mental picture of the man which suggests that reverence should forbid a close and objective scrutiny of the words which he wrote down for men to read and understand, does his fame little service; and seems to me

[1] It is translated in full by D. W. Lucas, *The Greek Tragic Poets*, p. 115.

*Sophocles and Oedipus*

as regrettable as the opposite tendency, now appearing from some quarters, to explain difficulties by calling Sophocles incompetent or careless.

The prevalence in England of this pious attitude to Sophocles and in particular to his best-known play is reflected in two events which took place in the last quarter of the last century. The first was the publication in 1883 of R. C. Jebb's edition of *Oedipus Tyrannus*; the other, the inauguration in 1890 of the Bradfield College Greek Play.[1] Both these events expressed a proper impulse to do honour to a great poet; and both have contributed greatly to the understanding and enjoyment of Greek drama. Yet both have helped to induce in readers and in audiences a kind of mystical reverence[2] which has blunted rational criticism. One illustration will be enough at this stage. Jebb in his edition gives at the beginning of each episode a short summary of the action that is to take place in that episode. A fair summary of the second part of the First Episode, lines 300–462, would read thus: 'Teiresias declares that the murderer is Oedipus, and that Oedipus is living "in shameful intercourse with his nearest kin"; questions his assumed parentage and predicts his blindness. Teiresias makes specific charges of parricide and incest, and departs.' To have printed such a summary would have made it hard for Jebb's readers to follow his exposition of the rest of the play without being uncomfortably aware of a whole series of anomalies and dramatic contradictions. Let us admit at once that Sophocles may have been aware of, may even have intended, such contradictions; but here is Jebb's summary of this passage: 'The prophet Teiresias declares that the murderer is Oedipus.' That is all.

The interpretation of the play which Jebb presented was supported by, and to some extent depended on, his curious (and surely unconscious) *suppressio veri* in his note on lines 216–462. This was also, as far as I know, the generally accepted interpre-

---

[1] Bradfield College, in Berkshire, has produced a Greek tragedy, in Greek, every two or three years since that date until the present time, in a fine open-air 'Greek' theatre constructed for the purpose.

[2] See, for example, Jebb's appendix, pp. 201–6.

tation in all previous centuries. It might, however, have been expected that the acid criticism of more recent years would bite into this; but no. For three more generations the faith has survived unimpaired, to be given a striking testimony in the programme which was printed for the performance, in Greek, of *Oedipus Tyrannus* by Cambridge University in the Cambridge Arts Theatre in 1965. To help a non-Greek-reading audience to follow the action, a fairly long synopsis was provided. Here is the sentence which summarised the action of the passage I have been referring to: 'Teiresias refuses at first to reveal what he knows, but when pressed points to Oedipus himself as the murderer.' No more. Here, exactly as in Jebb's note of eighty-two years earlier, all mention of Teiresias' more horrifying revelations is omitted. Such is the tenacity of a tradition in which reverence has replaced reason.

There is a story preserved by Plutarch, near the end of his *Life of Nicias*, that some of the Athenians captured in 413 B.C. at Syracuse, and enslaved, subsequently earned their freedom by reciting for their masters' pleasure choral odes from Euripides' plays. A few years later Aristophanes in *The Frogs* entertained his audience for nearly one-third of the play with a series of quotations from Aeschylus and Euripides. More evidence could no doubt be collected to show, what in any case it seems only reasonable to believe, that in the second half of the fifth century copies of the tragedies were in circulation at least among the more educated Athenians. They were a nation of conversationalists; and passages in Plato where the talk turns on the interpretation of this or that line of poetry suggest that in Athens and elsewhere people must often have discussed lines of dialogue or lyric from the tragic poets. All three dramatists, moreover, convey a strong sense of knowing exactly what they were about, whether in the general structure of a play, the invention or omission of a feature, or the choice of expression; of writing not only for the spectator, who divided his attention between listening and watching, but also for the reader whose eye would notice, compare and evaluate word, phrase and emphasis. This is at least as true of Sophocles as of the other two, and it is certainly true of *Oedipus Tyrannus*. The close exactitude of verbal texture which has been revealed in this play by B. M. W. Knox in his *Oedipus at Thebes* shows that the poet's mind gave as much attention to the careful, reflective reader as to the absorbed spectator. There follows from this, perhaps, an objection to the whole thesis of this book, namely that there is no written record of such arguments ever being raised in antiquity. This must be fully admitted at the outset; and the first answer is that all our records cover only a small fragment of the intellectual life of those centuries. The second answer is that the words as Sophocles wrote them are here before us, with their meaning clear enough to demand rational understanding. Absence of records does not absolve us from the duty, or debar us from the delight, of pursuing our study whither the matter itself leads us. That, and nothing else, is attempted in this book.

The traditional view holds that Oedipus at the opening of the play believes himself to be the son of Polybus and Merope; that he has never thought of connecting the man he killed on the road from Delphi with Laius, king of Thebes, or of suspecting that Iocasta is his mother. It is obvious that this will generally be the impression given by a good performance to the absorbed spectator; and it would seem that this was the effect intended by the author for the majority of his popular audience. The thesis which I hope to establish by a detailed examination of the whole play is that Sophocles intended the *careful reader* (and perhaps some unusually acute spectators) to see Oedipus as having been aware of his true relationship to Laius and Iocasta ever since the time of his marriage. The main problems in the play, if logically followed through, lead to this conclusion; and such an interpretation is the only one which comes near to answering all these problems.

There are two ways in which such a thesis may be expounded. The first is to take several of the hitherto insoluble problems in the play, and show how an analysis of them leads to a single new supposition. The other is to go through the play line by line and scene by scene as a developing experience, pausing at crucial points to take a more general view. The former method is perhaps preferable for readers who already know the play well either in Greek or in translation, and this book is certainly addressed to them. But it is also intended for those readers, whether university students or not, who have a general interest either in poetic literature, or in the ancient world, or in the theatre; and for their sake I chose the progressive method. This means that I must ask the more instructed reader to be patient for a while and hold judgement in reserve.

Every interpretation of a play must be based primarily on the facts of the text; only these may be used as arguments. But every text contains also many words, phrases and passages which are as they are because of the assumptions underlying the whole work; they do not prove these assumptions, but they illustrate them. In a scene-by-scene exposition it is inevitable that, for example, the four or five illuminating nuances to be found in Oedipus' second speech, 58 ff., should be referred to before any of the cogent arguments arising from later scenes have been set forth. The undertones of Creon's remarks in the Prologue, and the relationship with Oedipus which underlies their encounter in the Second Episode, have to be discussed before the revelations of the Third and Fourth Episodes have provided the material necessary for understanding them fully. And this, of course, is part of Sophocles' intention. The 'hidden play' was meant to be hidden from an audience not ready for it. The spectators were not intended to drag their attention away from the Corinthian shepherd in order to recall exactly what Teiresias had said; but the reader, looking back and forth again and again, finds in the whole work a structure so complete and coherent (though often eluding the rapt citizen in the theatre) that to attribute it to chance or carelessness becomes impossible.

The three Greek tragedians, and this play in particular, belong to world theatre, as Shakespeare and Racine and Chekhov do. They certainly suffer more in translation than plays written in prose; possibly less than Racine or Shakespeare. Like all world drama, they are bound to be constantly at the mercy of actors, directors, managers and audiences, as well as of scholars and translators; and they will survive everything because there is the text, which will always draw thoughtful students back to itself as a source of unfailing newness and surprise. Unhappily a Greek text is, and will remain, a Sleeping Beauty guarded by a formidable hedge of linguistic difficulty. Translations inspire varying degrees of confidence. In our generation, the nervousness which the English-speaking theatre so often shows in dealing with Greek drama arises partly from the knowledge that the public hates being offered what is good for it, partly from the feeling that they are trespassers in a field which has always been the private property of classical scholars. Where there is not nervousness there is apt to be insensitivity, of the kind that makes Helen in *The Trojan Women* appear as an expensive whore, or dead Pentheus in *The Bacchae* be carried on as a tray-load of butcher's meat. The root of the trouble is lack of communication between scholar and producer or actor. Perhaps no comparable classical scholar ever made more resounding mistakes than A. W. Verrall, whose name modern scholars are too apt to treat without respect; but at least Verrall saw Greek plays as theatre, and knew that the theatre was and is a public place of entertainment and not a dons' den; and he liked to see Greek plays produced and to hear people argue about what they saw. His appointment as first Professor of English in Cambridge University was a just tribute to his outlook as a Greek scholar; and one of the things this book attempts is to offer *Oedipus Tyrannus* as a subject of serious study to English-speaking students of literature and drama. That is the purpose of providing a literal as well as a literary translation: so that the student with no Greek can to some degree feel that the text itself is open to him for study.

In discussions about this play I have many times been told that my arguments rest on material which is strictly outside the play and are therefore invalid. This is too easy a parry, and not one to be used without discrimination. How far outside the action of *Hamlet* is the murder of Hamlet's father? How far outside *Oedipus at Colonus* are the events of *Oedipus Tyrannus*? Which matters are in, and which out, a dramatist knows when he is at work; and a student can discover, in so far as he gains insight into the dramatist's mind. That is a reasonably cautious way of putting it, and I would hesitate to make so general a statement as Kitto's (*FMD* 88), that 'everything that is implied by the play is in the play'. Let us examine this question further.

The length of *Oedipus Tyrannus* is 1530 lines. At line 1185 Oedipus goes into the palace to find Iocasta dead and to blind himself; after that point there is no more to be discovered. Of these 1185 lines, 230 or more (about one-fifth) are specifically occupied in providing detailed information about events that occurred either at the period (some seventeen years earlier) when Oedipus as a young adventurer came to Thebes, or eighteen or nineteen years before that, at the time of Oedipus' birth. There is no other extant Greek tragedy which contains a comparable proportion of lines devoted to circumstantial narrative of past events. Some of the details given (e.g. the story of the drunken guest at Corinth, Laius' mode of travel, the Shepherd's request to Iocasta to be allowed to live away from the city) appear to be inventions of Sophocles, introduced for his own purposes; others, such as the story of the Sphinx, the piercing of Oedipus' feet, and the oracle given at Delphi, were parts of the tradition which could not be omitted. Who can doubt that the selection and disposition of all this material, and the relative emphasis given to different features, were the subject of exact planning and construction on the part of the playwright? Many Greek plays have a background of myth which is fairly familiar and largely irrelevant, perhaps touched on pictorially in the choral odes but not contributing to the plot. The case here is different; in this play a whole history of relevant past events is built into the action, and the plot consists in the gradual process of 'fitting them together' – a phrase which the Chorus use in 902. Therefore we cannot study the play properly unless we construct for ourselves, with all the clarity which Sophocles has made possible, the whole fabric of previous events, covering at least thirty-six years, on which the action of the play rests. This history, its main features and many details, had to be clear in the poet's mind before he could begin to write the dialogue; since what each character remembers, knows, wants to forget, or wants others to believe, about those events will colour the way he says what he has to say, will affect what he omits or emphasises, and the degree of truth or false-hood, of firmness or vagueness, in his statements. To an audience, either then or now, only fragments of the whole story would appear; but the author's concept of it, which must have been more nearly complete than we shall ever perceive, is embodied in the text and awaits our discovery, and only as we discover it can we hope to understand much of the meaning of his work.

In recent years hundreds of pages have been covered with print to prove that *Oedipus Tyrannus* is, or is not, a play about an innocent man caught in a cruel trap by relentless Fate; that it is a play about the justice, or the injustice, of the gods; that the play's aim is to show man's nobility, or man's helplessness, or simply to fascinate the audience with suspense or provide aesthetic satisfaction. As we study scenes, themes and characters, we shall find that all these things are there. It seems almost certain that the view expressed by Oedipus himself in 828–9, 'Then would it not be a just estimate of my case to say that all this was the work of some cruel unseen power?' was the view accepted by fifth-century audiences, as it has been in the theatre of our own day. It was the poet's duty – and why not his pleasure? – to present on a popular occasion what the people could accept; and as for theology, there is truth enough – both poetic and religious truth – in the concept of a world where an inexorable principle of balance and proportion in events can override con-sideration of what is fair to the individual: an environment to which ordinary men, and wise men, respond with acceptance, but which rouses heroic natures to defiance. Human freedom of choice has always been and will always be a box of mirrors to bewilder each new generation; the whole tangle is here in this story – prophecy, chance, heredity, self. The play offers to each spectator as much as he is capable of seeing. My contention is that in addition to all this it offers the careful reader one thing more, and perhaps the most important thing of all to the poet who used such skill and subtlety in weaving it into the total pattern.

The almost incredible thing is that it should not have been

perceived before. So many recent scholars – Kitto, Waldock, Knox – have come so near to perceiving it, and turned away at the last moment. I shall make frequent and grateful reference to Knox's invaluable study of the play's words, themes and images in *Oedipus at Thebes*. To Kitto I am indebted for – among other things – his many vivid statements of the principles which should govern the study of Greek drama; here are a few of them, quoted from *Form and Meaning in Drama*:

> Every detail . . . is seen . . . to arise out of, and contribute to, one single conception. Nothing is there simply because Sophocles got interested in a character or a situation. (p. 210)
>
> . . . a very simple hypothesis, namely that Aeschylus knew what he was doing, and that everything that he does in the play is a logical part of a coherent plan. (p. 87)
>
> There are other facts that we have to contemplate, hoping that they will arrange themselves into a significant pattern, or structure, since Sophocles, presumably, invented and disposed them for this purpose. (p. 184)
>
> Analogy suggests that it is in the greatest plays that we should expect not only the greatest skill and care in technique, but the greatest daring too. (p. 92)

All those are admirable passages. The attitude implicit in them is my attitude in studying *Oedipus Tyrannus*, and has led directly to my conclusions.

Kitto writes (*FMD* 95), 'If [an interpretation] is an ingenious one it is probably wrong.' This is a rash statement. There is no doubt that my arguments will to some readers seem ingenious; but what in fact is ingenuity? Ingenuity is what every critic has been exercising for generations, to explain those glaring discrepancies which pass easily enough in performance, as the author knew they would; which when met by traditional reverence merely induce genuflection but, if subjected to the kind of study which a great work of art demands, cannot be explained in terms of any orthodox view of the play.

It is worth digressing to give one good example of ingenuity, from A. J. A. Waldock, *Sophocles the Dramatist*, p. 146:

Suppose Polybus and Merope were not really his parents; then he will not be securing himself by abandoning Corinth but will be rushing into unknown perils.

This is promising; he is on the point of seeing something that is really there – but ingenuity intervenes:

But the oracle has placed the emphasis so cunningly that Oedipus does not appear to us to be stupid.

The words he is referring to are in 791 ff.: '[Phoebus . . . revealed . . .] that I was fated to have intercourse with my mother, and to show to men a progeny they could not bear to see; and that I should be the killer of my father who begot me.' It is not clear what 'cunningly placed emphasis' Waldock is referring to here; but it is no matter, since in any case the words are not the actual words of the oracle, but Oedipus' report of them; so that any emphasis is placed by Oedipus, not by the oracle. Yet in spite of this alleged cunning, Oedipus does in fact here appear to be stupid; for when a man's belief in his parentage has been so shaken that he leaves home without word to either parent and goes to demand the truth from Apollo, an outrageous answer from the god concerning 'his parents' is hardly likely to have the effect of immediately restoring that shaken belief – least of all when distressing evidence of a mystery connected with his infancy is physically present in his scarred feet. If at this point (794 ff.) Oedipus makes the unconvincing statement that he kept away from Corinth to avoid his parents, we must conclude that the dramatist wished to present him either as stupid or as having a good reason for saying what he says. Since the play insists that Oedipus has intelligence and reasoning power, we must choose the latter; and a good reason is there waiting to be found, as we shall see in Chapter 4. What does Waldock say about this?

[Oedipus] does not possess, as far as we can make out, an intelligence of piercing quickness or very remarkable reach. (p. 144)

And a little before this there is a naïve parenthesis:

It is odd that he should have untangled the riddle.

Very odd. There are things which even ingenuity cannot explain.

The action of *Oedipus Tyrannus* shows one feature which has not often been commented on, which distinguishes it from all the other Greek tragedies, and which affects the question how we are to relate the play to any definition of tragedy. Let us look for comparison to two other plays which may fairly be called 'standard' tragedies. In *Antigone* the crucial act is Creon's insistence on carrying out the sentence he has pronounced against Antigone; if he had repented in time, if he had responded to Haemon's appeal, catastrophe would have given place to reconciliation. In Aeschylus' *Seven Against Thebes* the crucial act is Eteocles' obduracy against the appeals of the Chorus and against his own sense of piety; if he had curbed his pride and changed his military dispositions, the worst disaster would have been avoided even if he had lost his life; and the city would have been free from pollution. In *Oedipus Tyrannus* the case is different: the crucial act, or acts, took place seventeen years earlier. If Oedipus had not insulted Teiresias and demanded Creon's death and expressed disbelief in oracles, even though the truth of his identity had remained undiscovered, still a further catastrophe must have followed in the destruction of Thebes by the plague; and in any case safety was precarious, since the palace contained a guilty king and queen, and not far away were a prophet who knew the truth and a shepherd who had seen Oedipus kill Laius. In other words, this play contains no crucial act having the same significance in the tragic pattern as the two crucial acts just referred to, only the discovery of crucial acts committed long before. Other tragedies open with the hope that something at least, if not all, may yet be well, if only the hero or heroine will behave with *sōphrosynē*, moderation; at the opening of *Oedipus Tyrannus*, though the audience and the Chorus do not know it, there is already no hope. The suspense that operates in this play arises from our uncertainty as to how the truth will be discovered and how the discovery will affect Oedipus and Iocasta. That the truth must be discovered sooner or later cannot be in doubt.

Now, if we are to accept with literal exactness the rule that nothing outside the action of a play is really part of the play, a curious result follows. Knox (*OAT* 14–26) gives an admirable analysis of the many qualities which comprise the character of Oedipus. He then says (*OAT* 31), 'The catastrophe of Oedipus is the product not of any one quality of Oedipus but of the total man. The decisive actions' – he refers to Oedipus' resolute prosecution of his inquiry – 'are the product of an admirable character . . . their source is the greatness and nobility of the man and the ruler. Which makes the play correspond fairly closely to Aristotle's description of what tragedy should avoid: "the spectacle of a virtuous man brought from prosperity to adversity – this moves neither pity nor fear; is merely shocks us".' And a page further on, 'He has brought it about himself, and the actions which produced these results proceed from a character which is in almost all respects admirable. It is shocking because it seems to suggest that what he does and suffers is meaningless.' This is very true, and Knox's answer to it, which I shall consider in the next paragraph, does not carry conviction; and this unsatisfactory estimate of the drama is not the only consequence of insisting that we must find the cause of the catastrophe inside the action of the play. Another consequence will be – unless we are ingenious in avoiding it – a view which implies that, if Oedipus had desisted when Teiresias told him to, all would have been well; that the mistake Oedipus made was to demand the truth. Sophocles has emphatically forbidden us this view by his picture of the plague which dominates the first 300 lines of the play. The plague insists that all is not well; something is rotten in the state of Thebes, whether truth be neglected or pursued.

Knox's answer to what he calls the apparent meaninglessness of Oedipus' acts and sufferings is that the parricide and the incest were divinely predicted; that, but for the prophecies, Oedipus' cry of agony would be 'an echoless sound in an indifferent universe. . . . The hero's discovery of his own unspeakable pollution is made tolerable only because it is somehow connected with

the gods'; Oedipus' 'one consolation' is 'the fact of divine prescience' (*OAT* 43). But where is this notion supported in the text?
Here are the statements which Oedipus himself makes about his
relationship with the supernatural world: 'These things came
upon me from a cruel *daimōn*' (828); 'Apollo, Apollo brought
about my sufferings' (1329); 'To the gods I have become most
hateful' (1519). There is no hint of consolation found in divine
prescience, either for Oedipus or for the audience. The fact is
that, when the play is seen in its traditional interpretation, its
events are indeed as meaningless, in a philosophical sense, as
Knox says they seem to be.

The new interpretation offered in this book will suggest new
meanings for all the events of the play; but Sophocles created
both levels of meaning, and wrote for his first popular audience
as well as for his later readers. Even on the simple view with all
its contradictions, this is not a depressing play. What Sophocles
offers for consolation, what gives sublimity to the spectator's
experience, is a combination of several qualities: the orderly
pattern in which events unfold themselves; the pattern of human
characters (including the Chorus) whose wide variety contains
much goodness and no real evil; the sense of the infinite unknown surrounding the visible world at every moment, demanding piety yet making no promise in return; above all the figure
of Oedipus, braving destiny with the eloquence of an invincible
spirit and asserting his right to live in spite of everything. These,
in general, are the qualities which won the admiration of the
first audience, and have given the play its unique fame ever
since. Their brilliance is seen as the more notable because, when
we analyse the action, we find it to be hardly a tragedy at all in
any accepted sense; a drama whose crucial act took place seventeen years earlier, whose hero is guilty and condemned before the
play opens, whose suspense consists in the slow recognition of a
truth plainly stated in the First Episode, and whose catastrophe
holds one surprise – the hero's resolve to live blind rather than
yield to Fate and die.

Yet I do not believe that these brilliant qualities would have
sufficed to preserve for so many centuries the pre-eminence of

this play, had there not also existed the aura of special reverence for Sophocles and for this particular work which I noticed at the beginning of the chapter. For the peculiar nature of the action, as described in the last three paragraphs, is by no means the only feature which leaves a sense of uneasiness in the mind of the reader, and even of the thoughtful spectator. When people talk about discrepancies in this play, they usually refer to the fact that Oedipus finds it necessary to ask Creon how Laius died, and that both Oedipus and Iocasta seem to be telling each other for the first time in seventeen years of marriage about important things that happened before they met. To my mind these passages are no problem, but a natural and necessary convention. The audience must be given these facts; and the whole style is formal enough for us to feel no surprise. There are, however, other discrepancies which are really disturbing. Here are six questions which I think have never been properly answered.

1. In the scene between Oedipus and Teiresias, the prophet tells Oedipus, first, and in plain terms, that it was he who killed Laius; next, by clear implication, that he is not the son of the king and queen of Corinth, but of Laius and Iocasta. These hints and statements are repeated two or three times and finally summarised in clear and emphatic detail in Teiresias' last speech. During the scene that follows, Oedipus admits that the first of these statements, that he killed Laius, is only too probably true; yet neither he nor the Chorus make any comment on the other statement, but continue to talk as if no such thing had been said. Why?

2. In the Prologue Oedipus is presented as a man of exceptional, even godlike, dignity and goodness, one who for many years had earned the love and veneration of his whole people. Why, then, does he so quickly descend to such extravagant and groundless accusations against Teiresias, and why, in his scene with Creon, does he not only behave with puerile vindictiveness, but lose control of himself to such a degree that the scandalised Elders say to Iocasta, 'Madam, why don't you take him indoors immediately?' – as if Oedipus had lost the power of movement?

3. When Oedipus is telling Iocasta about his visit to Delphi and

the oracle that Apollo gave him, he says, 'When I heard this, I resolved to go as far away from Corinth as possible, so that I might never see the fulfilment of this shameful oracle.' That statement might have made sense, if he had believed that Polybus and Merope were his parents; but in fact he had come to Delphi because he had strong reason to doubt if they were. Therefore that statement makes no sense. Was Sophocles, when he wrote it, aware of this?

4. The Second and Third Choral Odes have never yet been given an exposition which I can find satisfactory. If the splendid cadences of the Second are as vague and general in their application as scholars say, then it is dull; if the Third is as naïve as they say, then it is hard to avoid calling it silly.

5. When the Corinthian Messenger arrives and tells Oedipus and Iocasta that Polybus is dead, Oedipus is already nine-tenths convinced that the man he killed on the road from Delphi must have been Laius; and that he is therefore, by his own edict, accursed and banished from Thebes. Even if he still thought that Polybus and Merope were his parents, Polybus' death makes no difference at all to his present dreadful situation, banished irrevocably from his home, throne and city; yet he and Iocasta suddenly forget all about that, and begin first to rejoice with relief, and then to worry over the absurdly remote danger – which after all he has lived with for seventeen years – of his going off and marrying the aged queen of Corinth. Why?

6. When Creon, in the Prologue, tells Oedipus how Laius met his death, he says that one of Laius' attendants escaped and brought the news to Thebes. Oedipus immediately institutes an inquiry; but does not send for the one surviving eye-witness, nor does Creon suggest it. Later when Oedipus is making his public announcement he talks of the possibility of a clue, or of someone who knows who the killer is, and in discussing it with the Chorus says, 'But the man who saw the murder no one sees.' Still he does not send for the eye-witness, nor do the Elders suggest it. Not until exactly halfway through the play does Oedipus at last send for the one man who could identify the killer by sight. Why?[1]

[1] See Note at end of chapter.

A quick provisional outline of the way these questions will be approached can begin with Oedipus' story of his fight by the roadside, and the account given, mainly in various lines spoken by the Priest, by Creon and by the Chorus, of what happened in the days following. A proper initial assumption is that when Sophocles wrote the numerous lines that refer to the events of those days, he did not choose his words in any haphazard way. He needed to give only a few key details here and there, but he can hardly have conceived these details without knowing in his own imagination the story as a coherent whole. Since he makes his Oedipus on the stage recollect and recount incidents from that period of his life, how can we doubt that the complete sequence was clear in Sophocles' own mind? Whether he intended everything to be equally clear to the audience is another matter. We are readers; and to understand the full significance of the words he wrote for Oedipus, we must reconstruct that sequence, treating Oedipus not as a historical personage, but as a dramatic personage whose history Sophocles has created for us in considerable detail.

'The driver of the carriage was pushing me out of the way,' Oedipus says, 'and in a rage I hit him. When the old man saw that, he watched me as I passed by him, and leant out of the carriage and hit me over the head with a two-pronged goad. However, he got more than he gave; a swift blow from my stick, and he rolled right out of the carriage on his back; and I killed every man of them.' (Let us digress a moment to ask, Why does he say he killed them all? This question will be dealt with in its proper place, in Chapter 4.) Oedipus was going to Thebes; the travellers came from that direction. Oedipus had noted (802) that the carriage was preceded by a herald; this meant that its occupant was probably a king. If Thebes now contained an eye-witness to the killing, it was a dangerous city for Oedipus to enter. Why did Sophocles make Oedipus mention the herald, unless to suggest that even on the day of the encounter Oedipus may well have asked himself, Could this man possibly be the king of Thebes? Oedipus did not change his plan. When he entered Thebes, how long could he have walked in the streets before he

heard what everyone was talking about? We are given the whole
conversation in 732–54: The king was killed two days ago –
where? – On the way to Delphi, at the corner of the Daulian
road. Wasn't he attended? – Of course; there was a herald, and
three servants; the king rode in a carriage. What age was the
king? – In his forties; greyish. What appearance? – Much like
your own. On Sophocles' deliberate showing, could there have
been for Oedipus the slightest doubt? If Sophocles wanted to
insist on Oedipus' innocence, could he not have made the evidence
a little less damning? Need he have shown us Oedipus asking
those questions, and receiving those answers, which he must
inevitably have asked and received on the day he entered Thebes
– unless he wished to bring to our minds that scene from the
past? When, in the play, Oedipus hears those details from
Iocasta, he says, 'Alas, all is now utterly clear.' Was not everything even clearer to him when his memory of what happened was
still only three days old? Is all this 'outside the play', or has
Sophocles taken meticulous care to put it in?

However, the text makes it plain that this was not the only
thought beating in Oedipus' mind on that day as he entered
Thebes. There was also the memory of the words of Apollo's
priestess: 'You shall marry your own mother and breed children
from her; and your own father, who gave you life, you shall
kill.' There was a fate which a pious man would be justified in
trying to avoid, as Oedipus himself says (796–7). There is no need
for us to reconstruct (though we can be pretty certain Sophocles
did) Oedipus' reflections during those days. We can go straight to
the next fact given us, namely that Oedipus went to confront the
Sphinx, answered her riddle, and received from a grateful city
the vacant throne and the hand of the widowed queen (35–9,
130–1, 383–4, 396–8, etc.). In other words, he married the widow
of a man he had every reason to believe he had killed, who was
old enough to be his father; and he did this within a very short
time after being told, by the most impressive of all authorities,
that he was destined to kill his father and marry his mother. To
say that a less damning way of presenting the facts could have
been found, is an understatement. And the man who acted in this

way was no fool, but gifted with adequate reasoning power; nor was he an insensitive scoundrel, for on hearing that shocking prophecy he had resolved to do all in his power to avoid its fulfilment. What, then, had caused a decent young man to commit these two crimes, in spite of divine warning? He had been driven to the first by rage, with some excuse; to the second by ambition, backed by courage, with only a thin thread of excuse, namely that his relationship to Iocasta was (considering the infallible authority of Delphi) a strong probability rather than a certainty. All these facts are strictly documented in line after line of the dialogue and are unquestionably a part of the play. To accept them as such is simple, straightforward criticism; to deny or elude them must tax the ingenuity of any reader.

One more argument can be briefly alluded to here, less immediate but still relevant. Throughout the dialogue there is frequent reference (see Knox, *OAT* 150 ff.) to measurement both of time and space. The question 'How long is it since . . .?' occurs twice, in 558 and 735. Knox has shown that the verbs *exisoun*, 'to equate', and *symmetrein*, 'to measure one thing against another', provide a recurrent image which is a feature of the plot. There are present on the stage a number of Elders who are well aware of the chronology of events since the marriage of Laius and Iocasta. It is at least natural that a reader, sharing their concern in the inquiry, should feel himself entitled, even bound, to ask: When Oedipus decided, for the sake of a city and a throne, to take the risk of marrying Iocasta, did he not learn how many years it was since Laius and Iocasta were married, and find that they had been married a year or less before his own birth? (The answer may be, that this is a point the dramatist expected us to ignore; and this is acceptable, provided we do not make the unwarranted assumption that the dramatist ignored it himself.) If, then, he knew what might be involved in marrying the widowed queen, it was ambition that swayed him to reject the clear but fantastic truth in favour of the easily accepted improbability, that he was after all the son of Polybus, and that all the evidences to the contrary were mere coincidence. In line 480 the Chorus, still assuming Oedipus to be innocent, picture the unknown killer of

Laius in words which exactly describe this deliberate choice of belief and disbelief, this effort on the part of Oedipus to convince himself that the oracle given at Delphi had not been fulfilled and could still be avoided: 'Seeking to put away, to separate from himself, the prophecy spoken at the earth's centre'. And they add, 'but that prophecy still lives and hovers about him'.[1]

How could Oedipus live with such knowledge? Sophocles shows us in a number of passages the sort of defence-system which Oedipus had built up for himself; a façade, a version of his story which made plausible sense, and which he trained himself and others to accept. This version said that on leaving Delphi his one concern was to get as far from Corinth as was possible, to avoid his parents (795); the knowledge that Polybus was probably not his father was suppressed (827). The version said that when he reached Thebes it never occurred to him to connect the man he had killed on the road with the king of Thebes – in spite of the herald; or to connect the widowed Iocasta with the widowed mother Delphi had assigned him as his wife – in spite of the doubt cast on his parentage in Corinth (1484). The version said that there did not exist in Thebes a man who had seen him kill Laius – Oedipus had killed all the four servants of the man in the carriage (813). The version said that he had never thought of comparing his age with the time that had passed since Iocasta married her first husband; that the one thing in life he must fear was going back to Corinth, killing Polybus and marrying Merope (988). Was it difficult to get away with this story? We know that it was not; for we too have accepted it uncritically.

Fortified by this necessary fabric of fiction, Oedipus lived as an adored king and a devoted husband and father. Yet, even if he was the son of Polybus and therefore not polluted, he was still guilty because he had ignored Apollo's warning and taken risks it was criminal to take. Aware of his guilt, he tried to atone for it; for seventeen years he gave himself to the care of his family and city and earned love and veneration. Then the plague came; and

---

[1] A letter from Professor Wilson Knight gives me this reminder: 'It is worth remembering how often it happens that a murderer really believes in his own innocence.'

Oedipus knew that the unforgetting gods were at work, that his happy life was at an end, and his ordeal before him. There was only one way to save Thebes: to have the truth brought out, and the polluted man banished, if not killed. But, to reveal to the citizens that their beloved king had for all these years deceived them, and was by his own fault responsible for the plague, would be an unnecessary cruelty. That part of the truth belonged to Oedipus alone. The other part, the bare facts, must be disclosed as it were by accident, as the result of an inquiry initiated by Oedipus himself. To further this end, he sends Creon to Delphi; and on the day when he is expected back, summons Teiresias to the palace. Here the play opens.

Did Sophocles ever conceive and consider such a version of the story?[1] I believe that the numerous details he has given us in the play make such a conclusion necessary. That such a story has both dramatic power and psychological significance, is no argument; that it illuminates many passages whose point is otherwise obscure, is an argument we shall examine as we study the play. It is a story which, by its very nature, could hardly be put on the Athenian stage within the existing conventions. Attic tragedy is above all explicit; everything is said. This story is about a man utterly unable ever to speak to another person the truth which he knows lies at the centre of his life. Even if he could speak, his words would be beyond the understanding of all but a very few in the audience. I suggest that Sophocles decided to write his play in a form which would appear to most of his audience, and perhaps to most readers, to present the traditional story as convin-

---

[1] There was a wealth of material available for Sophocles to study when designing and composing his play, including the two epics *Thebais* and *Oedipodea*. Surviving fragments are largely concerned with Oedipus' two sons and the Argive expedition against Thebes, or with the earlier history of Laius. Sophocles' selection and arrangement of the various elements in the saga, and his concentration of interest on the sequence of events between Oedipus' departure from Corinth and his marriage with Iocasta, would appear to be his own; though according to Tucker (see below), thirty-six tragedies are known to have been written on the Theban legends. Accounts of the material are to be found in Powell's edition of Euripides' *Phoenissae* and Tucker's edition of Aeschylus' *Seven Against Thebes*.

cingly as possible; and, at the same time, to weave into its fabric, from beginning to end, his consciousness of the other – perhaps the more sophisticated – view, containing all that the accepted view contained and something more. This, I believe, is the only interpretation of this supreme work of art which gives a satisfactory answer to its well-known problems. Kitto calls this play 'an unsurpassable masterpiece of construction'. On the usual interpretation I would say that this claim is exaggerated – though it remains a powerful and beautiful play; there are flaws and discrepancies, skilfully concealed, perhaps unnoticed in a good production, but challenging the careful reader on every page. Once we have understood the double level of meaning which the poet is expressing, then indeed we find ourselves contemplating 'an unsurpassable masterpiece of construction'.

A reasonable objection which I have sometimes met is that this thesis attributes an improbable degree of subtlety to a fifth-century Greek, even if he was a dramatic genius of the stature of Sophocles. It is true that the 'play beneath the surface' can hardly be said to 'complement' the play as traditionally accepted, since in a main point it contradicts it. But arguments about what is probable are at least partly subjective. For the student of this play only one question matters: is the 'second play' there or is it not? If it is, the fact must be accounted for. What degree of subtlety does a critic find improbable in Sophocles? Surely, before deciding this question, he ought to make a thorough study of the text of *Oedipus Tyrannus*; and when he has followed not only the arguments set forth in this book, but also Knox's exposition (in *OAT*) of the themes and images forming the fabric of this text, he may then ask himself where he should set a limit to the subtlety of which Sophocles was capable.

It now remains to study the whole play scene by scene, and in particular to examine the role played by the Chorus of Elders. As we proceed we shall note passages where Sophocles has taken care to make easy and acceptable the traditional version of the story; the most remarkable of these is found in Iocasta's speech, 711–19 (see pp. 181–2). Neither view of the play interferes with the other; neither is false; both were created as one organic

whole by Sophocles; and to take what he provided for his indis-
criminate audience and miss what he addressed to those who he
hoped would understand, is a pity. What does take some imaginative effort to realise, is the emotional stress which the writing of
this play must have imposed on the writer. To conceive of
Oedipus' marriage as entered upon with open eyes; to attribute
such sin to a good man, to show the cruelty of chance offering to
ambition the one slender thread of valid excuse in a slight but
definite element of uncertainty; to depict the agonised struggle,
the spiritual courage, by which Oedipus had to free himself from
the self-inflicted blindness of seventeen years, in order to reveal
the truth to others as well as to himself; to be sure in his own mind
that in such a story there was true psychology, true morality and
true religion – to be sure of this in a generation obsessed by war
and unsure of all values, must have been for the poet a costly
experience. It may well have been so costly as to inhibit him from
speaking of it to anyone; we can imagine him resolving that those
should understand it who would, and the rest should receive no
unasked enlightenment. The repeated insistence on Oedipus'
moral innocence that we find in *Oedipus Coloneus* – an insistence
which defies so many indications in *Oedipus Tyrannus*, and which
is in fact more relevant to the view proposed in this book than to
the orthodox view – this insistence may in itself suggest that
Sophocles at the end of his life, at the end of the war, and at the
end of Greek tragedy, was renouncing finally the attempt to
communicate to his fellows a vision of tragedy that was ahead of
its time.

*Note on the six questions, pp. 114–15.* An anonymous critic sent
the following note about questions such as the six listed in this
chapter: 'A much more economical explanation would be that
Sophocles hoped to take care of these oddities by showing them as
a direct consequence of Oedipus' very blindness. Oedipus doesn't
"put two and two together" precisely because he is blinded –
blinded with self-importance, with prosperity, with self-confi-
dence. It is the very heart of Sophocles' hypothesis that the man
who could solve the riddle of the Sphinx cannot solve the riddle

of his own, or of human, life. In terms of such an explanation, most of the "oddities" vanish or acquire a different meaning. The residue of "oddities" doesn't seem very impressive.'

This view is in itself reasonable and should be carefully considered. It is the conclusion which many thoughtful spectators must reach as the play progresses and the excitement of successive episodes erases the memory of the opening scene and prevents reflection on passing significances; and we should probably assume that Sophocles intended the play to give this impression to his popular audience. That he wished to suggest something different to those who could study his work at leisure, seems to me equally clear from a number of considerations.

First, if the hero at the centre of this drama were indeed this Oedipus blinded with self-importance, it is strange that more than 300 lines of the play should be spent on building up a figure of regal sublimity untouched by any noticeable human weakness. If the theme of the play is to be the folly of a wise man, we do not expect to wait until line 330 or so before receiving any hint of this contrast. When it comes, we accept it, and forget the kingly figure; but the unlikeliness of this structure should give us pause.

Secondly, in some of the most notable instances of this alleged mental blindness, there are lines which make us question it. Oedipus' blindness to Teiresias' accusations is fairly convincing through the violent dialogue and the two speeches, but then line 437 ('Wait – who *was* my father?') suddenly reveals the inner uncertainty, the awareness at least of doubt, which makes us suspect that the furious bluster was not, after all, genuine blindness. In the next scene, at 718, Oedipus' failure to notice Iocasta's mention of her son's scarred feet might pass for genuine blindness, were it not for the fact that in 716 Oedipus notices a much less noticeable detail, namely the mention of a crossroads. In 794–7 where Oedipus says that on hearing the prophecy he turned away from Corinth, we could perhaps accept that Oedipus as he spoke was blind enough not to see the illogicality of this; but are we also to accept that Oedipus at the age of eighteen, before he had become puffed up with prosperity, when the actual situation was vivid and urgent to him, was equally blind?

Thirdly, if the 'residue of oddities doesn't seem very impressive', it is at least considerable. Besides the three already mentioned, here are nine more (each of these will be dealt with in its proper place in ensuing chapters): Creon's evident distaste for the inquiry Oedipus is pursuing; the complete image provided in the text of what happened at Creon's initial inquiry; the Elders' failure to suggest summoning the eye-witness; Creon's inexplicable emphasis in 122–3; Oedipus' silent exit at 462; the sudden switch (825–6) from the real issue to an unreal one; the slowness of the Corinthian's responses; the exact meaning of the Second and Third Stasima; the plain implication of what Iocasta says (758–62) about her slave's request to be sent away out of sight of Thebes. We do not solve any of these problems by supposing Oedipus to be mentally blind as a result of pride.

# 2

## King and People

Professor G. Wilson Knight, in his opening chapter of *The Wheel of Fire*, on the principles of Shakespeare interpretation, defines interpretation (as distinct from criticism) as the study and exposition of that aspect of a drama which is 'spatial' rather than 'temporal'; which creates a world of emotional or spiritual experience, inside which the 'temporal' content, the actions and events of the drama, logically linked in a time-sequence, take place. 'Criticism', he says, 'is a judgement of [the poet's] vision; interpretation a reconstruction of vision.' He instances certain plays of Shakespeare in which the temporal aspect or the spatial is dominant, or in which the two are fused. There are some Greek dramas to which it would be hard to apply this distinction of two aspects; but *Oedipus Tyrannus* exhibits them fully. The history of Laius, Iocasta and Oedipus, covering thirty-six years and comprising details found on almost every page of the play, together with the speeches and actions of characters and Chorus, clearly define themselves as a 'temporal' structure. Discussion of the 'character' of Oedipus or of Iocasta, of their degree of guilt, conscious or unconscious, discussion of what Sophocles says about fate and free will, the power of gods and the functions of prophecy – all these are concerned with this 'temporal' element, which has naturally engrossed the greater portion of comment on this play, and will occupy most of the present study; but the other element is there, a definable sphere of human experience, enfolding alike the action, the thought and the poetry. When we have decided what this 'spatial' element is, we should be able to see what the play is about, and, in exploring this element, to reach an interpretation.

All great tragedies are about 'the human condition'. A play, however, is not a treatise; it is an emotional communication from author to spectator or reader, based on their common predicament in an intractable and mysterious universe. Those who expound Greek drama generally, and naturally, concentrate on describing the differences between the ancient world and ours; on showing how Greek social consciousness, and Greek religion, and Greek aesthetics and morals moved on different planes and in different modes from those we are familiar with. It is rare to find, in a book about the religion of the Greeks, discussion which seems to allow that their religion could satisfy the inner life of a rational person in our century. This is perhaps a result of the fact that during four centuries since John Colet, Dean of St Paul's, began to teach Greek, the study of Greek literature in England was for the most part pursued under the guidance of Christian clergymen or in schools and colleges having a Christian foundation – a situation which has begun to change only in the last fifty years. All the varied forms of Greek religion – the earth-cults of country communities, the mystery-rituals both popular and sophisticated, and the humanistic Olympianism of the tragedians – have been carefully described by scholars whose first unconscious premise is, more often than not, that these beliefs, considered as beliefs, are as dead as the centuries which practised them; that what they offered then as comfort or guidance to men and women facing chance, death, evil and the limitations of mortal existence, cannot speak to anyone's condition today.

This I believe to be an unreal critical attitude. Conditions of living have changed frequently and fundamentally in twenty-four centuries, and their variety in different parts of the world is still enormous; but 'the human condition', man in face of the universe, in face of himself and of society, changes comparatively little. The 'tragic' sense of the world in the awareness of articulate men and women remains broadly the same. It survives the deflections imposed on it by the powerful concepts of Christianity, as described by George Steiner in the opening chapter of *The*

*Death of Tragedy*. In the history of the development of the human soul, Oedipus and Peer Gynt stand close together, divided by less than a hundred generations, before a perspective of hundreds of centuries. What makes *Oedipus Tyrannus* worth studying afresh is not so much its position as a high artistic achievement of the celebrated Periclean age; rather it is the truth, comprehensiveness and force with which this play presents the unchanging human condition. It is conceivable that within the next few centuries an age of androids and genetic exploitation may change what has remained stable for many millennia; but as long as literary studies have meaning, the pattern of words which Sophocles created in his *Oedipus* will hold significance for man face to face with himself and destiny.

The world of human experience within which the action of *Oedipus Tyrannus* takes place is the world of knowing and not-knowing; of the choice and rejection of belief; the world which revolves between, at one pole, man's struggle with the knowledge of himself (this seems a more exact way of describing what is often called 'the search for identity') and, at the other, man's bafflement at what he cannot know, whether past, present or future. Between these poles come many different experiences of knowing, all illustrated in this play: the knowledge which a man wishes he did not possess, and tries to reject;[1] the knowledge which is near-certainty, but which, since proof is impossible, must be kept in reserve and not acted on; knowledge gained from mother-wit, from instruction, from experience; the incomplete knowledge which produces superficial judgement; the direct self-knowledge which is the centre of life yet can never be communicated to another soul. Dependent on these different kinds of knowledge are various kinds of belief, and these too are exemplified in the play: beliefs about oneself, about other people, about gods or prophecies, about this or that way of life; beliefs that have never been questioned, beliefs that make moral demands for action, beliefs chosen and defiantly held, beliefs adopted provisionally, or changed without understanding. What men know and do not know, believe and do not believe, constitutes a

[1] See footnote, p. 158.

dimension of life; and this dimension is the 'spatial' world, the atmosphere, in which the drama of Oedipus is enacted. And when we come to study the figure of Oedipus as he moves through the successive phases of the drama, we shall find that his words and moods are illuminated by reference to this dimension. Wilson Knight in the chapter just quoted says, 'The Shakespearian person is intimately fused with this atmospheric quality.' Such a fusion is hardly what we expect to appear amid the dramatic apparatus (so different from Shakespeare's) of Sophocles or Euripides (in Aeschylus such an idea would be irrelevant); there is something of it in Sophocles' *Aias*, perhaps something in the last scene of Euripides' *Heracles*; but Oedipus throughout the play, and especially in the Fourth Episode and the Exodus, exemplifies it in utterances which have a continuous double reference, one to the other persons on the stage, and one to himself and his conscious, incommunicable knowledge.

Again, later in the same chapter (p. 7), Wilson Knight warns the reader of Shakespeare against the kind of criticism which imputes 'intentions' to the author of a poetic drama. 'The intellectual mode', he says, having an 'essentially ethical outlook, works havoc with our minds, since it is trying to impose on the vivid reality of art a logic totally alien to its nature. In interpretation we must remember not the facts but the quality of the original poetic experience; and . . . we find that the facts too fall into place automatically when once the qualitative focus is correct.' This states with exactness what I believe to be true in the study of *Oedipus Tyrannus*. My own experience is that in reading or watching Sophocles' play I never 'accepted everything', as Wilson Knight says one does in reading or watching Shakespeare for enjoyment. What I have done in this book is to 'interpret my original imaginative experience' (plagued as it always was by dissatisfaction, doubt and refusal) 'into the slower consciousness of logic and intellect' (*Wheel of Fire*, pp. 2–3). As Knox has made clear (see *OAT*, e.g. pp. 183–4), the verb 'to know' is a bell which rings constantly throughout the play; and it is hard to believe that the poet, having addressed himself to this dimension of human experience, examined it only in the superficial degree implied by the accepted view. However, in pursuing the further view which I propose, we must take Wilson Knight's warning against the 'essentially ethical' outlook of the intellect.

That is to say, we should beware of inferring that Sophocles' primary intention in constructing the intricate double pattern of the play was to present his hero in a particular ethical light, to show him as a kind of saint expiating his own sin and giving his life for his people. It is obvious that our estimate of a man's ethical character is affected by the way he deals with knowing and not-knowing; knowledge or ignorance may itself constitute innocence or guilt, and in this play the ethical implications of knowledge are important. Yet it is not true that when we consider Oedipus as aware from the beginning our whole interest is transferred to the ethical aspect of his story. The scope of the situation is broader than that, just as it is broader than the question of men's belief or disbelief in the prophecies of Delphi. The supposition that Oedipus knew as soon as he had entered Thebes who it was he had killed, and was aware of his parricide and incest from the first night of his marriage – this supposition immediately raises also the further question of the knowledge or ignorance of other persons in the play, and so sets the predicament of Oedipus himself, and the various stages of ignorance and knowledge through which he passed in his pilgrimage towards self-knowledge, against the background of this whole dimension in the conscious life of human beings. It gives our imagination long vistas of human perception or blindness which transcend the possibility of praise or censure. It presents to us the world of knowing and not-knowing in its human and relative aspect, set in relief against the concept, so familiar to Sophocles' age, of that absolute and timeless knowledge with which Apollo was credited as the spokesman of Zeus. And the secondary place taken by ethical considerations in this dramatic design is illustrated by the fact that we are shown the central truth of Oedipus' awareness with complete clarity, and yet without any statement of it ever being uttered. Had its ethical implications been of first importance, they would surely have found words; as it is, even in the final scene with his daughters, Oedipus preserves to himself alone what he alone is capable of knowing and judging truly (1484; see p. 243).

This idea of a dimension of experience, the enfolding atmosphere or 'spatial' element of the drama, may be conceived in the form of a diagram, as a series of concentric circles. At the centre is the man himself. The innermost circle comprises what the man knows of himself. The next circle is what be believes, or would like to believe, about himself. Next comes what other people know of him; next, what they mistakenly believe about him. These circles concern the present and the past. Outside them comes the circle of timeless and absolute knowledge, which includes the future. Every man has a destiny; there is a chain of events which, whether it be known or unknown, will come (as Teiresias says, 341) as surely as tomorrow and next year. This circle, then, is the total pattern as known by whatever timeless powers the audience or reader may be assumed to believe in. Man himself, if his mind is simple, draws a clear line between what he knows and what he does not. If his mind is complex, events may drive him into a maze of uncertainty; for knowledge of ourselves and knowledge of events depend on each other. Sophocles has given us in one play both the simplicity and the complexity, both the surface and the depth of this tortuous world of knowing; and both are valid aspects of the story. Whether the drama is one of innocence or one of guilt, the atmosphere in which events proceed is the same; only the degree of apprehension varies. It is an atmosphere whose meaning for human beings is little changed in our century from what it was in the time of Oedipus; it is concerned with man's knowledge of himself, man's self-belief and self-deception, man's search for his own identity when a failure in judgement has caused him to lose it.

The text of a Greek play contained no stage-directions, and the theatre provided no programme. Information needed by actor, reader or audience was usually included in the text. 'Here comes Creon,' says the Priest of Zeus, 'wearing a wreath of bay-leaves and berries.' 'Why', ask the Chorus, 'has Iocasta gone rushing away in frenzied anguish?' Characters entering for the first time are, if necessary, identified or related by the address which another character gives them, as in the opening line of *Antigone*, 'My own dear sister Ismene'. The audience know the title of the play, so that Oedipus when he enters will not need to be identified; none the less, he does introduce himself, in line 8, with emphasis upon his unusual name which is to echo with significance throughout the action. Before he enters, we watch the stage filling with a varied crowd of people; and the stage-direction here is comprised in the opening lines of the Priest's speech. Statues of gods, with altars before them, flank the entrance to the palace. One of these is specifically mentioned by Iocasta in 919 as that of Lycean Apollo; Athene and Artemis, addressed by the Chorus in 159–61, would naturally be included; and a fourth, since the city is Thebes, will probably be Bacchus (211, 1105). The postures of the crowd express pitiful entreaty; hands are stretched out from right and left towards the central door in silence; the music of a flute speaks for them; and the king appears, and stands for a while taking in the nature and the composition of the assembly.

'My children', he says; and the first word of the play establishes the king's relationship with his subjects. The word 'children' is repeated a few lines later. The first line also establishes the place as Thebes and the time as several generations after its founder Cadmus. The postures of entreaty, the looks of suffering, are next confirmed in words, as belonging not merely to the small gathering on the stage, but equally to the whole population of the city they represent. The word-pattern then moves back from the distant parts of the city to its centre, the king; and displays as a verbal and visual tableau line 8: 'World-famous Oedipus, as I am called'. The two words *kleinos* ('famous') and *kaloumenos* ('called') are apparently from two different roots; but their point in this line is the similarity of their sounds, and both serve to spotlight the name Oedipus.

The popular derivation of the name Oedipus is and was familiar, from *oidein*, 'to swell', or 'be misshapen' – a root common in medical terminology today – and *pous*, 'foot': 'the man with swollen feet'. The name presents us at the outset with a point of major importance to the understanding of the plot.

There are three allusions in the text to the piercing of Oedipus' feet. One is in Iocasta's speech to Oedipus (718), another in the dialogue between Oedipus and the Corinthian (1031–6), and a third in Oedipus' lament in the final scene (1349–50). In 1033 Oedipus speaks of the mutilation as an *archaion kakon*, an 'ancient evil', or 'blemish' or 'misfortune' – the word is as vague as possible. In none of these passages is there any suggestion that this barbarous cruelty was exceptional, nor yet that it was usual. There is no doubt that the feelings of Greek parents towards children whom they had once accepted was full of tenderness; towards children whom for some reason they rejected, was callousness normal? Laius' shepherd pitied the child (1178); and Oedipus' indignation at the act comes out in 1037, where he exclaims, 'Did my mother do that to me, or my father?' The lack of other comment seems to suggest that foot-piercing had been heard of before, and that its purpose was known – perhaps to prevent the infant's ghost from walking.[1] Menander, whose plays are often about exposed infants, has no reference to such a practice; though this proves nothing, since only five per cent of his writing is extant. What is fascinating, is to surmise whether Oedipus, in the original version of his story, grew up knowing from the condition of his feet that he must have been a foundling. What is clear, is that Sophocles at no point overtly suggests this (though the Corinthian (989–1022) may perhaps hint at this possibility; see pp. 219–21), and therefore we cannot say that he intended such a situation to be imagined by his readers or audience. There is, however, the strange word *oneidos* ('re-proach', 'disgrace') in 1035. This may allude simply to the ugliness of misshapen feet, which would be felt by a small child (*sparganōn*, 1035, 'birth-tokens' – see note on that line) as a reproach among playmates whose feet were normal; equally the

---

[1] Compare the mutilation of Agamemnon's body referred to in Sophocles' *Electra* 445, Aeschylus' *Choephori* 439. I have been unable to gain any further information on foot-piercing from anthropologists.

word might refer to the reproach of having an uncertain parentage.

Two further points should be noted now. First, names from the heroic age were of course often related to the man's nature, person or destiny (compare Aiās, Pentheus); and the meaning of the name Oedipus was familiar to the average Athenian, as is clear from Aristophanes' *Frogs*, 1192. Second, although the first specific reference to Oedipus' feet does not come till line 718, yet the word 'foot' used in a figurative sense occurs four times before that (130, 418, 468, 479); and twice again in the Second Stasimon (see Knox, *OAT* 182–3). It is only in the Third Episode that Oedipus himself, following up his leading question to the Corinthian (1031), refers to his scars as the 'tokens for recognition' which were usually attached to an exposed infant – 'a strange [or dreadful] token this which I received'; but the tokens themselves, the scars, are there on stage whenever Oedipus is on stage, and it is to them that these repeated – and otherwise inexplicable – foot metaphors allude.

There is, however, a second derivation of the name Oedipus from the verb *oida*, 'know'. Knox says (*OAT* 149) that the name 'connects the knowledge (*oida*) of the confident *tyrannos* with the swollen foot (*pous*) of Laius' outcast son'.[1] This may be so; but the more immediate and obvious meaning is 'one who knows his feet' (i.e. who has not temporarily forgotten them at, for example, 718), knows the significance of them (and therefore may well have known from childhood that he was a foundling), and is known, recognised, by the evidence of their scars (1032). The line in which this meaning of the name is most clearly pointed is 397, 'I came, know-nothing Oedipus', *ho mēden eidōs Oidipous*; and this is also the phrase which most clearly hints that the man who 'knew nothing' to help him solve the Sphinx's riddle did in fact at that time know his birth-tokens, the scarred feet which could identify him. These matters will be looked at again when

[1] See the note on 397. Knox mentions two commentators, Earle (1901) and Masqueray (1929), who observe that the name suggests the man who 'solves the riddle about feet', i.e. the Sphinx's riddle; they evidently allude to 1525, and thus take *oida* to mean 'solve', whereas its more usual meaning is 'know'.

we reach the relevant passages. For the present we return to the Prologue.

The character of a man paternally concerned for his subjects, which the king's speech indicates, is confirmed and elaborated by the Priest of Zeus in his reply. He speaks for all those whom Oedipus has addressed as 'children', including both the aged like himself, small children, young men and the whole population of the city. All are storm-tossed and at the point of death. There is a blight on the fertility of man, beast and crop; the plague-god drives flaming through the city; Thebes is ravaged, while Hades, the land of death, is enriched. Can Oedipus, a man, save them from the onset of gods? Men may have 'dealings' with gods, and Oedipus is 'the first of men' (33–4), who once before saved Thebes from a supernatural enemy; what is more, the Thebans believe that he did this 'by the aid of a god'. So now, let him use whatever aid he can, divine or human, but chiefly his own experience of life. If he is not 'equal to a god', at least let him be 'equal to himself'; otherwise he will find himself king of an empty city.

Such is the Priest's appeal. He calls Oedipus 'ruler of my land', 'first of men', 'glorious in all eyes', 'best of mortals', 'saviour'; a man wise in his own experience and favoured by the gods. The portrait of Oedipus is so far consistent; his reply to the Priest confirms it further. Again he addresses his 'children', saying that he bears on his own heart the sorrows of them all, and has already been diligent to help them. Finally, Creon comes. His dialogue with Oedipus is full of interest, but for the moment we shall note only that it in no way contradicts the picture of Oedipus already given. Creon's words are strictly confined to business; they contain no compliment to the king – Creon, after all, is as royal as Oedipus, and a generation older – but his formal respect leaves nothing to be desired. So the Prologue ends; and Oedipus has been presented in a character which is ideal, almost saint-like. There is only one sentence in the Prologue which may be taken to foreshadow the violent proneness to suspicion which the king displays in the First Episode; this is in 124–5: 'Then how could the robber, unless there was some business with money from Thebes, have had the boldness to do it?' The question in its context is natural enough: political plots were for the audience a recurrent preoccupation; and a king's business was to be vigilant. These words cannot be called incongruous with the hero's character. In this play, as in *Antigone*, *Aias*, *Trachiniae* and *Philoctetes* (and so often in Shakespeare), the first scene in which a chief character appears may be taken as an indication of the qualities which are to determine how he fares as the play develops. We shall remember this established portrait of the god-like Oedipus when we come to consider the meaning of his behaviour to Teiresias, and still more to Creon.

The Priest's first sentence echoes the thought of Oedipus' opening lines; he brings before the king three generations of Thebans. In the course of the play three generations of the house of Labdacus will appear; Laius has vanished; and at the end of the play young 'inhabitants of our native Thebes' (1524), the contemporaries of Antigone and Ismene, will look back (49–50) on the finished reign of Oedipus. The Priest speaks next of a whole population sitting at altars of the gods, including the altar where Ismenus gives prophecies from burnt offerings. The world of the future, knowledge of the future, is all around on every hand, as yet out of reach. Creon will soon be back from Delphi; Teiresias has already been summoned. Oedipus commanded them, Oedipus will receive and communicate their reports. It seems as if Fate has laid upon him a role 'equal to gods'.

The Priest describes the blight. The processes of reproduction in plants, in animals and in humans are infected; the city is being deprived of every source from which life can be sustained and renewed. Next he describes the plague (which seems to be a separate visitation) as a 'fire-bearing god'. The word *theos* here signifies very generally a 'supernatural or cosmic power', and is equivalent to *daimōn* as used in 34.[1] 'Gods' in the more personal sense have already been mentioned – Zeus and Pallas and the river-god Ismenus, whose forms and faces are known by their statues; but this, the first use of *theos* in the play, suggests that the plague has some proper place in the pattern of events, a place

[1] Or perhaps Knox is right in assuming that the god referred to is Ares, whom the Chorus later name as the bringer of the plague, 189–202.

which neither Priest nor people yet understand, but which a man versed in the ways both of the world and of the gods (44–5) may understand and know how to deal with. Later when we discover that the king, the head of the body of the state, has many years since attacked the twofold source of his own life, destroying one parent and corrupting the other, we perceive that the nature of this *theos* is related to *dikē*, the principle of balance in nature and in human events (more simply translated as 'justice'), which Kitto calls 'the inevitable recoil', 'the way in which things work' (*FMD* 74). The present effect of the onslaught of this *theos* is that 'the house of Cadmus is being emptied'. The city with its streets, walls, people, the palace, everything which Oedipus had lacked when he first came and had won by defeating the Sphinx, everything which has been his life ever since – all this is now dying in his hands.

The Priest has mentioned, besides the fire-bearing god who destroys the people, several gods to whom the citizens look for help. 'We do not regard you as the equal of gods,' he says – to replace Zeus or control the plague[1] – 'but as the first of men, both in the chances of life and in dealings with supernatural powers.' Possibly a few members even of an average audience, holding the traditional view of the play, might reflect for a moment that the phrase should recall to Oedipus the two encounters which made him 'the first of men' in Thebes: a quarrel with a stranger on the highway – one of the 'chances of life' – and his confronting of the Sphinx. The Priest knows only of the latter; and goes on to recall how Oedipus won his victory 'without any special knowledge or instruction from us, but, as is said and believed, by the aid of a god'. The Priest is confident that Oedipus possesses knowledge from which he can 'find some deliverance for them, whether it is some utterance of a god that he has heard, or perhaps from some man'. In the Second Episode Oedipus will specify both: the oracle given him at Delphi (790 ff.) and the insult of the drunkard in Corinth (779–80).

[1] Herodotus has instances showing how kings, while enjoying some divine privileges, objected to being credited with divine powers. See also the Bible, 2 Kings 5:7.

We have reached the point where we cannot profitably go further without turning back to reconsider the whole Prologue in the light of the hypothesis outlined in Chapter 1 (pp. 116–20). On this hypothesis, Oedipus at the opening of the play has been aware of his situation ever since he became king, and during that time has rigorously repressed in his own consciousness the almost certain truth that he is married to his mother and guilty of his father's death. For his true identity he has substituted the persona with which he grew up, which he began to question as a young man in Corinth (or conceivably in childhood), and which on arrival in Thebes he discovered to be almost certainly false. This persona was a Corinthian, son of Polybus, conscientiously keeping away from Corinth for fear of the oracle, his memory clear of any uneasiness either about the men he once killed on a road near Delphi, or about his royal wife, or about the mystery of his scarred feet; convinced, like everyone else, that Laius' unexplained death had been contrived by private or political enemies in Thebes. This make-believe world has been brought to an abrupt end by the plague; for, as the Priest of Zeus says, a city without men is no city. It is clear now that the only way to save Thebes is to have himself, Oedipus, revealed as the killer of Laius; and that the least distressing way to achieve this is to have the truth brought out apparently by accident as the unexpected result of an inquiry initiated by himself. So he stands before his people, knowing how they love and revere him, how they remember the deliverance he brought them in the day of the Sphinx; knowing that they do not know how he deceived them then, that they will never know what he is doing for them today, but will shrink from him and spit at him. It is this knowledge which gives the tone to his voice when he calls the people, twice, *tekna*, 'children' – a more intimate and tender word than the *paides* with which he begins his second speech. With the phrase in line 8, 'named Oedipus the famous', he reminds them of the day when he had risked his life and won, when they had borne him in triumph to the palace through streets stricken with death and rejoicing in deliverance.

The Priest continues: 'I observe that, for men of experience, life's chances or encounters are the most valid of all counsels.' The word for 'chance' or 'encounter' is *xymphora*, which can also mean an event or accident. The Priest argues, 'Your encounter with the Sphinx should qualify you to help us now.' But, if Oedipus is aware of the truth, as *xymphora* in 33 may have suggested to him his encounter with Laius, so here in 44 it comes immediately after, and explicitly refers to, the 'utterance of a god or clue provided by some man'. So the chances or encounters which the Priest says should enable Oedipus, as a man of experience, to help the city, include not only the defeat of the Sphinx but also the drunkard's shout, the oracle and the meeting with Laius. Of course these incidents are not mentioned until later in the play, so that in the Prologue the audience is unaware of all this; but what we are studying is the mind of Sophocles as he wrote this speech for the Priest, for the words a dramatist writes arise out of, even when they do not reveal, what he knows to be the situation of the persons on the stage. In writing this speech Sophocles would be conscious of the man *speaking* these words, of his love for Thebes, and of his reverence for Oedipus; but still more the poet would be conscious of the man *listening to* these words; and we can now see that, line by line, they speak to the consciousness of Oedipus.[1]

This immediate appositeness intensifies as the Priest turns from recollection to appeal (46 ff.). 'Come, raise up our city! Come, take care; since now Thebes calls you saviour for your past devotion.' The next line, 'our memory of your reign' (echoed by the Chorus, 1221–2), unconsciously envisages the end of the play, when the reign of Oedipus – who should have outlasted the Priest by a generation – is already a memory. He continues (52 ff.), 'When you came to Thebes you brought us the favour of Fortune; now be equal to the Oedipus of those days' – this to the king who now, at the reckoned cost of his own life, is saving his city, and his own soul, by being utterly different from the man he was then. The appeal had begun (23) with the image of a ship labouring in a rough sea; it ends by recalling and applying the image: 'A city, like a ship, is nothing if it is stripped of men.'

[1] See the Note at the end of Chapter 2, p. 147.

Oedipus now replies; and his first few lines – if he is aware of the truth – are packed with double meaning. 'O pitiable children' – but only Oedipus knows how pitiable – 'Known to me, and not unknown, are the things you have come here to beg from me.' With what thoughts does Oedipus begin, 'Known to me, and not unknown . . .'? Could there be a more pregnant opening? The truth, known to the king, must remain unknown to the citizens. 'For I know well that you are all sick. . . .' The verb *nosein* (see Knox, *OAT* 139–47) describes an unhealthy condition either of body or mind, or of a city, of a relationship, of an enterprise, of almost any human concern. 'And, sick as you are, there is not one of you whose sickness is comparable with mine.' To his hearers Oedipus is saying, as Henry V says before Agincourt, that the king bears the burdens of all his subjects. To himself, Oedipus is snatching at whatever comfort can be got from telling some fragment of the truth, even if it is not understood. 'You are not rousing me as one sunk in sleep; be sure that I have shed many tears, and paced many paths in the wanderings of anxious thought. And, as the one remedy that careful search could find, I have sent Creon to Delphi.' Oedipus has been 'measuring the day with the time' of Creon's absence – the first of a number of passages in this play where measurements of time are mentioned (see Knox, *OAT* 150). Creon arrives, and the king calls on Apollo for an auspicious message. The pattern of concentric circles is nearly complete: Oedipus in the centre, with his knowledge of the past but not of the future; the Priest and the people next, with their 'image' of the godlike king; Creon, with a somewhat different opinion, and possibly with knowledge, guarding both in silence; but the outer circle is still faint, for the message from Delphi rests on conditions.

Our next question, before we hear Creon's message, is: 'What are the feelings with which, if our hypothesis is correct, Oedipus awaits Creon's arrival?' Surely uppermost is intense apprehension. Has the oracle denounced him by name, and told the whole truth of his double crime? or given some obscure hint of it? or spoken of entirely other things? Will Apollo make it easier, or harder, for him to carry out what he is resolved to do? The effect of this apprehension is hinted in a phrase which is easily missed. When Creon asks, 'Am I to speak before this crowd, or indoors privately to you?' he means, 'Would it not be more politic to receive and confer about Apollo's message in private, so as to start no rumours?' But Oedipus is so obsessed with the thought that the oracle will name him as guilty and demand his punishment, that he replies to a message which has not been given: 'Speak before them all; the grief which I bear is for them more than *even my own life.*' Again, in the speed of dialogue an audience would assume, and the Elders would assume, that Oedipus spoke of 'his own life' merely as a measure of his grief for his people; but if he is expecting a message that will bring his life to an end, the comparison has a further meaning. Creon ignores all emotional implications, is strictly formal. 'Apollo's commands to us were clear. He says there is pollution in Thebes, which we have cherished here. We are to drive it out, and not to render it incurable by still cherishing it.'

The questioning proceeds. Creon, when told to speak out, is slow to give his whole message, and does not name Laius until he has been prodded with two further questions. This is partly the convention of stichomythia (dialogue between two persons of one or two lines alternately); it is partly a contrivance to emphasise, by delaying, the crucial announcement when it finally comes; and partly it serves to establish Creon's character as a man of caution and reserve who never says more than he has warrant for (569) – even the purpose of Laius's journey to Delphi is given (114) with 'as he said' in parenthesis. Further, if there is any reason for supposing Creon to know the truth about Oedipus, this hesitation supports it. Possibly Creon's words in 110–11 contain a criticism of Oedipus for not seeking the killer of Laius at the time; just as lines 128–9 may show Oedipus throwing the criticism back at Creon. The two passages hardly make a firm basis for arguing that Sophocles intended to show suspicion and resentment already active between the two; but they are relevant to Creon's character, and later give some colour to the king's sudden attack on his loyal brother-in-law. What must be noticed now, however, is the curious sequence 114.–27, which neither stage convention nor Creon's character can fully account for.

The phrase 'as he said' in 114, and indeed the whole sentence, carries caution to a remarkable length, and hints at a distaste for the whole inquiry; and that this is not a casually given impression is shown by a couplet in the next Episode, 566–7:

*Oedipus.*   Did you not hold an inquiry into the murder?
*Creon.*   We held one, naturally; and we did not hear.

The brusqueness of this answer, and once again the absence of any reference to the eye-witness, are surely deliberate. (We shall observe presently that this distaste is shared by the Elders (278–9), who, like Creon and Oedipus, avoid making the obvious suggestion (292–5) that the eye-witness should be summoned.) When Oedipus asks (116), 'Did no messenger come back?' what makes Creon so reluctant to use any evidence that the eye-witness may have to give? We don't yet know; slowness to commit himself is part of his character; but his reluctance could also spring from knowledge. He replies, 'They were all killed – except one man; and he had nothing certain to say – except one thing.' No one could call this co-operative; and we may note in passing that 'they were all killed' is also part of Oedipus' account in 813 – part of his 'façade'. 'What was that one thing?' Oedipus now asks; and Creon's answer demands close attention: 'He said that robbers fell in with them and killed them, not with the strength of one man, but with a large number of attackers.' Why, after the loaded reluctance of 118–19, does Creon now lay so much emphasis on this one point? The reason usually accepted is that the statement refers forward to 842–7, where Oedipus says that if Laius was killed by 'robbers' the crime cannot be brought home to him, Oedipus, since he was alone when he killed the unknown traveller. But in 842 Oedipus does not refer to what Creon says here in 122–3, but to Iocasta's account in 716, 'Laius, they say, was killed by foreign robbers. . .'. Thus it is clear that Creon's emphatic statement here is not necessary to the plot; why then did Sophocles include it? It is usually assumed that Creon is pointing out that the large number of robbers will make it difficult to identify the killer. This may well be one reason; and it is consonant with the reluctance he has already shown, and with the fact that a few lines further on (130) he refrains from mentioning that an inquiry had indeed been held (see 567) at the time. Another and more dramatic reason, however, for the curious emphasis of 122–3 will emerge in the Second Episode; and for this we must wait until Chapter 4, pp. 177–8.

We should, however, in studying the behaviour of Creon, pay attention to another point. Sophocles, in constructing his outline of events since Oedipus' birth, clearly must have considered the question already referred to, whether Creon in the play should be in any degree aware of Oedipus' identity. It would appear that Creon had known Laius probably from his youth till the time of his death. Creon had lived (577–97) in close daily contact with Oedipus during the same period of life, from youth to middle age. The resemblance between Oedipus and his father is mentioned in 743. Like everyone else, Creon could measure the lapse of time between Iocasta's marriage to Laius and Oedipus' arrival as a youth of eighteen. Had he not known of the exposure of Iocasta's child, and was he not aware that the king had scarred feet? The author's meticulous provision of details in the family history makes it legitimate to ask such questions, and rash to suppose that the author did not ask them. The answer seems clear: that Sophocles' picture of Creon includes all these possibilities, yet establishes none of them as fact. This is what we would expect; for to establish any such fact would over-complicate the drama and divert interest from the main issue, while to establish the possibility increases the dramatic tension. Lines of dramatic irony such as 613, 'Well, you will know this clearly enough in time', and 569, 'Where I have no clear knowledge I prefer to say nothing', may be understood on either hypothesis. Lines 122–3 may, admittedly, be a superfluous labouring of a point, an unimportant oversight by the dramatist. If on the other hand they reflect the supposition that Creon had got the truth out of the eye-witness at the time (compare lines 758–64, which tell us that the eye-witness recognised Oedipus, but too late), and that he is here doing his best, with the best intentions, to divert the inquiry from its object, we see at once why he is in general unco-operative, and

in particular will not suggest sending for the eye-witness. This
in turn supplies a good reason why the Elders, who are not averse
to making suggestions (282), refrain from making this one, since
both Creon and the king are plainly avoiding it. The last piece of
evidence on this point only comes in 1152–66; the matter is
further examined below, pp. 177–8.

The very next line presents a further puzzle. 'How could the
robber be so bold?' Oedipus asks. Sophocles has just written the
over-emphatic line 123, 'not by the strength of a single man, but
by a large number of attackers'; then does he, immediately after,
write 'the robber', without having some reason for a straight
contradiction – especially when the difference between one robber
and many becomes significant later on? What could his reason be,
if not that he is showing us Oedipus at this moment absorbed in
his visual memory of the encounter, so that 'the robber' slips out
unconsciously? Two other points remain in this crowded passage.
First, when Oedipus asks (129), 'What prevented a full inquiry?'
Creon, instead of saying (as he does in 567) 'We held an inquiry,
but without result', says that they had been preoccupied with the
Sphinx, and the death of Laius was a 'mystery'; the eye-witness's
evidence is not discussed. Finally, Creon's reference to the
Sphinx must bring to mind what he and everyone else knew,
namely, that the 'champion' or 'helper' who delivered them from
the Sphinx was Oedipus; so that thenceforward it was Oedipus'
responsibility, as king, to pursue the inquiry. This hint of
criticism confirms the tone noticed in 111, 'That which is
neglected escapes'. It is safest to assume that what Sophocles
intends in this passage is what he in fact achieves: to suggest that
in Creon's attitude to Oedipus there is something hidden and
unexpressed. Certainly the tone of 103 seems to carry a dry
irony: 'There did exist a king in Thebes before you set the city on
a straight course.' Creon is a loyal subject, but – except when his
loyalty is questioned – an unemotional man with no time for
unnecessary politeness. When we come to the scene where
Oedipus accuses him, we shall study Oedipus carefully to see
what, if any, motive or occasion Sophocles provides for so absurd
a charge; and the character established for Creon in the Prologue

– stiff, critical, ironical, and quite possibly aware of the truth – will be a relevant consideration.[1]

Thus it now appears that in this brief scene Sophocles has not only announced the oracle which sets the plot in motion, introduced an important personage, and supplied essential information about the death of Laius; but in addition he has used these fifty-six lines of dialogue to set before us a part of the spectrum between knowing and not-knowing. The popular audience watches Oedipus the unhesitating inquirer, Creon the unjudging messenger and Apollo the unrevealing knower take their positions for the coming drama. As background to all this the careful observer sees taking shape the complex pattern traced by the mind of man as it weaves to and fro through layers of awareness, choosing this knowledge, rejecting that, holding the other in suspense; while over the emergent design broods the figure of the riddling Sphinx.

It was Oedipus himself who, in 116, asked the leading question which evoked the first mention of the eye-witness; and in spite of discouraging answers from Creon, he now concludes the scene with a promise to start from the beginning and bring the secret to light. He commends both Phoebus and Creon for their care in this matter and undertakes to be no less zealous himself. 'I shall dispel this pollution', he says, 'on behalf of no distant friend, but on my own behalf.' However, at this point the Prologue ends; the suppliants disperse; and now the Elders, representatives of the citizen-body of Thebes, summoned by the king in 144, enter the stage and perform the *parodos* or opening recitative.

They are not strictly 'representative'; they are leaders.

---

[1] It is right to mention at this point a notable piece of dramatic irony which operates in the traditional view of the play and is lost if Oedipus is aware. In 139–40 Oedipus says, 'Whoever was the killer of Laius might wish to take vengeance on me too': thus he foreshadows his self-blinding; but for the reference to have its dramatic effect it is necessary for Oedipus to be unaware when he speaks the words. There is no reason why there should not be instances (see also the discussion of the Fourth Episode on p. 234) where the 'hidden play' loses a dramatic point which is gained in the accepted interpretation; since no other passage is affected by the loss in this line.

Iocasta calls them (911) 'princes of the land', using the same title, *anax*, which is applied also to Phoebus and to Teiresias (284), to Creon (85) and to Oedipus (103). In 530 they cautiously disclaim authority; but in 278–9 they criticise Phoebus, and in 282 they offer the king advice unasked; in 649 ff. they plead strongly with the king, who yields to them; in 678 they even urge Iocasta to 'take Oedipus indoors' at once. They are responsible, experienced and involved; they are also, we shall observe, well aware of what concerns their own safety. They remember Laius as king. In 1051–2 the Leader implies that he was cognisant of events in the palace at the time of Oedipus' birth; and in any case it is reasonable to assume that at least some of the Elders belong to Creon's generation and think of Oedipus as a young man and perhaps as a newcomer.

When they enter, they know that Creon has returned with an answer from Delphi, but do not yet know what the message is. The Parodos begins with expressions of extreme fear and distress; includes a description of the plague, repeating what the Priest has already told us; and closes with appeals to five of the gods by name, to help them against Ares, the god of death. The Elders' religious attitude is fervent and unquestioning and (as Knox repeatedly points out in *OAT*) contrasted with the attitude of Oedipus, who is at first formally pious but soon is heard abusing Teiresias and refusing to accept Creon's oath, and with the scepticism of Iocasta. The Elders begin by calling the message from Apollo at Delphi an 'utterance of Zeus'. (In 284–5 they equate the word of Teiresias with that of Apollo, and use no such distinctions as Iocasta's in 712, 'not from Apollo but from his servants'.) To them the word of a god is 'immortal' and 'a child of golden Hope'. Later in the play we shall hear them actually lament that 'the ancient prophecies about Laius are fading' – which can only mean that they wish for fulfilment of prophecy even if it involves parricide; those words, however, must be studied in their proper place. For the moment, we observe that their piety is an unconditional dependence on divine aid.

Their description of the disaster in Thebes is expressed in the first person. It is regular for the Chorus-Leader to say 'I' when

speaking for the whole Chorus; here the chief Elder speaks not
only for his fellows but for all the citizens. All are united in an
agony of apprehension, waiting to hear what act of expiation
Apollo the Healer has prescribed. Last time the city was com-
parably afflicted was in the day of the Sphinx; then the ransom
demanded was the lives of young men, until Oedipus the deliverer came. Will today's demand be 'something new', or something
'fulfilled again with the circling seasons'? This last phrase is
intentionally vague, but surely recalls the toll exacted by the
Sphinx and still remembered. The inquiry was sent to Delphi in
hope; but the 'divine word, child of Hope', may equally, by
definition, be terror. The Leader appeals to Athene, Artemis and
Apollo: 'If ever in the past, when ruin swooped on us, you
banished from Thebes the fire of disaster, come now!' The image
of fire (perhaps carrying vivid associations for those who had
experienced the plague in Athens a few years earlier) is used both
for the pursuing plague and for the fleeing people as 'life after
life flies westward'; bodies lie unburied, spreading death;
prayers and mourning are mingled everywhere. Ares is named
as god of death and bringer of the plague, and the Elders call
upon Zeus to destroy him, and upon Apollo, Artemis and Bacchus
to be their 'ally against the god unhonoured among gods'.

Thus the character of the Elders has two main features:
unconditional piety, and fear not only of the plague but also of
what Apollo may prescribe to cure it. They are loyal to Oedipus;
but they do not like to have the past investigated – a feeling which
may bear some relation to Creon's evident distaste for this
inquiry in particular, which we shall consider in Chapter 4. Both
of these characteristics will influence and explain the attitude of
the Elders in subsequent scenes. From now on we shall forget
about the citizens whom these men represent, and become more
and more aware of the Elders as a united body of individuals.
Sophocles will also see to it that we forget entirely about the
plague whose effects he has detailed so vividly. The plague sets
the play in motion; but the play is not about the plague but about
Oedipus; the plague and the oracle open to him the final phase of
his pilgrimage, the fulfilment to which the last seventeen years

have led. The Elders are not pilgrims; they stay where they have always stood; and at the end they will have only a modicum of pity to spare for suffering which they have managed to escape.

*Note on lines 44–5, p. 4.* My interpretation of these lines 44–5, for which I am indebted to Mr T. L. Martin, differs from the usual one, elaborately defended by Jebb and followed by most scholars, including Knox, in which *tās xymphorās* is taken in conjunction with *tōn bouleumatōn* and rendered 'the outcome of their counsels'. But in fact these two phrases are separated by two significant words; and *tōn bouleumatōn* is immediately preceded by *malista*, which as a superlative gives an easier construction with a dependent genitive than *xymphoras* does. Further, the *xymphorai biou* have been mentioned eleven lines earlier, and the reference seems to be obvious. 'To men of experience, the chances or encounters they have been through are, in my view (*horō*), the most living, or valid, of all counsels.' This can either imply calling the chances themselves 'counsellors', and so mean that the chances of life are 'the most valid of counsellors', or it can mean, 'more valid than any counsel which might be given', just as *malista tōn prin* can mean 'more than the men of old'.

# 3

## The Outer Circle

In the First Episode Teiresias enters the stage, and with him the world of timeless and absolute knowledge makes contact with the world of relative human knowledge. In every scene of the play opinions about prophecy and prophets are variously expressed by Oedipus, by Iocasta and by the Elders. Discussion of prophecy, even in Sophocles' world, where the concept was familiar, must often have gone round in meaningless circles through lack of definition; and it is certainly so today, when the attitudes of ignorant and educated alike reflect many scientific assumptions, and perhaps some religious ones, with little experience or example available to keep argument concrete. So it will be well, before going further with our study of *Oedipus Tyrannus*, to ask, What was prophecy? How did prophecy as a Hellenic institution affect the life, thought and behaviour of individuals? Four questions must be asked and answered: (1) Was belief in prophecy an integral part of religious belief in Sophocles' time? (2) Why did not experience discredit prophecy? (3) Was it assumed that the gods, by foretelling a man's actions, took away his free will? (4) What does Sophocles say or imply about prophecy in this play?

1. Was belief in prophecy an integral part of religious belief? The plays of all three dramatists show characters making sceptical or abusive remarks about prophecy and prophets. Some intelligent people, like Herodotus, believed that oracles should be taken seriously — Socrates spoke of them with respect; others, like Thucydides, were sceptical. It is probable that many of those who expressed disbelief would, in a practical issue, prefer not to risk

acting on their disbelief. The dramatists were intellectuals, but they wrote for an audience easily persuaded to act on superstition. However, 'belief' in relation to the Delphic oracle was a mental attitude, and a different thing from the 'belief' demanded by the Christian religion in the New Testament, which was not only a mental attitude but still more an emotional one. For a Christian, 'believing in God' involves an attitude of reverence and of devotion, as well as an intellectual acceptance of dogma; the Olympian religion did not demand 'faith' in this sense, but formal acknowledgement. If a Christian is wrong in his beliefs, his 'soul' may be at stake; if a Greek was sceptical about oracles, he might find that he had acted imprudently in neglecting a warning, but such scepticism was not usually thought to be in itself a sin incurring divine displeasure.

2. Why did not experience discredit prophecy? There are three facts to be considered here.

First, a prophecy given to an individual may say that he will have good fortune, or have bad fortune, or commit some bad action. (I can think of no record of a prophecy that a man will commit a good action.) Of these, a prophecy of the first sort will tend to increase his enterprise or courage; of the second, to depress him and spoil his nerve; while the third will offer him a religious excuse for doing what he wants to do. Thus in all three cases there is often an inherent likelihood of fulfilment. Oedipus took his oracle as a warning; but the thought of an excuse may also have operated.

Secondly, if the oracle, for example, tells a young man, 'You will be killed by a woman', and if he is in fact killed by a woman, whether sooner or later, the story will spread throughout Greece; but if he lives fifty years and dies by natural causes the prophecy will be forgotten. Thus if one prediction in twenty, or in fifty, is fulfilled, the oracle will gain a reputation for being right, since the failures are of no interest and not recorded.

The third point is that oracles were sometimes ambiguous or symbolical, so that alternative events might equally be claimed as fulfilling them.

3. Was it assumed that the gods, by foretelling a man's

actions, took away his free will? Unreflective people have always tended to assume this; and even a modern intellectual may slip into such an assumption, as, for example, Bowra appears to: 'If they [the gods] force him to break their own laws, as he does when he kills his father and marries his mother . . .' (*Sophoclean Tragedy*, p. 176). The average man today would probably deny that foreknowledge exists; the influence of psychological and physiological ideas might induce him equally to deny the existence of free will, though in a practical issue he would be likely to insist, against all argument, that his own will was free. The Greek tragedians, and Sophocles in particular, saw their way clearly through these difficulties, though it is only in recent years that scholars have elucidated the relation of human freedom with divine prescience as it is shown, for example, in Aeschylus' *Agamemnon* and Sophocles' *Electra*. Kitto's exposition of 'double perspective', 'the dual plane' – of the concept of a divine *dikē* working through human agency – should be carefully studied in *FMD* 71–7 *et al.* To assume that foreknowledge implies compulsion is to forget that time is relative. The acts of gods, or of chance, do not infringe, but complement, man's freedom. In *Oedipus Tyrannus* the Corinthian Shepherd was a free agent and had his own motive for travelling to Thebes (1005–6), just as the Theban Shepherd was a free agent and had his own motive for sparing the infant he was told to kill; just as Laius had his reasons for travelling to Delphi, and Oedipus for braving the Sphinx. It is only when a series of freely performed actions reaches its conclusion that man looks back at them, perceives the pattern, and calls it *dikē*. Thus, when a man is warned by an oracle that he is destined to commit a crime, and takes measures to try to avoid doing so, these measures are neither *hybris*, 'arrogance', nor *asebeia*, 'impiety', but a natural and proper reaction. If in spite of the attempt to avoid it the crime is still committed, what is proved? Not that gods made a man sin, but that they rightly judged his character.

4. What does Sophocles say or imply about prophecy in this play? First, he is certainly not telling us that one instance of a true prophecy proves all prophecies true; no one would accept

that. Nor does he anywhere suggest that Oedipus acted wrongly when he tried to avoid fulfilling the oracle; writers on the play correctly describe the oracle as a 'warning'. He shows us the Chorus demanding fulfilment of a scandalous oracle so that traditional religion may be preserved; he shows Oedipus at one time claiming that 'a cruel *daimōn*' had lured him into killing Laius (828), at another that 'It was Apollo who accomplished my dreadful sufferings' (1330) – though this seems to refer to *the disclosure* of his acts rather than the acts themselves. Neither of these attitudes, still less Iocasta's unbelief, can be the poet's religious message. Knox says (*OAT* 43), 'The play is a terrifying affirmation of the truth of prophecy.' It is hard to see just what such a statement means; but it prompts the question, Was a play of this stature, of this human sensitivity and dramatic subtlety, created to persuade Athenians of 420 B.C. to believe in oracles? The scope of the play is broader, the thought of the poet more profound, than this banal purpose demands. Surely Sophocles was content to admit that the operations of Delphi, like other features of traditional religion, were a mystery, and discussion of them unprofitable. What he was interested in was the use a man makes of the mysteries which surround him; and what he says in this play about prophecy, is that its value lies in the use men make of it.

Oedipus and Iocasta are each haunted by a prophecy. Iocasta, a self-willed and proud, but not intellectual, woman, is resolute against belief in prophecy because she is afraid of it and resentful of it; just as those who are afraid of hell proclaim their disbelief in it and thus indulge their resentment. This makes sense in the orthodox view, but even better and more dramatic sense in the view now proposed. In his picture of Oedipus, Sophocles used the traditional story for his dramatic purpose with the average spectator, but even there invited further thought by displaying (984–90) the absurdity of Oedipus' belief in the oracle: 'Your father's death is a comfort' – 'Yes, but I must fear her who lives'. In any case, what is gained when either Oedipus or Iocasta has been persuaded to 'believe in' oracles? Iocasta is converted to belief, and hangs herself. Oedipus, though in one line, 1446, he perfunctorily and by implication admits that he now 'renders belief' to the gods, and in 1456–7 suggests a malevolent pattern in events, yet in the final scene shows no sign of any kind of conversion. His last word is still rebellious – 'Don't take them from me' (1522). He knows that his destiny is exile; and though he yields for the moment to Creon's authority, he clearly has not changed his mind about anything – certainly not about prophecy. He wishes that the gods had destroyed him at birth; but since they did not, he will not now relieve them of responsibility by killing himself. His words in 1454 are not a resolve to go away and die, but a resolve to live (*naiein*, 1451) in the mountains until death comes by a natural course. The exit of Oedipus is in an entirely different tone from that of the repentant Creon in *Antigone*.

Teiresias, who at the cost of temporal sight has gained eternal sight, has been summoned by Oedipus, to help both Oedipus and the Thebans (represented by the Elders) to escape from their different blindnesses. While he is on his way, Oedipus begins to prepare the Elders for the light they are to receive.

If Oedipus is unaware, his opening words (216ff.) show simply a kingly confidence and a formal exactness. If aware, the different elements in the lines are consciously balanced against each other: he knows that he knows all the facts which have to be revealed if Thebes is to be saved; but Teiresias must speak the words. Thus Oedipus feels himself in the position of a god in relation to the knowledge which he hopes Teiresias will publish. This shows clearly in the first three lines: 'You pray; and, for the answer to your prayers, if you will hear and receive my words, and minister to your disease, you will perhaps find help and relief from sufferings.' His confidence in his own knowledge, in his godlike power to manipulate the knowledge of others and to direct the events of this day – this confidence must not betray itself; so Oedipus at once counters his confident tone with assertion of his ignorance: 'I was a stranger to Laius' death and to the reports of it. However,' he goes on, 'I will now speak to you all, for if I were making the search alone I would not get far, if I did not have some clue.' This

last phrase is of particular interest.[1] The sentence is complicated
by having *two* conditional clauses, the second depending on the
first; this obscures the fact that 'having no clue to guide me'
implies – in Greek more than in English – 'if I had no clue, which
in fact I have'. In this ambiguity lies the dramatic irony of the
words.

Then follows the proclamation – on any view a moving piece
of eloquence, but enhanced and illuminated at many points if
Oedipus has knowledge. There are two appeals he must make:
first, to anyone who knows the killer of Laius, to come forward
and speak; secondly, to the killer himself, to avoid the penalties
of detection by giving himself up voluntarily, in which case
neither his person nor his property shall be threatened, but he
shall quit Thebes. As though he wished to give an opening to
every suspicion, Oedipus adds, 'If anyone knows that the killer is
a man from another country, let him not keep silent.' Then the
king pronounces a comprehensive curse and excommunication on
anyone who knowingly conceals the truth, and on the killer if he
does not confess, and on himself, should the royal palace with his
knowledge harbour the guilty man; and charges all Thebans to
carry out his commands. Finally he recalls that what he is doing
now is what should have been done seventeen years ago when
Laius was killed, and emphasises that, as successor to Laius'
throne and husband of his queen, he is the proper person to take
upon himself the place of a son in avenging his father.

Among the impressive cadences of the Greek there are several

---

[1] Jebb's detailed note on 220 ff. should be studied; but a second point
also arises in this line, in the words 'A stranger to this report, a stranger
to the deed'. This is the only statement of Oedipus which can be called
a plain denial that it was he who killed Laius. Can it be reconciled with
the supposition that Oedipus knew the truth? Several points may be
considered. First, for seventeen years Oedipus has chosen to 'know' that
he is innocent; at this moment the presence of his people tends to confirm that 'knowledge'. Secondly, when he killed Laius, each was a
stranger to the other; and when he first heard the report, he was a
stranger in Thebes. Thirdly, this contradiction – if it is that – cannot
cancel any item of the evidence for Oedipus' awareness; the responsibility for it lies with the author, who was certainly aware, and had his
reasons which it is for us to explore as best we can.

phrases whose meaning draws special attention. First there are those touching on the affection which unites him to his people. He could not undertake this task without them (220–1); he and they are fellow-citizens (222); those who help will earn not only reward but his gratitude (232); he appeals to them to help first 'on my own behalf' and then 'on behalf of the god and of our country' (253); and the final line of the speech looks to the future when he will no longer be with them, and gives them his last fervent blessing before the ordeal which opens twenty-five lines later with the arrival of Teiresias. Then there is the little clause in lines 261–2 with its pathetic double meaning: 'If offspring had not been unfortunate in his case'. The words would mean to the Elders, 'If Laius had not died childless'; but to Oedipus the word *genos* also means himself. Still more significant is the sentence beginning in 264: 'In return for which . . .'. Jebb's note properly explains that the logical phrase would have been 'In return for all this', alluding to lines 258–62, but that the parenthesis in 263 ('but as it was, fate leapt upon his head') broke the sequence of argument. That is true; but there is more to it. The use of the relative, 'in return for *which*', directs attention sharply to this same parenthesis which immediately precedes; so that 'which' means also the occurrence mentioned in the parenthesis, namely the killing of Laius, which is an obsessive picture in the speaker's mind. On that occasion there had been a battle to the death, and the son had fought against the father. 'Now,' says Oedipus, *'in return for this* I will fight *on behalf of* Laius, and will go to all lengths' in seeking his murderer. The compound verb 'fight on behalf of' (*hypermachesthai*) is only here found in this form; and the significance of the image as reflecting Oedipus' remorse at the recollection of that scene is reinforced by its use in 245 ('so stout an ally (*symmachos*) am I to the man who was killed') and in 274, where the same word calls upon Justice herself to be an 'ally' to Thebes in carrying out Oedipus' purpose. Finally, there is the list of royal ancestors, 267–8, which links in thought with 264, 'as for my own father's right', and gains in poignancy if the speaker is, in his own mind, claiming his true lineage.

In response to the king's proclamation the Chorus-Leader, as giving an example to the citizens in general, makes a formal denial of complicity; and adds a point which forecasts the shape of the scene now about to open. If the Delphic oracle knew that the polluted killer was living in Thebes, could it not have named him? The question must leap to Oedipus' mind, What if Teiresias follows Apollo's cue and will reveal nothing further? 'No man living', he says, 'can compel gods against their will' (280–1). The Elders, one step behind, suggest that Teiresias be called; and then comes a very curious piece of dialogue contained in seven lines, 290 ff.

*Chorus.* Indeed other [sources of information] are obscure and old.
*Oedipus.* What reports are these? I am examining all evidence.
*Chorus.* He was said to have been killed by certain travellers.
*Oedipus.* I too heard this; but the man who saw it no one sees.
*Chorus.* Well, if he has any particle of fear in him, he will not stay, when he hears these terrible curses of yours.
*Oedipus.* A man who does not shrink from a deed is not frightened by a word.

Now, it is true that the Elders were not present to hear Creon's story (122–5), 'He said that robbers – not one, but a strong party of them, met Laius and his men and killed them.' Iocasta (850) may perhaps be exaggerating when she says that 'the whole city' heard the servant's report, but surely the 'princes of the land' heard it. 'Travellers' for 'robbers' is not a serious discrepancy, but it is curious. Creon had referred to an eye-witness but had not suggested sending for him; the Leader has now referred indirectly to him, disparaging and slightly altering his evidence. What, if anything, have these two at the back of their minds? The question is not one which would ever arise in performance; equally, it would not arise in study, if Sophocles had not put it there. I take it as an axiom that nothing is here by chance, or through careless or confused conceptions on the part of the poet. Sophocles either devised such details for his own satisfaction, or included them intuitively because his vision of the whole story was complete and coherent. The theatrical experience does not demand this detail – though it must surely have exercised some directors; but the student must deal with what he is offered.[1]

Only one explanation seems to make sense. As Sophocles constructed, in all its wealth of detail, the narrative framework on which he built his play, he cannot have avoided pondering long and carefully the events that would have followed Oedipus' arrival in Thebes. If inquiry into Laius' death was at first prevented by the Sphinx, why did not Oedipus pursue it later? (Before Oedipus' arrival, Creon had held an inquiry (567); see pp. 177–8 ff.) Surely because he did not want to be confronted with the eye-witness, or to have the man's false story questioned. The servant himself had got out of Thebes as soon as he could (758–763), and his reason for going, namely that he had recognised Oedipus, but too late, is barely under the surface. The Chorus-Leader knows him both by face and character (1117–18), and knows that he was the same man who exposed Iocasta's child. These last two points are not to be used as the basis of an argument to explain the passage now being considered (290 ff.), since both occur much later in the play; but it is legitimate to note them as confirming what may already be surmised on other grounds, namely, that Sophocles thought of both Creon and the Chorus-Leader as being likely to have had, at the time of Oedipus' accession, a suspicion, either of his connection with the late king's death, or even of his identity – supported both by calculation of time and by his personal appearance (742–3). This fits well, for example, with Creon's words in 569, 'I don't know; in matters that I don't understand I prefer to say nothing', and with the brusqueness of 574, 'If he says this, you yourself know'. It fits the failure of both Creon and the Chorus-Leader to suggest sending for the eye-witness, since the reawakening of that long-suppressed suspicion is too dangerous to contemplate; and it fits the opening

[1] In recent years there appears to be a tendency, among scholars who are at last acknowledging the existence of serious anomalies in this play, to explain them by saying that Sophocles was careless or even incompetent. The difference between this view and, for example, Kitto's statement that the play is 'an unsurpassable masterpiece of construction' is interesting.

words of the Parodos (151–7), which express extreme fear of what Apollo's oracle may lead to.

Let us return to 293. If neither Creon nor the Chorus-Leader will make the obvious suggestion, why does not Oedipus now say, 'Let us send for the man'? Because, having begun his operation on the principle that the truth is to be revealed by the agency of others, so that he himself may appear to be unsuspecting, he is defeated for a moment by this surprising obtuseness. When in 293 he almost puts the words into the Chorus-Leader's mouth, that astute diplomat performs a remarkable side-step.[1] Stalling at Oedipus' prompt, he answers – nothing about the eye-witness, but about the murderer: 'But, if he has any fear in him. . . .' Sensing opposition, Oedipus does not press his point about the witness, but accepts the Elder's shift of ground; besides, Teiresias is already at the door. The Leader formally introduces the prophet, and in unmistakable words (298–9) commits himself for the second time (see 284–6) to belief in his unique infallibility. We should remember this when in 500 ff. we find him carefully contracting himself.

To Oedipus the arrival of Teiresias means the beginning of final self-discovery; it is a measuring of his strength against impersonal eternal powers. Creon and the Chorus-Leader may hold repressed suspicions; Teiresias knows all, or is reputed to. And yet Teiresias is also a man; his omniscience operates under certain human conditions. On the supernatural plane his reason for refusing to name the guilty man is doubtless the same as Apollo's – on which it is idle to speculate. On the political plane his refusal can only mean that he will protect the *status quo* in despite of truth and the dying city. Why does the city's own prophet take this unhelpful position? Since he knows who the guilty man is, and knows

---

[1] See Jebb's note *ad loc.* The use of the singular verb, in speaking of the man who actually struck Laius, is natural enough. But the Elder switches from eye-witness to murderer not because the latter 'is foremost in his thoughts', but because he is determined, for his own peace of mind, not to be drawn into talking of the eye-witness. There is, incidentally, a second ambiguity here: does 'he will not stay' mean 'he will come forward and confess', or 'he will fly the land'? I see no answer to this; but the former seems more appropriate to the eye-witness, the latter to the murderer.

that by exposing him he can serve the city, why does he refuse
to speak, and warn Oedipus to inquire no further? This question
seems as hard to answer in the old interpretation as in the new.
Teiresias apparently feels that to preserve the royal house is more
important than to preserve the people; in this he disagrees with
the Priest of Zeus (56–7). Another consideration, however, needs
to be taken into account. In Sophocles' design for the drama the
plague has a clearly limited function; it dominates the first 300
lines and fully motivates Oedipus' inquiry; once the inquiry is
afoot, it is quietly forgotten. The last specific mention of the
plague comes in line 307; allusions and echoes are heard in 406,
515–16, 636; in 1428 the mention of 'earth and holy rain' may
carry an implication that the normal processes of nature are now
restored in the fields of Thebes. And it is clear that, once Teiresias
has accused Oedipus of parricide and incest, the plague is no
longer needed as motive for an inquiry. Further, since it will
become clear in due course that Sophocles' picture of events at
the period of Oedipus' marriage included certainly Creon, and
probably Iocasta, as being aware at that time – but just too late –
of Oedipus' identity, it is natural that the dramatist should see
their decision to keep the whole thing quiet as being shared by
Teiresias. It would seem, then, that the question, Why did not
Teiresias wish to save the city from the plague by exposing the
guilty man? is a question – indeed the only question of any
importance – to which Sophocles did not offer a probable answer.

We should remind ourselves, moreover, that Teiresias' role in
the drama is not primarily a moral one, or comparable to that of
Nathan before David in the Old Testament. He may be the
repository of truth; but his first intention was to suppress the
truth.[1] He is not slandering himself when he says it is anger that
moves him to change his mind and speak. Teiresias is a true
representative of the world of gods, of the outermost circle in the
pattern of knowledge. There is in him, as in that world, no

---

[1] 'I knew this well,' says Teiresias (318), 'but I destroyed it.' As
Professor Whitman has pointed out to me, this is perhaps the clearest of
many indications that Sophocles in this play is using the suppression of
unwanted knowledge, and the notion of varying levels of knowledge,
as part of the material of his plot.

observable reason, no moral ground for action or for change of attitude; no pity or sympathy or recognisable goodness; but there is a plain appearance of the effects of anger. His two positive qualities are, first, that he claims to represent *dikē*, the impersonal principle of balance and proportion, of the payment of debts; because he sees the end from the beginning he is sure of *dikē*, and because he is sure of *dikē* he sees the end from the beginning. Second, that he expresses this principle in a form – here the medium is the poetry of the Greek language as Sophocles wrote it – of unanswerable majesty and beauty. These are also the qualities of the gods and of their world.

What are the qualities with which Oedipus faces him – man versus the gods? There are three, and they are all human and temporal qualities, irrelevant to the eternal world of omniscience. First, there is compassion for his suffering people, shown in the first word (*polin*, 'the city', 302) of his appeal to Teiresias. Secondly, there is the intelligence which gained him his throne, enabled him to live ever since in a precarious world of half-reality, and is now guiding him along the agonising path towards truth and release. The third quality is the pride and courage which, inflamed and poisoned in his early youth by resentment at his nameless and disinherited state, has now matured into the heroic firmness which though broken for a while in the scene with Creon will recover and nerve his resolve to suffer life rather than death at the end of the play.

This scene is probably, on any interpretation, the chief difficulty in the play for modern readers; and the difficulty is increased for those who have first grown familiar with its scenes and its poetry in the (literally) plausible guise of the popular tradition, in which the reverence accorded to 'the Parthenon of literature' invites the critical faculty to retire politely. We should first describe as exactly as possible what happens, according to the text, and examine how the persons concerned react to these events. Then we must state why these events and reactions are hard to understand, and look at possible explanations. We should do this with reference both to the traditional view and to the other view proposed in this book. Let me remind the reader that much of the evidence for the new view will be found in Chapters 5 and 6, and that references made to it in earlier chapters are largely illustration rather than argument. It is useful also to say here, in anticipation, that when we come to consider one of the more obvious problems of this scene, namely the motive for Oedipus' attack on Creon, we shall find that even when the play up to this point is read on the usual assumption of Oedipus' ignorance, a clear motive is discovered by close attention to the text; and this motive must influence our view of subsequent scenes. The trouble with the orthodox view has been that it skims over gaping problems without noticing them – or, even worse, assumes that this is what Sophocles did.

First, then, to describe what happens. In a speech of sixteen lines the king lays the city's need before the prophet; then in eighteen lines of dialogue Teiresias admits that he knows the answer to Oedipus' question, and refuses to give it, while Oedipus progresses from entreaty to reproach, and at 334 bursts into abuse. Abuse has no effect. Teiresias in 341 gives a moment's hope, and the king's moderate reply snatches at it – to be met with defiance. Then all moderation ends. The accusations are absurd, even childish; but they work. Teiresias.gives the answer he was asked for: '*You* are the unholy polluter of this land.' The king insists on his repeating it; he does so, and adds that Oedipus is living 'in the most shameful intercourse with his nearest kin'. But Oedipus' reply to this statement seems to take no account at all of its content; it is merely a further threat: 'Do you think you can go on saying these things unpunished?' Then, still ignoring the extraordinary charge of incest, with an expression of contempt for the prophet's blindness, he suddenly switches his attack to the absent Creon, insisting that Teiresias is in Creon's pay. He recalls how he, Oedipus, and not Teiresias, had saved Thebes from the Sphinx. The Chorus interpose, reproving both king and prophet for speaking in anger; but they too refrain from making any comment whatever on Teiresias' statements. Teiresias, ignoring the Elders, replies to Oedipus. He again alludes repeatedly to both parricide and incest, and asks Oedipus who his parents were. Oedipus' answer again is mere abuse and threats; and Teiresias once more mentions his parents. This time Oedipus takes notice, and asks, 'Who was my father?' but gets no reply. Teiresias in his final speech repeats all his former statements with explicit emphasis, including for the second time the prophecy of Oedipus' blindness. He then goes home, and Oedipus without another word retires into the palace.

About Teiresias we were told only one thing before he appeared: that everyone believes him to be the infallible mouthpiece of Apollo. Apart from that, his character in the drama is simply what he shows us in this scene. Oedipus, however, has been presented to us in a clearly defined character as noble, intelligent, serious-minded, and zealous in service of the city. We are therefore to consider his behaviour during this scene in the light of what we would expect of such a man; and numerous points require elucidation, chiefly the following eight:

1. Oedipus' accusation of Teiresias in 346–9 is absurd, childish, and therefore out of character.

2. His reaction when twice charged with Laius' death, 353 and 362, is irrational, blustering, and therefore out of character.

3. His reaction to the charge of incest, 366–7, is even more unnatural.

4. The sudden accusation of Creon in 378 demands clearer motivation than a jealous and suspicious nature.

5. The impotent rage of 429–31 is surprising in a man who has just listened to lines 413–25; but when that man also knows all that is recounted in 788–815 it is so incredible as to demand further search.

6. In 437 Oedipus, as if caught off his guard, reveals that the certainty about his parentage which he has hitherto implied, and which he is still heavily asserting in 827, and with which orthodox comment credits him, is not certainty at all.

7. The lines which immediately follow, 439 and 441, show Oedipus suddenly sane and quiet; and his statement that Teiresias' words are 'enigmatic', when they are already extremely clear, again demands scrutiny.

8. At 462 Oedipus leaves the stage without a word of reply to the final explicit statement of Teiresias. He knows that the Elders

regard Teiresias as infallible. If he believes in his innocence it is the Elders whom he must convince (cf. Creon's departing words, 'These men know I am innocent', 677): a crushing disparagement of venial soothsayers would be easy; yet he says no word – and after 430–1 we can hardly put this down to his sense of dignity.

These are the chief points calling for explanation in this curious and complex scene. We should begin by recognising that the traditional interpretation is a perfectly fair one, that Sophocles made it possible, even easy, for his first audience (after all, we did not see his production) to yield to the excitement of the performance and skate rapidly over the difficulties I have just enumerated. As one violent line follows another we feel this insensate anger to be fully explicable; the man who saved the city, who has for many years been its loved and honoured king, is suddenly told by one whom he would naturally trust that he murdered his predecessor. Provisionally, at least, we can feel that this shock is enough to throw any man off balance for a while; for what could be the prophet's motive, if not to overthrow him? There is no doubt that the eloquence and rhythm of the dialogue make it convincing in performance; but we must remember also that the play we are studying is not a primitive or natural product but a sophisticated work of art consciously constructed, word upon word and phase following phase, by a master of the medium. Either the succession of moods, revelations and reactions was designed and executed by the author with clear and consistent intention – or the play is hardly worth the generations of study that have been spent on it.

Let us consider first the fact that the encounter between Oedipus and Teiresias takes place in the presence of the Chorus of Theban Elders. The Chorus are both in the play and out of it. They are in it, as men who have a specific relationship to Oedipus, to Thebes and to other characters; they are personally involved in what is happening. They are out of the play in virtue of their relation to the audience, on whose behalf they are there to provide a permanent point of reference; to hear, to understand as much as the audience understands, and to remember. They are fifteen shrewd and responsible men; they have been in touch with events since Laius was king, and remember all that happened in the days of the Sphinx. They are now in danger of death from the plague; they look to Teiresias for the word which will tell them how to end the plague; and they regard him as infallible. Teiresias says that the guilty man is Oedipus. Plainly the Elders dare not, in the king's presence, appear to have understood; but they know that Oedipus first came to Thebes shortly after Laius' death; so that if they ask themselves, Can the prophet's word be true? they know that it can. Oedipus has no alibi, and he has been twice named by the prophet whose authority they equate with that of Apollo. Before they have time to reflect, they hear the second accusation (366–7), that of incest. Could even this be true? The Elders' choice is between Oedipus, whom they have respected as a man for seventeen years, and Teiresias, whom they have revered as the mouth of a god for as long as they can remember. During the rest of the scene the Chorus make only one remark, four lines of remonstrance to the two men; they have all the time they need for listening, remembering, calculating. Knox has shown (*OAT* ch. 3, par. 4, esp. 150) how significant is the constant recurrence in this play of such words as *exisoun, symmetrein*, 'to equate', 'to measure one thing against another'. Measurement, calculation of time – these are of the essence of the plot, as they are reflected in the imagery. How old was Oedipus when he first appeared? About eighteen. How long had elapsed then since Laius and Iocasta were married? The Elders know; it was about nineteen years. Whether or not they had known about the royal birth and the exposure (line 1051 says they had, but since that comes later in the play it is not to be used as an argument), this calculation must surely have shaken them. When Oedipus is accused of incest, they hear him, instead of making any direct answer, first redouble his threats and insults, then suddenly turn to attack Creon. This the Elders must certainly resent, since their loyalty was to Creon before ever they heard of Oedipus. When Teiresias, replying to this, has repeated his former statements, and mentioned Oedipus' parents, they hear the king ask (437), 'Who was my father?' and the prophet's reply, 'You will learn today'. Finally they hear Teiresias repeat yet again, with amplification, all he has already said; and they see the king go indoors without answering. They will make their comment in the First Stasimon; for the moment their function as Chorus is to remind the spectator that this is not real life, where words may be mis-heard, ill expressed, or forgotten; but a play, where all words are heard and understood – or if not, there is a significant reason. At the same time we should remember that, even if an author has in his own vision a clear picture, he may not wish to make everything explicit in his poem; just as an eloquent drawing may include blurred lines and blank spaces.

Let us begin with the first three of the points listed above. Oedipus' words accusing Teiresias, 346–9, are in the first place patently absurd; secondly they are accompanied by gratuitous insults which belie the character established for Oedipus. It may be said that this shows the insidious power of anger to corrupt a good man. This argument seems unsound for two reasons: (1) It makes Oedipus' anger into a significant fault, and leads the audience to think of it as at least one cause of his downfall. This again means that we accept *the revelation* of his guilt as the real disaster, rather than *the incurring* of it by his two crucial acts (see pp. 111–12); a view which will pass for performance but should not satisfy reflection. It will also lead to confusion in interpreting what the Elders say in the Second Stasimon about the Olympian laws (see pp. 203–4). (2) If Sophocles had been concerned to show us a noble king falling into unworthy anger, he would surely have provided more convincing and significant provocation. He has in fact taken care to show us that Oedipus knows how useless it is to try to force a god to speak against his will (280–1); and Teiresias has been equated with Apollo by the Elders (284–5) and addressed in the most reverent terms by Oedipus. We should, then, look for a further reason for the phenomenon of Oedipus' fury.

Next, Oedipus' reaction to Teiresias' repeated charge, 353 and 362, is strange. First, it seems unnatural that the man of intelligence, who gained his position by *gnōmē*, should make no reasoned reply. Secondly, if Creon knows how to receive a wild accusation in a dignified manner, it is strange that the Prologue gives no hint that Oedipus is incapable of similar dignity. Thirdly, in 334–49 Oedipus' anger is roused by Teiresias' obstinacy; the obstinacy then yields, and the prophet's statement completely changes the situation on the stage; yet the irrational anger continues without any change of mood, though its cause is now entirely different. This is a subtle and important point of dramatic technique and, no less than the first two observations, suggests that the anger is not spontaneous, but is affected for a purpose; that in fact Oedipus, being aware of the truth and resolved to have it known, is goading Teiresias to reveal the rest, and inviting the Elders to give full play to their suspicion.

Let us look further at Oedipus' answers to Teiresias. When told he is the killer of Laius, he says, 'Are you so shameless as this, to start up such a notion? Do you think you will escape punishment?' To the repeated statement he replies, 'You will be sorry for this.' When told he is married to his mother, his words are: 'Do you think you are going to continue saying these things without suffering for it?' Now, there are at least three considerations which make these answers inexplicable on any orthodox view. First, the authority of Teiresias was by tradition immense, as Oedipus' own words acknowledge; even if he quarrels with him, even if he disbelieves him, it would be natural for the king to show him some shred of respect. (In *Antigone*, Creon at first reviles Teiresias; but afterwards believes him, though he came unsummoned.) Secondly, if the king's respect for the prophet is limited, that of the Elders is not; and there could hardly be a more certain way of convincing the Elders that the charges are true, than to ignore them and resort to insults and threats. Thirdly, it is already established that Laius was killed shortly before Oedipus appeared in Thebes, so that the first charge could be true; and it is well known that Iocasta is old enough to be Oedipus' mother, and Oedipus in 437 admits uncertainty about his parentage; so that the second charge could also be true. And when Teiresias says, 'You are married to your mother', and Oedipus replies not with denial or refutation but with vague threats, we cannot simply say, Oedipus is so angry that he does not hear, or does not take in, what is said. That might happen in real life; but it is inconceivable in the work of an ancient dramatist.

The usual view of the play assumes that Oedipus is meant by Sophocles to have no suspicion that the first charge is true until 716, 'at a junction of three highways', and no suspicion that the second charge is true before 1016, 'Polybus was nothing to you in blood'. This view I take to be totally untenable. Even if Oedipus is presented as innocent of any knowledge or suspicion when the play opens, the only thing that can motivate his behaviour in this scene is his immediate perception that both of Teiresias' accusations may well be true. This will affect the interpretation of all subsequent scenes; it must also mean that if Oedipus perceives this possibility the Elders probably perceive it too, since more evidence is available to them than to Oedipus; and this must affect our understanding of the First and Second Choral Odes. Then, if Oedipus knows in a flash not only that the charges could be true, but that the Elders, watching him intently and receiving the prophet's words as those of a god, know equally that they could be true, it follows that he must know in the same flash that there is also one man, whose correct deportment never betrays a thought (87–131, 569), but whose piercing eye, open to numerous facts which we shall note in due course (pp. 177–8), may always have suspected both charges to be true, and who may be ready, if sufficiently provoked, to betray his suspicion. Even on the orthodox view, we can see here a credible motive for the sudden attack on Creon. This interpretation makes sense, and could be convincingly acted; and would account well for the extremity to which the quarrel proceeds in the following scene.

It seems, then, that when Oedipus leaves the stage at 462 enough has already transpired to warrant us in assuming that his last lines spoken to Teiresias, 445–6, are virtually an admission that both charges have shaken him. Even so, his failure to offer any refutation of them is surprising; but we are to learn in the next two scenes from Oedipus himself a number of facts about his past life, each clearly recorded in his memory, which make it both more and less surprising. He had been conscious ever since childhood of the reproach of his maimed feet (1033, 1035). As a young man he had been given cause to be doubtful of his parentage, and his supposed parents would give him no information. He had been told by Apollo at Delphi that he would marry his mother and kill his father. He recalled clearly the occasion when he had killed 'an old man' (*presbys*, 805, 807) with grey hair, of similar build to himself (742–3), who was travelling with a royal retinue (802) from Thebes towards Delphi. He remembered entering Thebes soon after, defeating the Sphinx, and receiving as his reward the throne of Thebes and the newly widowed queen as wife. The man who in Episodes 2 and 3 remembers all this in such detail, in Episode 1 listens to the clear and repeated statements of Teiresias without uttering a word to suggest that he connects one thing with another, or indeed that he even hears what is said. Surely Sophocles intended that the successive charges of regicide, parricide and incest should be seen to give, as it were, the first shake to those slumbering memories which in the next scene Iocasta's story will rouse to full consciousness. Even if, as is usually assumed, Oedipus had never suspected that the old man he had met travelling from Thebes in a carriage preceded by a herald was the king of whose death he learnt as soon as he entered the city, it is hard to accept the idea that Teiresias' denunciation in 353 and 362 could strike no chord in the memory of one who half an hour later was recalling in vivid detail his roadside battle and its outcome.

For these reasons it seems impossible to accept lines 429–31 ('Intolerable! To hell with you! Get out, this instant! Turn your back and go! Away, away, away!') as a spontaneous burst of rage natural in a quarrel. To the popular audience it will appear to be this, and the excitement of the scene will forestall reflection, since there has been no mention yet of the prophecy given to Oedipus at Delphi. But if we consider these lines as the work of a dramatist who knew exactly how to convey in words the mood as well as the meaning of each speaker, and then consider that here the speaker has just been told clearly for the second time two things which were prophesied to him many years ago and which he knows are vouched for by both reason and evidence, then this rage, if genuine, must spring either from guilty knowledge of the whole truth, or from panic fear of it. The other interpretation possible is that this is a pretended rage, but reinforced by the agony of the underlying situation; that Oedipus' intention is not to clear himself, but to convince the Elders of the truth of everything the prophet has said. The idea of such a strategem is strongly supported in the text: three times Oedipus, as though unsure whether his assumed anger were convincing enough, explains and excuses it (334–5, 339–40, 345). Spontaneous anger is not so self-conscious. The angry outburst of 429–31, then, taken with 437 ('Who is my father?') and with his silent exit in 462, should produce suspicion in the Elders' minds, if anything could. In fact they resist stoutly and cautiously for another 300 lines. Oedipus has to watch their reaction and at the same time to play his part as an innocent man outrageously slandered. On the Elders' faces he reads the caution of courtiers trained to believe only what it is expedient to believe. For their sake he insists (359, 361) that Teiresias shall repeat his words. He repeats them, and again the well-drilled Elders register a proper imperviousness, which they will put into words as soon as the First Stasimon gives them the chance. Teiresias then adds the second charge, which makes apparently even less impact on their minds than the first. What is the use of a prophet whom no one heeds? The king's famous insult with its hammering alliteration,[1] 'You're blind, not only in sight, but blind in hearing, blind in brain' (371), is a virtuoso line for the actor; it fits equally well the fury of indignant innocence blind with self-righteousness, and the much more complicated exasperation of an Oedipus who is at once aware, frustrated, and bewildered by the difficulty of what he is trying to do. The heat of feeling is there, and a wealth of motivation for actor and audience to choose from.

The supposition of Oedipus' awareness, then, leads us to interpret the scene, and to explain the attack on Creon, along lines already suggested for the orthodox view, as far as 377; with this difference, that the king's anger is seen to arise as much from frustration at the obtuseness of the Elders as from the sense of being slandered. From 378 on, Oedipus' motive is partly his

[1] *Typhlos ta t'ōta ton te noun ta t'ommat' ei.*

inveterate fear of Creon, partly perhaps a hope that Creon, like Teiresias, may be stung by insult to speak what he knows. We have to remember that Oedipus' guilty knowledge has through his whole adult life been the secret of his solitary thought; so that to hear it suddenly brought out into the audible, visible, political world – even though this is his own doing – must at first make it seem unreal and confusing. In fact, his situation when confronted by the prophet's assertions is so extraordinarily complex that one can hardly call this speech or that reaction likely or unlikely. The scene in performance electrifies by its matter, by its form, by its poetry; the technique of the artist may exercise our percipience but does not abide our question. However, the attack on Creon here is only an offshoot of the conflict with Teiresias, and we shall study it further when Creon himself appears in the Second Episode.

A few further points in this scene are worth noting before we turn to the comment by the Chorus which follows it. First, the poet skilfully uses Oedipus' speech 380–403 to furnish yet more details about relevant past history: the Sphinx's riddle and Oedipus' triumph (393–8, 440–4), the gratitude of the city and the invitation to the throne (383–4), the long-tried loyalty of Creon (385). Secondly, when Teiresias, already on his way out, alludes to 'your parents', Oedipus calls him back and asks (437), 'What man was my father?' This line alone would make it clear that in this First Episode Sophocles already thinks of Oedipus as the man who remembers the day when Polybus of Corinth lied to him for the last time, and he resolved to go to Apollo for the truth. This line is our first hint of what the Second Episode will make explicit, that Oedipus, when in a rage he pulled Laius from the carriage and killed him, was *not* securely certain that his father was safe at home in Corinth; to kill this grey-haired stranger was to take a risk which no pious man in those circumstances would have taken, and which, if what he says in 796–7 is honest, he had surely sworn on leaving Delphi never to take. This thought has further implications which are not fully relevant to the understanding of the play, except in that they suggest aspects of the life-story of Oedipus which Sophocles must have considered when composing his play, and which have already been outlined in Chapter 1 (see pp. 116 ff.).

Thirdly, in 397 Oedipus says that he, *ho mēden eidōs Oidipous*, overcame the Sphinx – 'Oedipus, the man knowing nothing': a statement ironically uttered and pregnant with meanings both conscious and unconscious. First, when Oedipus faced the Sphinx he had, as the Priest said (37), no special knowledge from the citizens to help him solve the riddle; he is also stating that he did not then know he had killed the king of Thebes, and did not know that the prize he would win by defeating the Sphinx was his own mother; and he is replying now to Teiresias, who has three times already charged him with want of perception; besides all this, the phrase coming next to his name reminds us that even if he knew nothing else, yet he 'knew his feet', i.e. knew that their scars were a warning of his uncertain parentage. Fourthly, when Teiresias in 456 pictures the blind Oedipus as 'feeling the ground before him with a stick', he reminds us that this play shows the life of Oedipus – infancy, youth and three-footed age – as an illustration of the Sphinx's riddle about the three stages in the life of a man.

Finally, we should observe exactly how the scene ends. So that no one should imagine that Oedipus leaves the stage before Teiresias has finished his speech, Sophocles gives us 'Go indoors' in line 460, which would be absurd if Oedipus had just gone indoors. Since scholars whose work commands the highest respect have assumed that Oedipus enters the palace at line 447 or 448, this point needs to be laboured. In the first place, the phrase *legō de soi*, 'And I tell you', is theatrically awkward if addressed to a retreating back. Lines 449–60 are all in the third person; so that the reversion to the second person in 460 becomes still more improbable if Oedipus is not there. Finally we should remember that the Chorus in this play are not mere onlookers but personally involved in everything that happens; and they cannot avoid hearing and understanding Teiresias' parting speech. Their appalled avoidance of all reference to it in the first half of their ensuing Ode is the best evidence of how clearly they heard it; and for the Elders to hear crucial words which, through an accident

of timing, were unheard by Oedipus, would be an intolerable
feebleness in the plot. In any case there is nothing in lines 449–62
which has not been said earlier in the scene and much of it two
or three times over. An exit for Oedipus at 447 would demand
cogent evidence, and there is none. The relentless clarity of these
fourteen lines is presented to a man who heard Apollo's prophecy
at Delphi seventeen years ago and has not forgotten it. The
Elders watch him listen to those threefold reverberations in
458–60; then they watch him walk into the palace without a
word. Now it is their turn to speak.

The king is not within hearing; it should be possible to make
some comment on the scene they have just witnessed, and the
words they have heard; either to say – as was so often said – that
prophets are not to be trusted, or to reflect that a good name is a
precarious possession, or to recall that Teiresias has never yet
been proved wrong. Instead, their opening words show them
perfect in the practice of politic deafness; they speak as if this
scene had never occurred. When the last question asked is too
terrifying, refuge can be sought in the last question but one.
'Who is the man of whom the prophetic rock of Delphi spoke, as
having committed with bloodstained hands the unspeakable of
unspeakable crimes?'

The terror has pursued and confused them. The rest of the
strophe and antistrophe show that the man they are talking about
is the unknown robber who killed Laius, and they picture him as
a fugitive living in woods and caves like a rogue bull. We can
understand their referring to his 'bloodstained hands'; but why
do they call his common act of violence 'the unspeakable of unspeakable crimes'? Because, resolved though they may be to
forget them, Teiresias' words about parricide and incest haunt
their minds. They try again to banish the thought which gives
to this imaginary outlaw the form and name of Oedipus. 'He will
try to escape,' they say, 'he will run with a foot swifter than
horses . . .' – and the word 'foot' echoes (as in other passages
throughout the play) the name of the king whom the prophet
named as guilty. They speak with poetic enthusiasm of the hunt
which the prophet's words have started: 'Apollo goes forth armed

with fire and lightnings, accompanied by the dread, unerring Fates.' Surely, if the killer were an ordinary robber, a squad of armed men could go out from Thebes and look for him? To demand this divine armament, the hunted man must be in their imagination more than some wretched bandit or hired assassin. Thus, though the Elders are resolved to ignore all that Teiresias told them, and firmly refer to the killer as 'the man who has not been pointed out' (*ton adēlon andra*, 475), three times in twenty lines they fall into phrases which show that the man has indeed been pointed out to them, and they cannot ignore or forget. And in 480–1 they use a phrase carrying a dramatic irony of which they themselves are not aware, but the audience is – for the story of the oracle would be familiar: 'Trying to keep at bay the prophecy spoken at the earth's centre' describes well enough the supposed outlaw; but it describes even more vividly the man who received a prophecy at Delphi seventeen years ago, who after defeating the Sphinx had had to decide whether to accept the prize or flee from it, who today is overtaken by the consequences of his decision. However, who is to blame the Elders? Their eyes have been opened by Teiresias, and what they saw has naturally confused and terrified them. With this fabrication of the fugitive haunting the mountains they carefully blind themselves to the true picture of the killer of Laius which the prophet showed them: a king living in a palace, surrounded by obedient servants and a loving family. So eloquently do they reassure themselves that they did not hear what they heard, that they have persuaded centuries of audiences and readers to agree with them; 'but these things still living hover around' (482).

Thus self-comforted they gain courage, in the second strophe, to make a cautious reference to the visit of Teiresias. 'Certainly what the learned augurer told us is disturbing, deeply disturbing. We can't accept it, we can't refute it; we don't know what to say. All is uncertainty and surmise, whether we look to the present or to the past.' It was the very certainty of the prophet's pronouncements that had shattered the old certainties of their familiar world. So far their words seem honest; but the question which follows again reveals that they are disingenuous. 'What feud ever existed between the house of Labdacus and the son of Polybus, which would justify me in attacking the public reputation of Oedipus in order to avenge the mysterious murder of Laius? I never heard of any, either in the past or recently.' This remark, which on the surface sounds intelligent, actually disposes of one possibility, that Oedipus had set out from Corinth in pursuance of a family feud to kill Laius and take his throne – an idea which no one has even thought of yet. It pretends that parricide and incest have not been mentioned; it is a face-saving formula. They agree that a serious charge like regicide must be 'tested with a touchstone' (493); so they invent a non-existent question to which the touchstone can be safely applied. Their real reliance is neither on Teiresias nor on rational possibility, but on public opinion, the 'nationwide reputation' of Oedipus. Unhappily for their peace of mind, the Elders heard everything that Teiresias said. Now they must decide, and their decision is for the moment to ignore everything: the challenge is too severe, too sudden for mortals; it must be left with the gods. So they conclude by asserting, first, their piety: 'The whole truth is known to Zeus and Apollo'; then, their common sense, verging upon impiety: 'One man may be cleverer than another, but I question whether any man is a better prophet than I am'; then, their caution – after all, Teiresias and the Sphinx both represent the unseen world: when the Sphinx 'came against him', Oedipus 'was seen to be skilled'; he may win again. Lastly, they affirm their loyalty: 'Oedipus won his throne by his services to Thebes; I will never think evil of him without proof.' And there they leave it for the present.

The last stanza of this Ode, then, epitomises both the character of the Chorus and the 'spatial' element in the drama. It is about the degrees of human wisdom and the absoluteness of divine knowledge. It keeps before our minds the pattern of the whole action, which has at its centre Oedipus answering the riddle (itself concerned with the nature of man), and at its periphery the past and future known to the gods. These lines recant, for the comfort of the moment, the Elders' former profession of faith in Teiresias as Apollo's infallible spokesman; and pit their human wisdom against his divine vision. They assert as the only sure fact what they and all the Thebans once witnessed – that Oedipus defeated the Sphinx and saved the city. That is the familiar creed; and in spite of prophecy, memory, calculation, and the present evidence offered by Oedipus' behaviour, they will not venture outside it.

# 4

## *The Second Episode*

The closing note of the Chorus was: Oedipus' past services to the city are proof enough for me of his innocence; without full evidence I will never think evil of him. Now immediately enters the man whose loyal service in the past the king has ignored in condemning him. Oedipus' injustice recoils upon himself. The first nineteen lines of this scene serve to establish an atmosphere of serious and genuine discourse; Creon is evidently innocent of conspiracy, and the Elders show that they believe this, while avoiding criticism of the king. Both they and Creon allude to the unbalancing effects of anger. Then in bursts anger personified; and serious discourse vanishes. If Oedipus believes in his own innocence, he is sure that Creon will not believe in it, once the words of Teiresias are reported to him. His suspicions of what Creon may always have suspected are just beginning to take form, moulded by his memory of the prophet's repeated statements. If on the other hand Oedipus is already aware, and is engaged in a deliberate self-betrayal, then he has for years been sure – whether rightly or wrongly – that Creon knows the truth, and that the whole security of his life and reputation has been enjoyed on sufferance.

We should be exact in assessing Oedipus' fault of behaviour in this scene. The Greek word for it is *akrateia*, 'want of self-control'. If Oedipus had carried out his threat and killed Creon, it would certainly have been an act of *hybris*, 'arrogant violence'; since it was confined to words, though it expressed the mind of a tyrant, it was hardly a definite act of *hybris*, for Greek morality did not generally equate the intent with the deed. Aeschylus' *Agamemnon* gives an illustrative parallel. Agamemnon earned his fall by two deliberate (and figuratively connected) acts of *hybris*, the sacrifice of Iphigenia and the annihilation of Troy; and these unseen crimes are reflected on the stage by the folly of treading on purple silk, a symbolic act of pride which draws from Clytemnestra her cry of triumph. So, in this play, the man who before the action began has twice defied Apollo's warning makes his *hybris* visible on the stage in an action which is folly rather than crime. The visible sign has no dramatic validity unless or until the audience are aware of what it represents. In *Agamemnon* they are made aware by the Chorus, the Herald and Agamemnon himself; in *Oedipus* they are – or should be – made aware by Teiresias, and by the Elders' equivocating refusal to consider his words. Later, when the Elders have made up their minds, Oedipus' folly in accusing Creon is given its true place in the dramatic pattern by their firm statement, 'Arrogance begets the tyrant' (873), which will be discussed in the next chapter. In the present scene, Sophocles surely intended Oedipus' behaviour to Creon to come as a puzzling shock to the audience; it is certainly that to the Elders, whose moral level is far below that of Oedipus. The audience gradually translate this shock into meaning as the reality of Oedipus' guilt reveals itself during the course of the Second Episode.

'Oh, there you are! You have the face to come here? You dare to come to my house?' The house was Creon's before Oedipus came to live in it; the words are picked to challenge. In 534–5 the choice of words recalls recent exchanges: Oedipus calls Creon a 'killer', *phoneus*, which was Teiresias' word for Oedipus in 362, and a 'robber', a word which Oedipus used in 124 referring (consciously or unconsciously) to himself. 'Did you think me a coward or a fool?' he asks, harping still on his ancient exploit, or knowing how different his own fault is from either cowardice or folly.[1] 'Isn't it you who are the fool, to think you can go hunting

---

[1] The 'crucial act' (see pp. 111 ff.) in the whole tragedy was Oedipus' decision to confront the Sphinx; for in that decision he committed himself almost irrevocably, in the event of success, to marrying

kingdoms without friends to back you? For that, you need a
strong following, and money.' This is a taunt at Creon as the
merely average politician; Oedipus had gained his throne without
following or money, with only brains and courage.

In the first twelve lines of stichomythia Creon's tone is
moderate or conciliatory; Oedipus displays his anger by twice
(548, 551) repeating in his answer the words just spoken to him.
Lines 559 and 574 indicate that Teiresias' words have not yet
been reported to Creon; but there are lines in this dialogue which
fit exactly the supposition that Creon long ago put two and two
together, keeping all such thoughts strictly to himself. First,
Creon's allusion to the inquiry he had held after Laius' death
(567) has a curious and recognisable tone: 'We held an inquiry,
naturally, and we did not hear.' What it reminds us of is his
unco-operative reply to Oedipus in 118–19: 'They were all
killed – except one; and he had nothing definite to say, except. . . .'
The brusqueness of 'We did not hear' suggests that of a man who
dislikes being forced to lie. What did they hear at that inquiry?
Creon has told us; in 116–31 he gives the evidence of the only
available witness – but gives it as if he wished to imply that as
evidence it was worthless. Oedipus, naturally dissatisfied with
this, then asks (129) what has prevented a *full* inquiry (*exeidenai*);
and Creon tells him – the Sphinx. What did 'a full inquiry' mean?
Sophocles did not need to tell us, because everybody knew, how
evidence was taken from slaves; but in case we had forgotten he
gave us a reminder (1152–3): 'For God's sake don't torture an
old man!' In so serious a matter as the assassination of a king,
when a political plot was suspected (124–5), torture or the threat
of it would soon change the evidence from 'a large band of
robbers' to 'one lone traveller' (846); and almost certainly would
elicit the identity of the traveller. That this was known to the
witness is clear from the fact that soon after the inquiry the man
begged Iocasta for permission to go and live in the country, 'as
far as possible from sight of this city' (762); for Sophocles could
have no reason for putting that in, unless to tell us that the man

---

Iocasta. Thus the act which most severely tested his courage and his intelligence was also his one real crime.

had recognised Oedipus when it was too late. (Iocasta's nervous assurance that 'he cannot revoke his evidence' (848–9) suggests that she too knew what happened at the inquiry, and agreed with Creon that the Shepherd would find it easier to hold his tongue when well away from Thebes.) The account which was current in the city (716, 850), and which Creon so superfluously insists on (122–3), was the one given by the eye-witness at the first questioning, and, credibly enough, the only one which Creon allowed to get outside the inquiry room. None of this, of course, makes legitimate ground for the interpretation of the play; but as corroboration *post suppositum* it illustrates again how many of the details contained in the text fit exactly the presumption of a complete and coherent history existing in the mind of the dramatist. Secondly, when Oedipus after some delay at last tells Creon that Teiresias had named him as the killer, one would have expected Creon to show some surprise and ask for further information. Instead he simply says – as though it were a thing that ought never to have been repeated in front of the Elders – 'If he said that, you best know; but now . . .' and then firmly seals off that line of inquiry by starting questions of his own.

In the stichomythia 555–82 several details are worth observing. First, Creon's interruption in 559. The dividing of a sentence to preserve the pattern of line for line is an occasional but accepted feature of tragic dialogue. Here, however, the effect is more stilted than usual, and it is hard to believe that Sophocles could not have managed better – unless he had some definite stage-effect in mind. We have twice already been shown Oedipus betraying by his words that he is absorbed in thoughts beyond those he is uttering at the time (see pp. 140, 143 on lines 94, 124). It seems possible that here too the original production, directed by the poet himself, may have shown Oedipus pausing, suddenly rapt by memory at the name of Laius;[1] while the yet more stilted next line ('Did what deed?' rather than 'Suffered what fate?') shows Creon, as always, instinctively diverting the inquiry from its object – an end he still pursues in the vagueness

[1] Exactly this is done in the magnificent film of *Oedipus* made by the Shakespeare Company of Stratford, Ontario.

of his next answer, 'That would be a long and distant time to measure' (561). The significance of 567 we have already noticed. Lines 569–74 contain the verb *oïda*, 'know', four times. They show Oedipus baffled by the silence (569) in which Creon prefers to mask what he knows and what he does not know; Oedipus baffled by not knowing whether the two men who perhaps knew his secret had conferred about it (572); and still more baffled, surely, when Creon, by his total lack of interest on learning that Teiresias had accused Oedipus, shows that the notion of the king's guilt must have been long familiar to him; so baffled, in fact, that in 576 Oedipus actually tries to get him back to the subject ('I shall never be found guilty of murder'), but in vain – a point which ought to prove puzzling to those who hold that the orthodox view is the only view. Then suddenly, after declining to show interest in the killing of Laius, Creon says, 'You are married to my sister?' – and immediately Oedipus sees his second crime as on the point of disclosure; and the ponderous suspense of 578 ('There is no denial of the question you have asked') is punctured when Creon, instead of making any accusation, merely says, 'And you are as much ruler of Thebes as she is' – an emphasis which Oedipus acidly corrects in his reply.

The main tenor of Creon's apologia (583–615) points two contrasts between him and Oedipus. First, Creon's mind is royal, but unambitious; Oedipus has chosen 'rule with fears' (585). Secondly, Creon honours and demands justice; Oedipus is acting unjustly. The whole speech is moderate and persuasive in tone, as befits a wise elder addressing a headstrong younger man. The Chorus listen to it, and gain a little in confidence from its realistic good sense, so that in 616 they dare to hint a warning to the king to 'beware of falling'. Oedipus apparently does not listen to a word that Creon says; when the speech is over, he demands his death.

The emotional state of Oedipus between 618 and 676 should be studied carefully. In 623 he is demanding the death of a tried friend and brother-in-law. With this demand he has so far held the initiative in the altercation; but in the rapid exchanges which now follow Creon gains the initiative with a series of intelligent points, while the king's answers are ineffective, and end with his appeal to the city (629) to witness that he is confronted by treason. The suggestion of hysterical impotence (*akrateia*) in this appeal is confirmed by the fact that it is followed by Creon's firm reply, the rebuke of the Elders, the entry and domineering speech of Iocasta, and the statement of his case by Creon – all without a word from Oedipus, till in 642 he says, 'I confirm that', *xymphēmi*; the word is a rearguard action, and the words that follow ('for I have found him plotting against me') show that he accepts Iocasta's right to arbitrate. He has suddenly found himself in the position of a younger man before two older people. His two lines 642–3 are his sole attempt to present his case against Creon. The heroic task to which he has addressed himself is proving even harder than he had expected. The inherent weakness of his status as son and nephew has brought him to his knees in the first round; he is almost out for the count. Yet before the scene is over he will again be on his feet, in charge of the situation, and pursuing his purpose to its end.

Iocasta begs him not only to believe Creon's oath, but to 'respect me and these Elders in whose presence you are'. The word 'respect' here (*aidestheis*) means primarily 'yield to our entreaties'; but it also hints that the king's manner and appearance have embarrassed her. At her shocked tone Oedipus' force – though not his fury – collapses. In 650 and 653–4 he sullenly yields; that is to say, he agrees not to press his demand for Creon's death.[1] Then in 658–9 he says to the Chorus, in effect, 'You realise that if I spare Creon, he and Teiresias will press home this accusation that I killed Laius, and I shall suffer either death or banishment, according to the instruction from Delphi and my own edict.' He repeats this statement in 669–70; and is evidently assuming that if the charge is pressed he will be found guilty. Why does he assume this? It can only mean that, even on the orthodox supposition of his ignorance at the opening, he has had time since the departure of Teiresias to discover that (in the words of the Chorus, 902) 'these things fit'; he has reached that

[1] I cannot agree here with Knox, who says (*OAT* 60) that Oedipus' yielding to the Elders illustrates his democratic exercise of royal power.

degree of knowing which is the second stage away from true ignorance, but is still several further stages from full knowledge – the last of which stages will come when he sees the last sight of his life, Iocasta dead.[1] This doom of death or banishment is closing in on him, and half of his consciousness welcomes it as just and necessary, while the other half shrinks from it in dread. The cause of it will not be Creon; but it is natural for Oedipus, in the agony of his self-revelation, to feel that his present confused misery, and his approaching fate, are both taking their course under this cool, correct and inscrutable eye, so that even Creon's loyalty is a reproach to the treason which Oedipus has committed against Thebes. Creon's departing words do nothing to mitigate this bitterness: 'Such natures are most painful for themselves to bear' (675). Oedipus knows that this stab has touched the very nerve of truth, and he reacts with a cry of utter despair and defeat, 'Will you not leave me alone and get out?' It is after this that the Leader says to Iocasta, 'Hadn't you better take him indoors at once?' The fact that Iocasta answers, 'Yes, when I have learnt what happened', makes it certain that at this point Oedipus is in a state near to nervous collapse; lines 687–8, 'You see what you have come to, though you're a well-meaning man, in slighting my purpose and frustrating it', fully confirm this; so does Oedipus' tone in 700–1. In 702 Iocasta is still doubtful whether he is capable of giving a plain account of the quarrel; and the half-truth of 703, with Oedipus' self-correction in 705, complete the picture of a man struggling for composure.

Now we must look at the attitude of the Chorus in this lyric passage (the *kommos*, 649–96). They plead with the king to reflect and be reasonable; and their argument, summarised in 656–7, is: When a friend has bound himself with a curse (Creon had said, 'May I die if I am guilty of conspiracy', 644–5) you should never bring a dishonouring charge against him on unproved report. (Exactly the same situation is found in Euripides' *Hippolytus* when Hippolytus protests on oath to Theseus that he

[1] For a study of the meaning and stages of knowing in another play, see Euripides' *Bacchae*, and the valuable exposition of its ideas contained in Winnington-Ingram's *Euripides and Dionysus*.

is innocent.) As Creon is to Oedipus, so Oedipus is to the Chorus. A dishonouring charge has been laid against Oedipus by Teiresias, whose word is as yet an 'unproved report'; and the Chorus, regarding Oedipus as a 'friend', have rightly refused to uphold this charge against him (511–12). Oedipus, they say, should now show the same fairness to Creon. When they hear him reply in words which seem to say that he expects to be found guilty of the death of Laius (658–9) they are profoundly shocked, and their reply (660–4) is their most emotional utterance yet about anything other than their own fears, and does them credit; seventeen years of close association do not count for nothing. However, in protesting that – for the moment – they do not believe Teiresias' accusations, they invoke the Sun, from whose presence all uncleanness must be hidden (see Creon's words in 1426); and this suggests that in thinking of Teiresias' words they recall the charges of parricide and incest as well as that of regicide. The next stasimon will show how mistaken it is to suppose that they did not hear or did not understand what the prophet said. For the present they say, 'We defend Creon, not because we support Teiresias' accusations – nothing could be further from our thought; but because when Thebes is suffering from the plague a quarrel between her rulers can only make things worse.'

After Creon has gone, the Elders have to deal with Iocasta. Oedipus has surprised them momentarily into protesting that they don't believe a word that Teiresias said. This, however, is not the case. When Iocasta asks, 'What was the point at issue?' they hedge, and say again, 'Thebes has enough trouble; let this matter rest where it is.' Oedipus' ambiguous remark 687–8 they seem to interpret as implying, 'You see, you *do* believe what Teiresias said'; and their reply is fully revealing. They cannot bring themselves to say, 'We do not believe what Teiresias said', because they are predisposed to believe him in any case, and have not been given good reason for doubting him in the present instance. So they repeat with distressful emphasis, 'We would be both mad and foolish if we wanted to get rid of you. You saved our dear country in its former troubles; and you will probably guide us out of our present difficulty.' They are polite and con-

siderate, but entirely non-committal; and it would not escape
Oedipus that their last sentence is – whether or not the Leader
intended it so – ominously double-edged. For Oedipus will
indeed 'guide them out of the present difficulty' by being found
guilty, and taking the city's pollution away with him into
banishment.

By this time the steadying presence of Iocasta has in some
measure restored the king's self-control. His first three speeches
are, in effect: 'Creon has been plotting against me'; 'He says that
I killed Laius'; 'Or, at least, he sent in a corrupt prophet to say so,
being careful not to involve himself in slander'. After this comes
Iocastas's crucial speech of nineteen lines, containing two statements which, if Oedipus was unaware at the beginning of the
play, should make everything now clear to him; and if he was
aware, remove his last hope of uncertainty. Faced with this
knowledge, he remains calm and restrained and considerate to
Iocasta, even polite to the Chorus-Leader when he makes his
single remark in a passage of 165 lines. In fact, this is the point
where the two plays enter on the process of merging into one;
even if the play began with the orthodox assumption of ignorance,
it should now be clear to many in the audience, as it certainly is
to the Elders, that Oedipus knows and is facing the whole truth,
though Iocasta is still resisting; that Iocasta, having helped him
to recover from his emotional crisis, from this point on retreats
into impotent terror. Oedipus is now not only in command of the
situation on stage, but, especially towards the end of this scene,
he is protecting and comforting Iocasta, and trying to soften for
her the shock of knowledge which must inevitably come.

Before we examine the crucial developments which occupy the
rest of this Episode, we should give some time to looking at the
figure of Iocasta, the part she is given in the story and the way
she plays it. First, between her and Oedipus there is a deep
affection; it is this which lies behind the confidence and godlike
dignity which impressed us in the Prologue. Equally clear is his
tendency to yield in authority to her: she tells him what to think
and believe (707–9, 857–8); and when the Chorus-Leader urges
her to take Oedipus indoors, she replies, 'I will do so, when I have

learnt what happened'; and she proceeds to question – not Oedipus, but the Elders in Oedipus' presence. But on that occasion there is good reason; and she can also show due deference to him (769–70, 862). At 857 she tells Oedipus that, as for prophecy, she would not – as we say – cross the road for it; yet her next appearance, after an interval for reflection, shows her somewhat shamefacedly ('since you are nearest', 919) suspending this unbelief, as she comes with offerings for Apollo. Her changeableness partly springs from present apprehension, and partly reflects the philosophy which she expresses in a memorable phrase, 'To live at random is best' (979). This is a principle which might be upheld with rational argument; but Iocasta is of an opposite temper to Oedipus, and reasoning is not her strong point. To begin with, when she tries to comfort Oedipus by telling him to pay no heed to prophets, the example she quotes is of a prophecy about the future, while the question at issue concerns knowledge of past events – a very different matter, not necessarily involving supernatural powers at all. The clearest evidence of her irrational mind comes in 848 ff. 'This at least he cannot now revoke,' she says, referring to the eye-witness's account of Laius' death, 'for the city heard it, not only I' – a pathetic *non sequitur*. She continues, 'Even if he were to deviate somewhat . . .' – a phrase of naïve self-deception; and in the next eight lines her argument amounts to this: 'Even if you are proved to have killed Laius, and thus to be accursed and banished from Thebes, at least we know that the prophecy given to Laius thirty-five years ago was false.' This conclusion, even if it were sound, could not possibly bring any comfort to Oedipus, nor could Oedipus at this stage possibly think so, though Iocasta's tone in 857–8 shows that she thinks she has said something helpful. This must surely be the most unintelligent speech given to a royal heroine in any Greek tragedy; and the foolishness of 987 ('At least your father's death is a comfort') matches it closely. The folly arises first from panic, for which there is ample cause. There is, however, another explanation and excuse for Iocasta's inability to reason: she is obsessed with a hatred of oracles. The origin of this hatred is not far to seek, and furnishes another instance of the thoroughness with which Sophocles constructed for himself, and wove into the fabric of his drama, the whole life history of his chief characters. As a young wife Iocasta had her firstborn son taken from her and exposed on the mountain, because her husband feared an oracle.

We now return to the scene; and Iocasta begins her speech to Oedipus by bidding him take comfort and learn from her. She tells of the oracle given to Laius, and emphasises that it was given by Apollo's servants – implying that Apollo himself might know the truth, but his servants could only guess. (How, one might ask, could any god communicate his knowledge, if not through his mortal instruments?) The way in which she continues her story is worth observing. Instead of saying, 'So, as soon as the child was born, Laius had it exposed', she leaps forward eighteen years and says, 'Laius was killed by robbers at a crossroad.' Then she goes back again and says, 'Two days after the child's birth Laius bound its ankles together and had it thrown on the pathless mountainside.' This odd order is not noticeable in performance, and may possibly have no significance; but it does in fact enable a director to pass off as credible a detail which might otherwise seem incredible. I have seen a film version of *Oedipus* which made the point very clear. When the king was listening to this speech he followed Iocasta with close attention as far as the phrase 'a place where three roads meet'. Then he started, turned away from her, and walked slowly towards the camera with a brooding face. Behind him we saw Iocasta continuing the speech which Oedipus was obviously not hearing. The two lines 718–19 which Oedipus did not hear contain some scope for emotion on Iocasta's part (the plain verb 'he threw' which begins the line, the rare tribrach in the fifth foot, and possibly the somewhat emphatic *keinos*, 'that man'); but none of this reached Oedipus, who was absorbed in memories of the road to Daulia, and heard no word to remind him of what he knew all too well (see 1033), that he was standing on two scarred feet.

That is easy in a film; the screen showed only the two figures and faces. It is feasible in a theatre, ancient or modern; for an audience accepts what it is looking at more quickly than what it hears, and at this moment it sees Oedipus engrossed in recollection, and deaf to words which, had he heard them, would have stopped the play then and there. And in real life it might happen that a man would fail to hear, even though spoken directly to him, just those words which could have told him the truth he was seeking. But this is not real life, it is art; a play written by a man who chose every word he wrote. Sophocles knew that audiences would happily accept this anomaly; he was writing for the mass of his fellow citizens on a national religious occasion, writing the play they wanted and could accept. Why, then, should he include this anomaly at all? It was not necessary for Iocasta to mention the maimed feet at this point. Why should she address to Oedipus crucial words which are not essential here to the traditional story, for Oedipus to ignore and for the audience to forget? Is there another such instance in Greek tragedy?

Let us first, for argument's sake, accept the passage as it has always been accepted, and admit that it is conceivable for such significant words to be spoken, and to be ignored by the character to whom they are spoken, to whom they are vitally relevant. The question still remains, Why did Sophocles write these words? And the answer must be, that he intended careful listeners or readers[1] to consider what situation arises, if Oedipus hears and understands the words Iocasta speaks to him. We remember that his name is Oedipus, *Oidi-pous*: he knows his feet and is known by them; and we see that his only possible reason for not bursting in with 'I have scarred feet, I am the son of Laius!' is that he knows it already before Iocasta speaks; that his aim is, for the sake of Thebes, to secure his own banishment as the killer of Laius, and to spare Iocasta the exposure of incest; that Teiresias' words have taken matters beyond his control, so that he is now cautiously feeling his way, undecided yet whether full disclosure – of incest as well as regicide – is necessary or avoidable. So, in answer to Iocasta, he chooses to notice, not the uncommon detail so personal to him – the story of the maimed feet – but the commonplace, less dangerous detail of the road-junction. He has recovered from his confusion. The severance with Creon has

[1] For the *readers* of tragedies, see p. 103.

assured him that, in treading the lonely path on which he cannot now turn back, he is leaving behind him a world familiar and dear, but unreal, and entering a world dark and terrifying, but real. It seems that during the latter part of this scene he decides that his establishment of truth must not be partial; and Iocasta's allusion to his maimed feet has contributed to this decision. He must be exposed as not only the killer, but the son, of Laius; and this involves taking Iocasta with him into the darkness and terror. This last realisation is a further step in his achievement of knowledge. In 830–3 he expresses indirectly his horror at the thought of what awaits him; but he demands that the Shepherd be brought.

Oedipus asks Iocasta a series of questions (726–57) about the place of Laius' death, the time, the king's personal appearance, the number of his retinue, the carriage and the herald – whose presence would indicate royalty. (It has already been pointed out, p. 117, that Oedipus could hardly have avoided asking just these questions, and getting the same answers, on the day he first entered Thebes.) To complete the tally, Oedipus asks about the man who escaped, the eye-witness; and Iocasta's answer is to be studied. She begins: 'When he came from the place and saw that you were king and Laius was dead. . . .' This sentence gives a confused account of the sequence of events; and confusion would be natural, and could be deliberate, if she knew (as Creon knew) what evidence the man gave at the first inquiry (see p. 177). Iocasta's clear statement of the facts has been made already in 736–7: the servant brought this news to Thebes 'a little while before you became king'. During that interval, then, Oedipus went to the Sphinx, answered her riddle, and received his reward. From the information Sophocles gives us certain conclusions can be drawn about the conscious knowledge with which Oedipus at that time made his fatal decision; these have already been described on pp. 116 ff. Iocasta now provides a further detail, concerning the servant who escaped: 'He clasped my hand and begged me earnestly to send him to the country pastures, so that he might be as far as possible out of sight of the city.' In writing those lines Sophocles can have had no other purpose than to indicate that the servant had recognised Oedipus.[1] If Oedipus began the play aware of the truth, this detail is already known to him; if unaware, then it is for him, as it is for the Chorus, further confirmation of the knowledge already gained, first from Teiresias, and now from Iocasta's details about Laius and his servants.

Iocasta in her revealing speech to Oedipus tells him (717–19) that her infant son was exposed by Laius. We should now look at the institution of infant exposure and see what significance it has in this story. The object of it was, of course, to get rid of the child without incurring ritual guilt by killing one of kindred blood. A vivid belief in gods or goddesses who might take care of the abandoned child must often have countenanced the act; we see this belief cherished by Creusa in Euripides' *Ion*. The theory on which Laius relied was evidently that exposure on the 'pathless mountain' provided a ninety-nine per cent probability that the child would die, while reserving a one per cent possibility that it would live – and this possibility saved him from ritual pollution by kindred blood. The practice, though probably not frequent, was regular enough in Greek communities to occasion little or no critical comment on humanitarian grounds. I do not know of any passage from ancient writers which supports the assumption that infant-exposure would be regarded as a crime in either the heroic or the Periclean age. Fourth-century ethics began to be more sensitive, and there is a scene in Menander's *Periceiromene* where an aging father, meeting after eighteen years his miraculously preserved children, listens to their reproaches and expresses his penitence. The exposure of Oedipus, in any case, was not Iocasta's act but Laius' (718–19); and Laius has already paid his debt. The more surprising thing is that the added barbarity of piercing the child's feet has never, apparently, drawn upon Laius any of the infamy which attaches, for example, to Atreus for his treatment of his nephews. Iocasta in recounting the fact voices no overt censure of her husband (unless possibly the pronoun *keinos* carries a bitter tone). Oedipus himself expresses a natural indignation (1035, 1037); but the absence of other

[1] The significance of this in relation to what Creon says about events at that period is dealt with on p. 177.

comment suggests that foot-piercing was not unheard of in cases of exposure. Again, I have not yet come across any literary reference, any primitive custom known to anthropologists, to illuminate this point; which is an important one, since if foot-piercing were a traditional practice, however rare, the scars would mean that Oedipus grew up knowing he was a foundling. As it is, the orthodox view of the play has to insist that Oedipus, even after being told by the drunken guest that he was not Polybus' son, even after being refused enlightenment by Polybus, and even after being given at Delphi a prophecy which suggested something mysterious in his relationship with his parents, still did not think of connecting his scarred feet with the possibility that he was a foundling. To accept this demands the suspension of disbelief to a remarkable, but evidently not impossible, degree.

Someone once said of Tolstoy that as a novelist he was supreme because he knew fully the inner meaning, source and history of every little personal habit or feature of the characters who move over his vast stage. Within the 1530 lines of this play Sophocles shows us a comparable creative process at work. A complete structure, such as a novelist would conceive, exists in this dramatist's imagination; those of its events which are visibly enacted, those which are specifically narrated, are chosen with the strictest economy; but because the rest formed a clear and coherent pattern in the creator's concept, shadows and echoes of them occur again and again, some of them deliberately placed by the author, others probably unconscious. Here is a slight but remarkable example: Oedipus refers eleven times to his two parents; in two of these cases, the nature of what he is saying makes it inevitable that he should mention his father first (774, 1497–8); in 1372–3 he again mentions his father first; but in the other eight cases it is always 'my mother and my father'. Oedipus is a man to whom parental affection, given (see 1463–5) or received (1023), meant much; he grew up an orphan; but he thinks first of his mother, then of his father – and this trait shows itself in the way the poet writes the lines Oedipus is to speak.

So once again it should be remembered here that a thing legitimately to be attempted is to reconstruct, from the material

Sophocles provides, that outline of the whole story which must have been the source from which he created his characters and moulded the lines they were to speak. Now, following up the implications of the story of the exposure, we may infer that Laius lived the rest of his life gambling on a ninety-nine-to-one chance; and eventually he lost, when his son, in a quarrel with a grey-haired man, knew that he must heed Apollo's warning and not strike him, but reckoned the chance was not one in ten thousand that this could be his father, and struck. The pattern was reversed when Oedipus, after defeating the Sphinx, was faced with marrying Iocasta. Now the odds, backed by the authority of the Delphic oracle, were a hundred to one that he was indeed Iocasta's son; but he seized the slender possibility that his fears were groundless, that he was the true son of Polybus, and so justified himself in taking the risk in spite of Apollo's warning. These situations are the background to two notable moments in the play: Iocasta's pronouncement, 'It is best to live at random' (979), and Oedipus' 'I hold myself the son of Chance' (1080); as well as to the frequent use throughout the play of the noun *tychē*, 'chance', and its cognate verb (see Knox, *OAT*, 165–8, 176–9, *et al.*). Thus the story of the exposure provides material for the 'temporal' aspect of the drama; just as the story of the oracle, which perceives and adjusts the symmetry of the whole pattern, provides material for its 'spatial' aspect. These two opposed elements in the story of Oedipus, *Tychē* and *Dikē*, Chance guiding the events of life, and Justice balancing the long-term pattern, are the two basic elements in the human condition: chance events – the stuff of which a man has to make his life; and the symmetry of the pattern – the medium of every man's self-discovery.

Now comes Oedipus' story of the first crucial period in his life. He begins by telling Iocasta, 'My father was Polybus of Corinth, my mother Merope.' Of course it is unlikely that after so many years of marriage Oedipus would now be informing his wife, as if for the first time, who his parents were; but it is dramatically important that this whole passage should provide for the audience a clear and complete statement. This line supplies as briefly as possible what is needed, and the improbability is hardly noticed in performance. It is, however, surely perverse to argue from this instance that all, or that any, other improbabilities in the play are to be accepted as insignificant. This instance is dramatically desirable, but carries no implications which affect the plot; even if Oedipus had never told Iocasta his father's name, nothing would be implied about the degree of knowledge of his identity possessed by him or by Iocasta. On the other hand, the play contains elsewhere a dozen incredibilities which, like this one, pass unnoticed in action, but which, unlike this one, combine their implications to form a coherent picture of a real situation already known to Oedipus, a situation whose truth is in due time revealed. When we consider, for example, the improbability, loaded with significance, which is discussed in the next paragraph, we cannot simply dismiss it by referring to 774, 'My father was Polybus of Corinth'.

Oedipus then relates the incident at a banquet in Corinth, when a drunk man told him that he was not Polybus' son. Before relating this, Oedipus describes it as 'a surprising incident, but one that I ought not to have taken so seriously'. Does he really think that it was not a thing to be taken seriously? Polybus, he says, when questioned, was angry – and this was a comfort to him; but 'the matter was being widely talked of', and lines 775–7 seem to imply that Oedipus' standing in Corinth suffered as a result. He was worried enough to leave home secretly and question the Delphic oracle. The oracle gave him no assurance, but foretold a fate which reinforced the idea that there was a mystery about his parentage. Add to this the fact that he had grown up from infancy (1035, *sparganōn*) conscious of a 'terrible reproach' in the malformation of his feet – a thing for which Polybus could offer no explanation. If we consider all the details which Sophocles has supplied, that taunt at the banquet was not the beginning of a new suspicion but the confirmation of an old one. Apollo's refusal to satisfy him was further confirmation; and after all this, who can believe that Oedipus imagined himself as destined by Apollo to kill Polybus and marry Merope? The man who twenty minutes earlier in the play was told repeatedly by

Teiresias that he was not the son of Polybus, and then admitted
he did not know who his father was, now tells Iocasta that the
drunkard's taunt was not to be taken seriously. This is incredible.
Admittedly, Iocasta has not yet heard any report of what
Teiresias said; but the Chorus are there all the time; and is the
king's memory so short? No: when Oedipus says, 'I ought not to
have taken this so seriously', he is saying what he wants Iocasta,
for her own sake, to accept. She entered the stage at 634 imperi-
ous and domineering; but by 746 she is afraid; and Oedipus
already sees that she is unequal to the ordeal that awaits her, and
instinctively adopts a protective attitude. Even on an orthodox
interpretation it is impossible to suppose at this stage in the play,
after all that has passed, that he himself believes there was no
significance in the drunkard's shout. He is in fact presenting to
Iocasta and to the Elders the carefully constructed façade behind
which he has lived for seventeen years, the version of his life-
story which was forced on him as the result of his rash blow on
the Delphi road, and still more rash yielding to ambition when
he accepted the throne of Thebes. He is the pious and innocent
son of Polybus.

After recounting the twofold prophecy that Apollo gave him,
in terms which spare nothing (791–3), he continues: 'When I
heard this, I resolved for the future to measure my distance from
Corinth by the stars, and I fled, towards any place where I might
never see this evil prophecy shamefully fulfilled.' We must
remember that he is speaking to Iocasta, who did not hear
Teiresias, rather than to the Elders, who did; but the Elders are
listening. Even Iocasta, though not an acute reasoner, might well
be struck by the fact that his story, like hers, contains a prophecy
of parricide; but there is such a wealth of cogent evidence
establishing the first charge, of regicide, that this coincidence
pointing directly to the second, of parricide and incest, merely
hangs above the action as a threatening cloud.

These few lines (794–7) are of central importance. The whole
of the orthodox interpretation depends on assuming that this
statement of Oedipus to Iocasta is still his genuine belief. In
performance the intensity of feeling is such that an audience will

readily accept this, and if qualms remain they are dispelled by
the ever-growing excitement. I have to record that I was myself
conscious of such qualms since my first reading of the play as a
student; but the dramatic interest always carried me safely to the
end of the scene. This undoubtedly was the poet's intention – for
the majority of his audience. But if it had been his only intention
there would have been no qualms. Why should there be? The
banquet in Corinth was, as far as we know, not a part of the
traditional myth; even if it was, it could easily have been
omitted or replaced; Sophocles could have found another motive
for Oedipus' visit to Delphi. Instead he selected, or invented, this
motive, one which makes it plain that when Oedipus left Delphi
he regarded as probably untenable the belief that Polybus was
his father. That is to say, he knew very well that to avoid Corinth
would not save him from the crimes predicted; he might meet
his parents anywhere in Greece. He continues: 'In my journey I
came to that place where you say this king met his death. And,
my wife, I will tell you the truth. . . .' The next thirteen lines
will be the very truth – all except the last word; but surely that
phrase, 'I will tell you the truth', marks the transition, whether
conscious or unconscious, from fiction to fact.

The sequence of events described by Oedipus is, I think,
rightly interpreted (except on one point) by Jebb in his note on
804,–12. Oedipus first met the herald, who was walking in front;
Laius, in the carriage, and the herald 'were for driving' him
forcibly from the path; at their bidding the driver, who was
walking by the horses, shoved Oedipus aside, and Oedipus in
anger hit him; as he passed the carriage the old man leant out and
hit him with the goad. Oedipus dragged the old man out of the
carriage; the herald and the driver came to attack him, and so
did two attendants who were probably walking behind the
carriage. Oedipus killed Laius and three servants; one servant
got away (Jebb says, 'unperceived by Oedipus', which is quite
groundless, and incredible considering the nature of the place,
and the danger Oedipus was in, which would make him take care to
ascertain whether he had dealt with all his enemies); but Oedipus
says, 'I killed them all.' In this he is reverting instinctively to his

protective façade, the version of his story which has enabled him to live in Thebes and which says that there does not exist in the city a man who saw him kill Laius. But this reversion is instinctive and not deliberate, for he has already asked for the man to be summoned.

The next ten lines contain two twin curiosities: twice Oedipus makes a statement and follows it with a reason which is no reason. In 815 ff. he says, 'What man could be more wretched or more hateful to the gods than I, since no one . . . may lawfully receive me . . .?' and in 823 ff., 'Am I not wholly impure, since I must be banished, and in banishment never see my parents or tread my native soil?' We should note that when in 813 he says, 'I killed every man of them', his tone is that of factual narrative scarcely tinged with regret, still less with guilt; he is speaking of anonymous travellers. The 'But if . . .' which follows considers an entirely different hypothesis, namely that the man he had killed was Laius, king of Thebes. What in Oedipus' reasoning constitutes the difference? The fact that his victim was a king? No, for he had already noted the herald whose presence indicated royalty. The actual meaning of Oedipus' words here has no moral content at all; he simply says, 'I am wretched because I have unwittingly cursed myself.' Something much more morally serious than this is suggested not only by the emotional tone of the passage, but also by the fact that the audience knows the truth; what we are half expecting him to say is, 'I am wretched and hated by gods because I killed my own father, as Teiresias said.' This he dare not yet say; but this is the truth which his agonised tone urges Iocasta to face. The simple meaning of his words in 823 ff. is, 'I am polluted, since in banishment I may not see my parents'; and the inconsequence of this (for banishment and the avoidance of his family and fatherland cannot make him impure) only underlines the cogent rationality of what we are half expecting him to say: 'I am polluted because I am married to my mother.' This he dare not yet say; but this is the truth which he must induce Iocasta to recognise, if he and she are to penetrate, in the brief time now left to them, the barrier of pretence which has separated them since the day they were joined in marriage.

Furthermore, these two appeals have been preceded by an even stronger one, which we find in the verbal pattern of 813–14, 'If there is any blood relationship between this stranger and Laius.' On the surface this is a cautious way of saying 'If this stranger [i.e. the man in the carriage] and Laius were one and the same person.' But though to Oedipus Laius had been a stranger, Oedipus too is himself a stranger – see 219, 452. Iocasta a few minutes ago was speaking of the son who had been destined to become his father's killer. A few lines later we find 'These hands of mine, which killed him, now defile his bed.' These words, even the verb *chrainō*, 'defile', may no doubt be taken to fit the supposition that Oedipus is the son of Polybus; but they recall so closely the words, only thirty lines back (791–3), in which Oedipus related Apollo's prophecy, that we should expect them to strike a chord in Iocasta's mind. That they should strike no chord in the mind of Oedipus as he speaks them, may be acceptable in performance, but to a reader must surely be incredible. The illogicality of the whole passage shows in a most poignant way the effort Oedipus is making to bring together two worlds, the real and the unreal, first in his own mind, and then, if possible, in the consciousness of Iocasta. A still closer look at this passage will reveal yet more.

At line 825, in the middle of a long sentence, comes a most surprising 'sleight-of-tongue'. Up to this point, more than half-way through the play, the issue of the plot has been perfectly clear: is Oedipus, or is he not, the man who killed Laius, and therefore banished by his own curse? This question is by now almost resolved; Teiresias has said that Oedipus is the guilty man, and a whole pattern of circumstantial evidence has since confirmed the charge, so that only one faint hope remains – the testimony of the eye-witness who has been sent for. Unless this proves favourable and strong enough to confute all the rest, Oedipus must within the hour quit his throne, home and family, and wander forth a shunned and penniless outcast. With this shattering prospect before him, Oedipus in 825–6 suddenly alludes to another prospect, admittedly a terrible one, but in comparison with his imminent exile quite remote: the possibility that he might one day kill Polybus and marry Merope. This possibility has been mentioned only once before in the play, 791–3, and is a burden which Oedipus has clearly borne for seventeen years or more without undue anxiety. Yet now, in face of immediate disaster, Oedipus switches his attention to this ancient prophecy; and in doing so makes no reference to the fact that less than an hour ago Teiresias told him it was already fulfilled. When, in 830, he prays to the gods for help, his words make it clear that what he is deprecating is not his banishment as the killer of Laius but his fulfilment of the Delphic oracle. Though the remainder of this scene is concerned with the real issue – whether or not he killed Laius – yet the first part of the next scene strongly suggests to us (947–8, 964–88) that the extreme agitation in which Oedipus spent the interval occupied by the Second Stasimon – described by Iocasta in 914–17 – was caused not by the real issue at all but by consideration of this remote and irrelevant hazard. Not only so, but it appears that Oedipus has managed to switch Iocasta's attention as well as his own in this unaccountable way, from the real to the unreal. What is the meaning of this?

First, is this new issue in fact unreal? Oedipus has lived for seventeen years taking care, presumably, never to kill an old man who might be Polybus, king of Corinth, and he has so far managed to avoid this – we have seen no sign in 800 lines that such a fear obsessed him. The danger of his marrying Merope is purely fantastic; she must be a good deal older than Iocasta, for she would hardly have adopted a foundling until she had been childless for some years; and Iocasta cannot well be less than fifty-one. In any case, the danger of Oedipus' committing these two acts is irrelevant to the whole issue of the play as established in the First Episode. This new issue, then, is unreal. So we must ask next, What is happening here? Our study of the play up to this point should make it clear. Oedipus is trying to get Iocasta to face the truth, to break through, before it is too late, the barrier of pretence. In 822–3 he has used the words 'defile', 'evil', 'impure'. As he speaks them he cannot tell what effect they are having on Iocasta – she has her refuge ready, and runs to it in 848 with 'But be assured that this is how the report was first published'; but all three words win an emphatic, if silent, assent from the Elders, who in the course of this speech have been finally enlightened, and have turned from sympathy to condemnation. To defy their hostility, and still plead with Iocasta to face the truth, Oedipus puts the situation into words: 'I am doomed to marry my mother and to kill my father.' Whether line 827, 'Polybus, who begot and reared me', is spurious as some editors say, or is a defiant lie to the Elders' faces, is immaterial; Iocasta resists what Oedipus is trying to make her accept. She accepts instead what appears, verbally, as a sudden switch on Oedipus' part from the real issue to the unreal one, partly because it fits her obsessive hatred of oracles, and partly because it offers a momentary refuge from total exposure of the truth; and finding some comfort in this she sticks to it (987, 'At least your father's death is a comfort') until the Corinthian destroys her illusion in 1016. Meanwhile Oedipus' lines 830–3 are an agonised utterance – 'Never, O pure holiness of gods, never may I see that day!' – but the danger which their literal meaning deprecates is in fact even more remote now than it has ever been, and grows more remote with the passing of each year. The agony springs not from this danger, but from the knowledge of the truth which is on the point of being revealed to all the Thebans and, worst of all, to Iocasta. It is a last plea for communication, after half a lifetime of severance by pretence.

What are we to make of the couplet spoken by the Chorus-Leader 834–5? What does he expect from the evidence of the eye-witness? Oedipus has not yet alluded to the discrepancy between 'a large band of robbers' and 'one lone traveller'. Is it possible that the Leader knows what happened at Creon's inquiry, and anticipates a summary conviction of Oedipus? On the surface the words imply 'Perhaps the servant will say that the killer was a man quite unlike you in appearance'; but this equivocal speech should be interpreted in the light of the Ode which is soon to follow. Certainly the Elders are moved by the dreadful nature of the whole situation – 'to us these things are full of fear' – but their counsel to 'have hope until the eye-witness comes' carries a very thin surface of comfort over a depth of

condemnation, and is even more likely to be ominous and malevolent, implying: 'Enjoy hope while you can; once the shepherd
comes your hope will vanish.' The Elders in fact already see
Oedipus' double guilt as evident; the coming of the Shepherd
will establish it and justify the indignation which burns in them.
Oedipus in his reply looks them in the face; he knows what is in
their mind, and knows that they do not know what is in his.
Meanwhile he provides Iocasta with a slender hope which at
least will enable her to turn her back on the Elders with dignity,
yet reminding her (846–7) that if it fails he is accursed and
banished.

Iocasta's reply has already been considered (pp. 184–5). It
shows a foolishness which can only reflect panic. 'He cannot contradict what he said then.' Why not? Any man can contradict his
former statement, however many people heard it. The rest of her
speech is of the kind which allows an actor to play infinite varia-
tions; it may indicate anything between complete innocence and
a fair degree of percipience. She has before her three clear
statements and one fact. They are: Apollo said that Laius would
be killed by his own son; it is extremely probable that Oedipus
killed Laius; Apollo told Oedipus that he would kill his own father
and marry his mother; Iocasta is married to Oedipus. All this
knowledge is now in Iocasta's possession. Did not Sophocles
postulate some limit, even in a woman, to mental blindness and
self-deception? If in face of all this Iocasta has no inkling of the
truth, perhaps she may still be a heroic figure. If on the other
hand she begins to perceive, but with an instinct to protect
Oedipus in front of the Chorus now makes her entirely irrelevant
censures on Loxias and on prophecy in general, her speech is at
once heroic, convincing and moving. If this is the case, does
Oedipus perceive that she perceives? Perhaps not. His reply, 'You
judge well', seems more probably to mark the point at which,
believing that she has finally retreated from the truth, he takes
over responsibility and emancipates himself from the maternal
authority whose power he felt for the last time at the opening of
this scene, 634–86. Even if Iocasta now begins to perceive, her
words seem to show that she cannot deal with what she perceives;

Oedipus must make decisions for her, and must support whatever frail defences she may find in her distress. As part of his reassuring attitude he accepts her assumption that she is the person who will give orders for the Shepherd to be fetched; at the same time, lest her panic should prevail, he makes his reminder a firm one: 'Do not neglect this.'

Before leaving this Episode we should carry a step further the study, begun on p. 183, of the place that Sophocles has given to Iocasta in the pattern of knowing and not-knowing. She has in common with Oedipus, first, an awareness of the 'outer circle' of timeless and absolute knowledge; for the opening of her adult life, as of his, was overshadowed and distorted by a prophecy – a prophecy whose fulfilment she must dread as a wife (though as a wronged and indignant mother she might even hope for it); secondly, an awareness, gained from experience, that what most people call 'knowledge' is hardly distinguishable from 'belief', i.e. it can be a thing chosen, either deliberately or intuitively, as a basis for living. She differs from Oedipus in that her suppression of truth has been more complete than his,[1] since in her the dominant side of life is the emotional, in him the intellectual; he is struggling to escape from his chosen unreality, she is clinging to hers.

With Creon she has little in common. Creon's deference to oracles (1438–9, 1518) seems to be a political rather than a religious attitude; Iocasta's antipathy to oracles is rooted in the injury which an oracle inflicted on her as a girl-mother. Creon's concealment of knowledge is fully deliberate; Iocasta's suppression of knowledge springs from fear and is barely conscious.

Perhaps it is only at this late stage, when the uncertainty of Iocasta's mental grasp has become apparent, that we remember the impressive brilliance of her first entry (634), and realise how her first lines, though convincing at the moment, betrayed her weakness. When from inside the palace she heard Oedipus shouting *O polis polis*, she at once concluded that the king and her brother were demeaning themselves in an 'ill-considered

---

[1] It is possible that in 436 Teiresias suggests that Iocasta's knowledge, though suppressed, is real.

dispute' over a 'trifling grievance'. This shows the arrogance of the kind of woman who acts and speaks on the principle that a quick judgement is more desirable than a careful one. Iocasta must feel the first shudder of the approach of truth during Oedipus' speech 771–833, and her innate unsoundness of judgement snatches at a crumbling hold in 849, 'He cannot revoke what he said'; by the time the Corinthian arrives she has reached an intuitive decision to forget the real issue entirely and pretend that everything hangs on the truth or untruth of prophecy. When we study the Third Episode we shall see that this pathetic move wins no conviction from Oedipus – though the opposite assumption, as part of the orthodox view, has always been taken seriously in spite of its absurdities. It is only when the Corinthian produces his unexpected information in 1026 ('Cithaeron') and in 1042 ('Laius') that Iocasta's last defences are swept away; and Oedipus, who must still harden himself for one more scene, has to turn suddenly from compassion to brutality.

This is not yet the whole account; we shall contemplate Iocasta again near the end of Chapter 6. For the present we go back to the close of the Second Episode. The Chorus, after the Leader's one equivocal remark, have listened in silence. The king and queen perform their desperate and hollow dialogue to make possible a dignified exit. Giving each other what affection and miserable comfort they can, both go into the palace, leaving the Elders with more to say than they can well contain.

# 5

## The Olympian Laws

The Elders' chief feeling is one of horror at what has been revealed; and the horror arouses their first concern not for Oedipus but for themselves. When the First Episode ended they were disturbed by the prophet's accusations but unwilling to believe them without proof, remembering the services Oedipus had rendered to Thebes. They then saw the king, without any evidence, accuse Creon of treason and demand his death, and this with a display of uncontrolled rage which shocked and embarrassed them; this was not the behaviour of an innocent man. Then, when Iocasta spoke of the death of Laius, they heard Oedipus recognise one detail in her account, ask for more details, recognise them all, and exclaim, 'Alas, this is now utterly clear!' They heard of the oracle which said that Laius would be killed by his own son – corresponding with what Teiresias had said; they heard that Iocasta's son had been exposed and was assumed dead; and knew that, if he had survived, he would now be of the age of Oedipus. They heard Oedipus' life-story: that in his youth his parentage was in question, and neither his supposed parents nor the oracle of Delphi would give him any assurance; that Apollo had destined him to the same two crimes of which Teiresias just now accused him, parricide and incest; and could they fail to notice that Apollo's prophecy of parricide given to Oedipus foretold the same crime by which, a generation earlier, Apollo had said Laius was to die? They heard that Oedipus on his way to Thebes had killed a man who almost certainly was Laius, and in circumstances which would make it probable that as soon as he entered the city he would know who it was he had killed. They had now learnt that he accepted the throne of Thebes, and the widowed queen as his wife, at a time when Apollo's warning was fresh in his ears, and in spite of the doubt about his birth, and other significant facts readily ascertainable.

All this, or most of it, the Elders should have intelligence enough to interpret. (We may pardon them for not going one step further to ask, 'Why then did the king pronounce a curse, knowing himself guilty?') They see before them a man destined by heaven to horrors, who did not flee from his destiny but through ambition embraced it. They see him as the cause of the plague which is devastating Thebes, and as the source of gross pollution in every part of the city's life. They themselves have been his close associates in government; and they know well that, when the gods destroy a sinner, those nearest to him are engulfed in the cataclysm. They are in mortal fear. Their lives have been circumspect and law-abiding; the plague has threatened, but they so far have escaped – are they after all to perish with the wicked? They have heard of the *moira*, 'destiny', of Laius, and the *daimōn*, or attendant fate, of Oedipus. What of their own? They know of the prizes Oedipus won; what prize shall be theirs, as men who desire purity and reverence the laws of Olympus? They begin with a prayer.

The prayer is spoken, as is usual in a Chorus, in the first person singular; and the order of words, though hard to preserve in English, shows clearly their train of thought. *Ei moi xyneiē pheronti moira tān eusepton hagneian* . . . *Ei xyneiē* expresses a wish or prayer, and *moi* is 'for me': the strophe is a prayer for themselves. *Moira* is one's 'destiny' or 'portion' in life. Oedipus enjoys the 'portion' of a king; the Elders' portion is that of subjects; but subjects may pray for innocence or purity as a portion for themselves (864) and for destruction as a portion (887) for the king (*moira* is the word in both cases). A portion may be partly assigned by fate, partly won by merit. *Pheronti tān eusepton hagneian* is 'winning that [coveted prize of] pious innocence or purity'. The rest of the long sentence is clear in a straightforward translation:

'May the portion that accompanies me through life be one that wins the prize of pious purity in regard to all words and deeds concerning which are established those laws of lofty range, laws brought into being in the clear regions of the sky, whose father is Olympus alone; laws begotten by no mortal human nature, nor shall oblivion ever lay them to sleep; divinity is powerful in them, and never grows old.'

The Elders are subjects of a king who has absolute power over their lives: it is natural they should shrink from speaking too openly; but their prayer for purity is, as plainly as they dare utter, a protestation to the gods that they wish to dissociate themselves from the polluted man who has broken the holiest laws of the universe. What, in fact, are the deeds forbidden by those laws which the Elders describe in phrases of such sublimity? In the next stanza they summarise them as *hybris*; and exponents of the orthodox view insist that what they say about *hybris* and its consequences, from 873 to 896, should be taken as general moral reflection. If this is so, *hybris* must refer to Oedipus' behaviour to Teiresias and Creon, and 'begets the tyrant' must be meant as a warning that if Oedipus continues such behaviour he will become a tyrant. If this is the case there is no special point in 'to no good end . . . things neither proper nor profitable' (874–5), and the doom foreseen in 876 ff. is also general in its application; and it must further be assumed that the Elders, despite their anxiety to find and exterminate the cause of the plague, and despite the mass of evidence which has been unfolded before their ears and eyes, are still ready to be persuaded that Oedipus is innocent of the death of Laius, and have not yet suspected whose son he is. But this Ode, following so eventful a scene, must surely bear some reference to what took place in it; the Elders are not singing a hymn chosen at random out of the book. It is most unlikely that they should speak in such terms of the Olympian laws, unless they felt sure those laws had been broken. What laws have been broken in the play so far? Two: one which says, Thou shalt not fly into a rage against thy kinsman, nor accuse him unjustly; and another which says, Thou shalt not express scepticism about the words of prophets. The first of these is an excellent rule, but one of ethical expediency rather than of fundamental morality; and a threat, which it is folly to utter, only becomes *hybris* when it is carried out. As for the second, the Chorus themselves came near to breaking it in lines 499–501, 'It is not proved that any mortal prophet knows more about the future than I do.' To suggest that these two faults (or, still more, the fault of Iocasta in allowing her son to be exposed) fittingly introduce the theme of *hybris* in the next stanza, is to stretch the argument beyond belief; as offences against heaven, they are simply not commensurate with the lofty splendour of these lines about the Olympian laws. The Elders speak as they do because they are convinced that Oedipus is guilty of two more heinous acts, which are not the less terrible for being unwitting. Their awe-inspiring phrases refer to two laws based in the very being of man: Thou shalt not shed thy father's blood; Thou shalt not enter thy mother's bed.

'Arrogance begets the tyrant.'[1] It is clear now what particular meaning they put into this general statement. The arrogance which ignored warning, calculation and probability, to secure a throne by marrying a queen, now after many years begets the tyrant who can insult a revered prophet, and demand the death of a tried friend and kinsman, on unfounded surmise. They continue: 'Arrogance, if it be surfeited to no good end [*or*, in its folly] with many possessions which are neither proper nor profitable, after climbing to the topmost ramparts plunges to the most miserable straits, where no service of the foot can serve.' (Again the imagery includes the word *pous* – the falling king will find no *foot*hold.) 'Struggle', or 'wrestling' (the literal meaning of *palaisma*) 'that benefits the state, I pray the god may never bring to an end. The god I shall not cease to regard as our protector.' Oedipus' 'possession', the city of Thebes, is perishing by the plague, and thus proves as 'unprofitable' as his possession of Iocasta is 'improper'. 'The most miserable straits' describes the outlawed condition which Oedipus has brought on himself by his proclaimed curse. Oedipus' victory over the Sphinx ('advantageous for the city') is set against his quarrel with Creon; and even

[1] For the meaning of the word 'tyrant', see Knox, *OAT* 53–60 *et al.*

for that victory (see 38) the god, and not Oedipus, will receive the Elders' praise and gratitude as the city's defender.

The second strophe becomes yet more outspoken; to any who were present in the Second Episode, every phrase indicts the king. Oedipus has *walked proudly in his words* (against Teiresias and Creon) *and in his actions* (against Laius); in accepting the throne of Thebes, which came to him through a violent act, he has *shown no fear of judgement*; if he had *felt reverence for temples of the gods* he would have heeded the twofold warning he received at Delphi. Because he did not heed it, the Elders now pray unequivocally, 'May an evil destiny (*moira*) destroy him.' It is still perhaps possible to take the seven condemnatory phrases of this strophe as general in their reference, a mere pious execration of evil-doers; but the catalogue of sins fits the case of Oedipus exactly. *Chlidē* means 'luxurious self-indulgence'; the Chorus use this word as a euphemism for incest, and call it 'ill-starred', or in Jebb's phrase, 'miserably perverse'. Oedipus had come to Thebes with empty hands, and he *gained his advantage unjustly*. He did not *keep himself from impious deeds* (parricide), and *in his folly he touched the untouchable* (incest). Taking courage from this battery of accusations, each supported by the evidence of the last scene, the Chorus abandon the pretence of a general moral reflection and summarise their indictment with 'in the case of these crimes' and 'actions of this kind'. Oedipus has for long enough escaped the arrows of the gods. 'If actions of this kind are held in honour, why should I dance?' This striking phrase has two layers of meaning. First, it is the Theban Elders speaking in character and asking, 'What is the point of religious observance?' For *choreuein* means any kind of religious ritual or procession based on prescribed movement and music. Then with the second meaning of the words the Chorus, as it were, momentarily step out of the play and appeal directly to the moral and religious sense of the audience, saying to them in effect, 'We, by our part in this Dionysiac performance, and you by your presence here, are alike committed to honouring the Olympian laws of Zeus, which are the same to you today as they were to Oedipus seven centuries before you.'

The final stanza, however, has a significance which is strictly dramatic, and not to be taken (as it has often been taken) either for a general lament over the decline of religious belief in the late fifth century, or for a mere reproof of the impiety shown by Oedipus and Iocasta in defying the oracles of Apollo. In fact the tone of the whole utterance is less that of religious-minded men deploring the prevalent irreligion, than that of the common man who is annoyed when his religion does not do for him what he wants it to do, and threatens to abandon it, saying that in any case other people are doing the same. To say this is not to call the Elders hypocritical or peevish. The firmly-stated condition with which the last stanza opens represents an accepted attitude in Greek religion, providing one of its notable contrasts with the modern Western idea of religion. 'I will go no more to worship at Delphi or Abae or Olympia, if these prophecies shall not fit together, so that all men point the finger at them. So, almighty Zeus, if you are truly called almighty, let these things not pass unnoticed by you and your ever-undying rule!' For Greeks the worship of gods was in one aspect a bargain that had to be honoured on both sides. If the gods receive worship they must give value in return, in matters which men are powerless to govern for themselves, such as the respect for moral principles shown by other individuals or by cities. This 'condition' addressed to Zeus by the Elders is also an echo of what the Priest of Zeus said to Oedipus in the Prologue (47 ff.), 'Have a care for your fame. . . . Let us not put it on record that under your rule we were raised up only to fall later.' So now the Elders say to Zeus, 'If you expect our worship, it is for you to convict the guilty man.'

There are two phrases which attach this stanza to the action of the play, showing that the Ode is not merely general in application, but is a demand for the immediate overthrow of Oedipus. The first is in 902–3, 'if these things shall not fit together, so that all men point the finger at them'. What things are to 'fit together' (*harmosei*)? The prophecies given to Laius and to Oedipus, and the statements made by Teiresias; Oedipus' killing of a king on the road from Thebes to Delphi, and his learning a few days later in Thebes that Laius had been killed on that road at that time;

the prophecy given him by Apollo, and his acceptance of marriage with the widow of the man he had killed; the clear statement of his guilt by Teiresias, followed by his wild attempt to parry the charge by turning to accuse Creon; and so on. What do the Elders mean by saying that they wish all these pieces of evidence to 'fit together'? There can only be one answer: they want the fact of Oedipus' double guilt to be openly established. They wish this, not because they want a prophecy of parricide to be fulfilled, but because they are sure Oedipus is guilty, and their indignation demands that he be unmasked and punished. The other phrase is in 906–7, 'The ancient prophecies about Laius are fading, and people now leave them out of account.' The prophecy about Laius was that he would be killed by his own son; Iocasta has said she is sure this has not been fulfilled, and the Chorus now resent her assurance, leaving us with the only possible conclusion, that they wish it now to be proved beyond doubt that this polluting act has indeed been committed. This should make it finally clear that at this point the Chorus are convinced not only that Oedipus killed Laius, but that Laius was his father. It is the king's guilt that has polluted Thebes, and this is why they want to see that guilt brought home to him, and proper punishment inflicted. The Elders are not models of sympathetic virtue, but at least they are not wicked enough (though Knox says they are, *OAT* 46–7) to lament simply that a prophecy of parricide has not been fulfilled. On the other hand, if they have discovered that such a crime has been committed, and know who the guilty man is, then – and only then – they are justified in wanting the fact disclosed, the prophecy proved true, and justice executed. That they reinforce their appeal to Zeus with the trite complaint that 'no one nowadays honours Apollo; religion is vanishing' may be taken partly as Sophocles' mild satire on indignant moralists, partly as preparing a contrast for the change of tone in the next stasimon, 1097, 'Phoebus, may this be pleasing to you!' But in so far as it relates to the actual situation in the play, the complaint is evoked not by the impiety of what Oedipus and Iocasta said about oracles, but by the realisation, now complete, that everything Teiresias said about Oedipus is true; and to this extent it is a genuine, and indignant, reflection; and its very commonplace tone suits exactly the character of the Elders.

Knox is right in saying (*OAT* 100) that the words of the Second Stasimon 'constitute for the editor or critic of the play a problem which is central'. A little earlier (99) he says, 'The problem lies in the fact that this stasimon . . . contains some phrases which can be made applicable to Oedipus only with great ingenuity.' His interpretation of the play marks an advance on previous views in that he perceives that in these lines the Chorus are condemning Oedipus; the question remains, condemning him for what? Knox says they condemn Oedipus for killing four men on the Delphi road, Iocasta for conniving at the exposure of her son, and both for disbelieving oracles. The notion that these faults could be serious enough to bring plague on the city, or to merit the prayer, 'May an evil destiny destroy him', seems to me so far-fetched as to be quite undramatic. In order to see each line of this stasimon as applicable to Oedipus, what is required is not ingenuity, but a reading of the play up to this point, and especially of the First Episode, on the simple assumption that *what is said is both heard and understood*. The confusion which results from neglecting this requirement is well illustrated in Knox's discussion of the passage in *OAT* 209–11; this, with other views which he quotes from other authors, shows what difficulties beset the attempt to make sense of this Ode on any other principle than the one recommended in this book.

Again, near the end of the same note, Knox says, 'The ode is magnificently functional; it puts the question raised by the situation (the validity of divine prophecy) in its larger framework, the validity of the traditional religious view as a whole.' The question of the validity of prophecy is not raised by the situation; it is raised by Iocasta in order to escape from the situation (see pp. 196–7). The question raised by the situation – if this is a tragedy at all, and not a treatise dressed up as a poetic dialogue – is: What is happening to Oedipus? How much does he know, and how will he act when he discovers everything? A tragedy must have for its centre a person. A question such as the validity of prophecy can be of central interest only if its answer depends on a person's performance or neglect of a crucial act. If the question in this play were, Will Oedipus go to confront the Sphinx, and so commit himself to marrying Iocasta? then it could be said that the play was about the validity or invalidity of prophecy. But in *Oedipus Tyrannus* this point has been reached and this question answered long before the action begins; the crucial acts were performed soon after they were foretold. Therefore the question of the truth or untruth of prophecy, or the broader question of the whole traditional religious view, though of some interest to the Elders, and though used by Iocasta as a refuge from the real issue, cannot be central to the tragedy of Oedipus. What answer is given to it does not matter to the play, or to Oedipus, or to the poet. What matters is how Oedipus will deal with events and discoveries. In the play itself the only act of Oedipus which has a prophecy behind it is his putting out his eyes; and this, besides being integral to the myth, is primarily something of poetic value in the design; as an issue of decision its point lies in being the chosen alternative to suicide.

The understanding of this Ode is therefore vital to the understanding of the play. These words of the Elders mark a point of no return, and make the orthodox interpretation of the Third Stasimon impossible for a reflective reader. Before going on to the next Episode, however, we should remind ourselves that, as centuries of study and performance have shown, a popular audience when absorbed in the speed of action is slower and less shrewd than the Elders of Thebes. Most spectators at this point have not yet seen how 'these things fit together'; the evidence has overwhelmed them with its completeness, they have grasped only pieces here and there. The play was written primarily for these spectators, and for them the plot is still in its middle course, with two scenes to come before the catastrophe. Even for those who perceive as much as the Elders perceive, the next scene begins with one surprise after another and ends with a shock – Oedipus' sarcastic scorn of Iocasta's family pride, and the defiant rhetoric which intimates that he will see the last scene of ritual disclosure through to its end.

Meanwhile the closing words of the Chorus, 'Nowhere is

Apollo honoured; religion is vanishing', pose a nice test for the theatrical director. If, as sometimes happens, he allows his composer to lead him with a bridle, those sententious phrases will be intoned as a nostalgic plaint on an all-too-familiar theme, and tension will drop; so that when Iocasta enters in a religious garb to make offerings before Apollo, the audience merely wait for her to get through her speech, and the scene really starts with the Corinthian. Only if the Elders' last two lines are spoken with a tone of superficial, resentful, matter-of-fact banality, is the proper effect obtained as the Leader turns from conventionally agreeing with his fellows that religion is as good as dead, to find himself addressed by a terrified woman who has come to worship Apollo.

# 6

## *The Third Episode*

The stage-direction is in the first sentence of the new scene: 'Enter Iocasta carrying wreaths and incense.' This in itself is a phenomenon, and will strike the Chorus as such; it comes ironically after their last words, 'and religion is vanishing'. It seems to strike Iocasta herself similarly, for there is a faltering, almost apologetic tone in the words she uses; so that lines 911 and 919, for example, may serve as another stage-direction: 'The queen has lost her air of assurance, and is anxious, bewildered.' 'The thought has occurred to me', Iocasta begins, 'to come as a petitioner to the shrines of the gods.' We gather that such a thought has not occurred to her for a long time past. That it occurs now is a measure of the crisis which she feels is upon her.

'For Oedipus excites his imagination too much with distresses of all kinds.' What exactly is the thought which Iocasta clothes in these words? If the argument we have pursued is valid, Iocasta has already been faced with strong evidence of Oedipus' guilt. But truth has a tendency to be unbelievable; and long-established comforting beliefs yield reluctantly to evidence. On the road to recognition of truth Oedipus is by this time some way ahead of her; she has guessed instinctively where he is going, and has told herself she cannot and will not follow him into the 'manifold distresses' which she can see are torturing him. 'He does not, like a man of intelligence, judge new things by old.' The 'new things' are, first, the statements of Teiresias, and next, the discovery that Oedipus killed a man who was probably Laius.

The 'old things' are, on the popular view of the play, the supposition – which Iocasta holds to be a fact – that her exposed son perished on the mountainside, and that the prophecy given to Laius is therefore proved false. Equally well the 'old things' may be those established facts on which the Chorus too relied to protect them from the first shock of Teiresias' words, namely, the services of Oedipus to Thebes and his long and successful reign. A man of intelligence, Iocasta says, would judge from Oedipus' courage, ability and fame that the present dreadful accusation must be false. Her words are unconsciously ironical; for 'judging the present by the past', inferring present guilt from former decisions and actions, is exactly what Oedipus has been doing; moreover, it was the fact of being intelligent, *ennous*, 916, which in his youth enabled him to calculate chances and justify a criminal risk, and which now is enabling him painfully to retrace his path and make what amends he can.

Iocasta has been giving him advice (918); but she has done this too often over many years (1067), and Oedipus will not listen. This frightens Iocasta, and she turns to the gods. The statue of Apollo stands near the door of the palace. Iocasta has twice, standing before this statue, affirmed the impotence of gods to foretell the future (720 ff., 852 ff.). That she now appeals first to him is in itself a direct apology,[1] yet even in her panic Iocasta keeps her pride, and conceals her act of repentance with the offhand phrase, 'for you are nearest' – a piece of subtle psychology, for she continues immediately, 'I come as a suppliant with these prayers.' The prayers are that Apollo 'will provide for us some release from pollution'. She is not thinking of the plague; it has not been mentioned specifically since 665. It is her own share in Oedipus' pollution that is dimly overshadowing her. Finally, this short speech of Iocasta performs the function of a 'messenger from indoors', *exangelos*, to tell us what is happening to Oedipus. He is 'struck out of' his usual character (*ekpeplēgmenos*), 'beside himself' with distress. Imagination will tell us that what is distracting him is not only his own fearful predicament but the impossibility

---

[1] For the notion that gods were open to apology, compare Neoptolemus' journey to Delphi in Euripides' *Andromache*.

of communicating in words to his wife the truth which she must inevitably learn very soon.

Iocasta turns to the statue of Apollo and stands with her back to the audience as the Messenger from Corinth enters. The verbal form of his opening question is remarkable, and has been well expounded by Knox (*OAT* 183-4). The line-endings hint at the connection of *Oidi-pous* with the verb *oida*, know; and the genitive *Oidipou* in 925 makes a pun with the adverb *hopou*, where. In addition to this the innocent question 'Do you know where Oedipus is?' has just been answered by Iocasta with a vivid picture: he is in the palace in a state of panic distress, like a man out of his mind; in no condition to interview strangers. The Chorus-Leader answers, 'This is his house, and he is indoors'; and then, as Iocasta turns at the stranger's voice, 'And this lady is the mother of his children'. This line, 928, has usually been called unconscious dramatic irony; but if the Elders at this point are unconscious, it seems hardly worth while to give any study at all to the words Sophocles so carefully wrote for them to speak and to hear. Moreover the word for 'lady' or 'woman', *gynē*, is also the regular word for 'wife'; so that the first half of the line can mean, 'and this wife is mother . . .' until the words 'of his children' safely cover the chasm. The hint is enough to remind us that the mood in which the Elders welcome the newcomer is not one of detached interest; they are waiting for their prayer, 'May an evil fate destroy him', to be answered. The Corinthian's greeting to Iocasta stresses the 'blessing' and 'fulfilment' that have come to her in bearing children; and Iocasta's innocent reply shows how little the threatening truth has yet penetrated her awareness: she thanks him for his 'kindly words'.

It has been often pointed out (e.g. by Kitto, *FMD* 73-4) how Sophocles likes to show his characters welcoming a new event in ignorance of its true import; and Kitto excellently expounds the way this is related to the part played by gods in human affairs. Here the Messenger says that his news will bring joy, and perhaps sorrow as well. This proves to be true; but neither the joy nor the sorrow is the same as that which the Messenger, or Iocasta, was thinking of; and Iocasta's question (938) about the 'double force' of his news is an unconscious forecast. Kitto's observations on the character of this Corinthian (*FMD* 212), his humour (1018–20), his purpose in coming (1005–6), and his function in the drama, should be studied, and will not be invalidated by certain further observations we shall make presently. The man is, of course, light relief for just over a hundred lines, which is as long as he has fair excuse for not perceiving that his jolly mood is face to face with tragedy. Even when he first meets the queen, however, he is sensitive and tactful, and does not blurt out, 'Polybus is dead', but carefully introduces his news with 'The Corinthians will make Oedipus their king'; and in 958 he is chagrined at being unable to use the same formality with Oedipus himself. His desire to be tactful serves a dramatic purpose which we shall notice presently in studying lines 989–1016; at the moment we see him mystified by Iocasta's reaction to his news – she is joyful, but for an incomprehensible reason. Iocasta may even think she is right in saying that 'Oedipus long feared and avoided Polybus lest he should kill him'; but that is certainly not what is troubling Oedipus now. In fact this fear was not mentioned until more than halfway through the play (790), by which time other fears far more urgent had occupied the whole of Oedipus' attention. The notion that fear of encountering Polybus and Merope had dominated Oedipus' life was examined in Chapter 4 (pp. 195 ff.). It is an unreal notion, which Iocasta seizes upon because (1) it fits with her hatred of oracles which began when Laius exposed her son, and (2) it offers her a refuge from the terror of the real issue. This accounts for her irrational joy in 945 ff., which seems not to be damped by the sober reaction of Oedipus in 960, 962.

The interview between Oedipus and the Corinthian shows with particular clarity the twofold story which the poet is telling throughout the play, and his consciousness of two different audiences. In spite of the compelling interest and detailed structure of the hidden version, and in spite of the *rapprochement* between the two versions which is already taking place, he still presents the popular myth with plausible continuity, easing the passage of the more improbable moments with dramatic qualities of speed, suspense or surprise. In response to Iocasta's joyful summons Oedipus enters, hears the news, shares her joy and her triumph over the one half of the oracle proved false, while retaining a pious caution in regard to the second half. It is this caution which elicits from the Corinthian the information that Oedipus is not the son of Polybus; and this leads, without any break to allow the audience to reflect, to the final revelation of the truth to Iocasta in lines 1026, 1032, 1042. It has been proved many times that this sequence can be fully satisfactory in performance. The painful excitement allows no time for questioning either Oedipus' baseless joy over the news, or his morbid anxiety about Merope, or his reaction to the mention of his feet, or the curious slowness of the Corinthian in parting with information. This last is acceptable as part of the old man's humorous character; the allusion to the maimed feet is acceptable as a useful clue for an audience – and a Iocasta – too slow-witted to take up a dozen clues already given; while Iocasta's joyful confidence in 945ff., and her philosophy of the random life in 979 are persuasively eloquent enough to carry with them both Oedipus and the audience until the Corinthian begins his questioning in 989. Now, however, let us give Sophocles the second hearing he demands, and change from spellbound spectator to no less absorbed, but reflective, reader.

Oedipus enters with an unusually strong expression (950) of affection for Iocasta (in the whole Second Episode he uses nothing but the plain 'lady' or 'wife', *gynai*); this accords well with the idea that he has now accepted the necessity for the complete disclosure which will involve Iocasta even more fatally than himself; and that he knows her as no longer the domineering older wife, but a frightened, helpless woman taking refuge in self-deception and completely dependent upon him. She has met him with a delighted face, and introduced the Corinthian as a herald of deliverance. What is Oedipus, looking at her in an agony of remorse and pity, to answer? Is he to crush her pathetic hopefulness with the obvious statement that this news can make no possible difference to anything? She has retreated beyond reasoning. He is not inhuman: he enters gently, and with what show of enthusiasm he can muster, into her brief comfort, found in the unreal world they have made and lived in together, which is about to be exploded. His exclamation, *Pheu, pheu,* in 964 may cover a variety of emotions; it can express sympathy for Polybus ('poor man', *ho tlēmon,* 962), or sadness at Iocasta's refusal to see, or at the irrelevance of news intended to be good news. The actor on a modern stage, and still more the actor on a screen, must commit himself at this point; the actor in a mask could play two parts at once. The last two words of his speech affirm that the oracles of Apollo are 'worth nothing'; and the phrase carries a clear double meaning. On the surface it states that Oedipus is no longer in danger of killing his father. This is the usual interpretation; but even if it is true, that danger is one which, for the first part of the play, Oedipus was not the least concerned about; and further, if he really believes now that Apollo's oracles are 'worth nothing' in this sense, why does he, in 976, 986 and 988, reiterate his fear of marrying Merope? This first meaning, then, is merely his attempt to give some seeming comfort to Iocasta; for himself, the phrase means that nothing, indeed, can be more worthless than a prophecy already fulfilled and seventeen years out of date.

Next comes a very curious passage, 975–90. Three times Oedipus insists that his great dread is lest he should find himself in union with Merope. The oddness of these lines passes in performance because we can feel them leading directly to the next revelation by the Corinthian; and it thus illustrates again what an expert dramatist knew he could get away with. But even in a good performance I doubt if the passage has ever carried conviction; the absurdity of 976, 'Surely I must fear my mother's bed?' when sense requires, 'What help is that to me, accursed and exiled?' demands some further explanation. What is the reader to make of this harping on Merope? The reason for it has already been given in Chapter 4 (pp. 196–7) as a comment on lines 824–33; and it is that Oedipus, who has accepted Iocasta's joy over the news from Corinth, knows none the less that time is running short; that Iocasta must, if possible, and as soon as possible, be helped to take a further step in the long process of knowing; brought to recognise, and face, a fact she may have been aware of for years, which it is impossible for Oedipus to state to her in so many words, whose full import Oedipus himself will not perceive until near the end of the play. He is apparently talking about Merope – but he does not speak that name. In 976 he says 'my mother', in 985 'she who bore me', in 988 'her who is living'. The Elders perhaps think he is talking of Merope; but he is looking at, and thinking of, and meaning, Iocasta; begging her to listen, to think, to reason and to have courage; to conclude for herself what he cannot express. Iocasta herself is clinging for safety to the make-believe world which for so long has protected them both, which she cannot accept as ended – the world where Oedipus is the son of Polybus. Oedipus, knowing there is now no safety anywhere, is begging her to come out and join him in the danger of the real world. Of all this there is, of course, no proof in the text – except that the literal alternative is in fact absurd; and we should remember that Sophocles directed the play himself.

But the real world, in which fear, caution, hope and purpose are based on principles won from experience, is a world that Iocasta rejects. Her famous pronouncement 977–9 gives the philosophy of Chance which has guided the fortunes of the house of Labdacus for two generations. First, Laius (if the prophecy was given him before he married Iocasta) ignored his warning and decided to chance doing what he wanted to do; when his son was born he decided that chance was too dangerous; but instead of killing the child exposed it, so as to give the chance of survival which cleared him of pollution. Chance found for Oedipus a home in Corinth, and revealed to him that his parentage was obscure. When chance confronted him with his father, Oedipus, like his father, took a chance and ignored the warning he had received; arrived in Thebes, and, warned again by events and by reason, took a far more dangerous chance and married Iocasta. The same story told from the opposite side, from the viewpoint of the gods, has a different pattern, an orderly sequence illustrating in two generations a constant principle – the principle enunciated by the Chorus in the Second Stasimon: that the man who for his own profit risks pollution will find his bluff called, and be guilty of the pollution when it comes. Oedipus lived until he was a man, and a king, in the world of chance. After that, at some time either soon or late – perhaps earlier under the sting of guilt, perhaps not until the plague compelled him – he changed his allegiance; in the Second Episode he won his freedom as a man; and is now about to pay his dues under the rule of *Dikē*, Justice. Iocasta is still a subject of Chance. Wisdom about the future (*pronoia*, 978), as she well knows, comes only from the experience and the acceptance of an ordered pattern in human events, from recognition of *Dikē*; that is another reason why she has rejected prophecy – because she belongs to the other kingdom. Today's developments have brought home to her the reality of this ordered pattern with a terrifying relevance; unprepared for the shock, she denies reality, defies *Dikē*, exalts Chance: 'It is best to live at random, whatever way one can. . . . Life is easiest to bear if you disregard all prophecy.' True enough – until the crisis closes in. But the nearer the crisis comes, the more blindly secure Iocasta feels in her imaginary refuge; so that she even dares to use the outspoken phrase *mētri xyneunasthēsan*, 'many a man has bedded with his mother'. She feels impregnable.

Meanwhile the Corinthian has been listening with curiosity to the king's earnest reiteration of his fears connected with 'his mother'. This old man is not a chance messenger; he knows a little more about Oedipus than most Corinthians – but only a little. When the promising and popular prince (775–6) so suddenly disappeared, it would be surprising if what was already 'a fairly widespread report' (786), that Oedipus was not Polybus' son, did not quickly become universal knowledge. That he was born in the neighbourhood of Thebes the old shepherd may well have kept to himself, as being of no significance; when he heard that Oedipus had become king of Thebes, it would seem to him natural that the young man had found his way back to native soil. When he arrives with his valuable news at the Theban palace, he is at first mystified by Iocasta's talk of prophecy, and by philosophical remarks which are above his head; but yet more mystified to hear Oedipus talking as if he still imagined that he was the son of Polybus and Merope. Again the Corinthian shows tact; if Oedipus in Thebes is calling himself the son of Polybus for his own reasons, the shepherd will take care what he says

before the Elders – or can it be that Oedipus is genuinely ignorant of the facts? The shepherd's incredulous question in line 1000,
'Was it really in fear of this that you lived as an exile from
Corinth?' is elicited by that same incredible (though habitual)
statement of Oedipus, 'That was why I stayed away from
Corinth' (997–8), which ought surely to have seemed equally
incredible to Iocasta when he told her his story (794–7). The
Corinthian feels his way slowly and carefully from question to
question, watching Oedipus' face for his cue to speak out. The
extreme slowness of progress, through seven successive questions
and answers (991–1014), itself produces a dramatic suspense;
while Oedipus on his part, talking guardedly with a stranger,
reverts to the line he has followed for so many years. At last the
fact which everyone but Iocasta knows comes out in words:
'Polybus is nothing to you in blood', 1016; and in 1019–23 we
have a man uttering and hearing uttered in words for the first
time a truth he has known, unexpressed, through his whole
adult life.

The next stage (1021–53) in the dialogue of recognition
(*anagnōrisis*) contains the three clues which makes clear to the
most uncritical audience the reason for Iocasta's agitation from
1056 until she rushes out after 1072. They are that Oedipus was
found exposed on Cithaeron, that his feet were pierced and
bound, and that the man who gave him to the Corinthian was a
servant of Laius. Again, in performance the intensity of feeling
is such that most members of an audience, though momentarily
uneasy, will postpone indefinitely the effort of reflection. To those
for whom (as for some of Sophocles' contemporaries) reflection
does not destroy dramatic enjoyment, it will occur that, though
these three clues convince Iocasta, they seem to convey nothing
to Oedipus, who still apparently thinks (1062–3, 1079) that he
may be base-born;[1] and that the only one of these clues which can
possibly tally with any knowledge private to Iocasta is the pierced
feet – and that is on the unwarranted assumption that Oedipus
did not hear, or did not heed, what Iocasta told him in 718, 'Laius

---

[1] The argument we applied to the study of line 718 applies again
here. See pp. 185–6.

pinned its ankles together'; and there is the further question, which it may or may not be legitimate to ask: Had Iocasta lived seventeen years as Oedipus' wife without knowing about the scars on his feet? What is in fact happening is that during this dialogue the two stories in the play merge into one. We are not now dealing even with a series of intelligible events, but rather with a pattern of intense emotion which, now that the climax is approaching, can pursue its way independent of rational considerations. Anouilh has put the matter well in the Prologue to his *Antigone*, where he explains that a person of heroic temperament, once involved in a tragic pattern, on the approach of a crisis plays his part ritually and instinctively, under the compulsion of that sense of Tragedy in which all the characters share.

This can be illustrated from lines 1030–1. The Corinthian says that he 'found' Oedipus in the glens of Cithaeron. It is obvious that anyone who 'finds' a baby abandoned on a mountain 'saves' it from death in one form or another; therefore his statement that he was the child's 'saviour', *sōtēr*, does not need any explanation. Nevertheless Oedipus' next words are, 'What pain had I when you took me up in your arms?' If Oedipus began the play unaware, and still does not guess that he is the son of Laius, he asks this unmotivated question simply by dramatic compulsion, as a part of the tragic ritual in which the time has come now for Iocasta to learn the truth and to go indoors and hang herself. If Oedipus began the play aware, since he has failed so far to communicate the truth to Iocasta by his own words, he now makes the Corinthian give her the information which she already has, and has had for years, but which until the last moment she has steadfastly refused to heed. The same two alternative processes can be observed at work in 1027. In the previous line the Corinthian has given the first important clue: 'I found you on Cithaeron.' Why does Oedipus here utter no word of surprise, as he does in 1017, 1021, 1023? If he is unaware, he is now so close to the moment of truth that the revelation of disaster no longer causes him surprise but appears as integral to a perfect pattern. If he is aware, then having forged one link in the word 'Cithaeron' he presses on at once to forge the next, which must be to identify himself by the 'strange birth-token' of his pierced feet.

Next comes at last – delayed for two-thirds of the play – the first clear mention of the scars. Line 1036, 'You were given your name because of them', links this passage with line 8, 'called Oedipus'; the phrase, 'joints of your feet', 1032, echoes Iocasta's phrase in 718 – which was clear enough, but then drew no word from Oedipus, whether he was conscious of its significance or not. Here the fatal words come in reply to a strongly leading question from Oedipus in 1031; and as if to deny that he had prompted the shepherd's answer, he exclaims *Oimoi* – which is usually an expression of grief but can also convey impatience; and this may be more in place here. In any case this and the next two lines spoken by Oedipus are there to show how Sophocles thought of the effect which this deformity had upon Oedipus' life. It was a thing he had always hated, an 'ancient evil', *archaion kakon*; from infancy he had carried it as a mark of disgrace, *deinon oneidos*. This is clear enough whichever meaning we attach to the word *sparganōn* (see note on 1035, and pp. 131 ff.). Knowing now that he is not the son of Polybus, he leaps to the question, 'Was this inflicted on me by my parents?'[1] – and at once a whole series of inferences appears which Sophocles cannot have missed but did not choose to make a part of his play; allowing us no more than an unwarranted surmise that Oedipus grew up to think of himself as a foundling. At least we are justified in assuming that when he was called bastard by a fellow-diner in Corinth he would link the taunt with the mystery of his feet; and now that he has told us how painfully conscious he has been all his life of those scars, we know that they were with him when he went to consult Apollo, and when he fought with Laius, and when he married Iocasta, and when he listened to her telling how she had lost her firstborn son.

When the third clue is given (1042, 'he was a servant of Laius'), once more a witness is summoned; but the threads are drawing together – the witness is the same man who is already on his way. The same man was agent when Laius tried to kill his

[1] Oedipus is not asking *which of his parents* did it, but *whether either* of his parents did it. The distinction is clear in Greek.

son, and witness when Oedipus killed his father. This is exactly right for the dramatic pattern; and since it will be helpful, once the man arrives, for attention to be concentrated on his answers to the questions the Corinthian will ask him, with no time wasted in identifying him with Laius' travelling-attendant, the Chorus make the point clear now. This is a piece of competent dramatic design; but did its further implications escape the dramatist? In any case this was the way he wrote it; and we need only observe that, while the Elders could have inferred Oedipus' guilt from the numerous other facts offered them, their inference was confirmed if, as is implied in 1051–2, they were aware at the time that Iocasta had had a child and that Laius had exposed it. And, since the present scene has now triply confirmed their previous belief about both the crimes of Oedipus, it is difficult to acquit them of some vindictive satisfaction when they say (1053), 'Here is Iocasta; she is the best person to tell you about that.' It echoes the tone of line 928, 'This wife is mother . . .', and of 835, 'Till the shepherd comes, have hope.'

One more small point in the dramatist's art is worth noting before we leave this part of the scene. When Oedipus asks the Corinthian (1025), 'Did you buy me or find me?' he answers, 'I found you.' Later in 1040 he has to correct this. Sophocles wrote 1025 in the form of a leading question in order to ensure a simple answer. Of the alternatives offered, the Corinthian chooses the nearer to the truth; to have to answer, 'You were given to me by another shepherd, a Theban, who found you on Cithaeron', would blur the clear line of revelation, hurry the audience, and defeat the artistic function of stichomythia, which is partly to clarify communication by regulating the flow of facts. The incorrectness of 'I found you' in 1026 does not worry the audience at all, nor does the correction that follows later; but 'I found you' has a second function in illustrating again the sensitive, anxious-to-please character of the Corinthian, who to avoid seeming to contradict returns the answer suggested to him. And this sensitive character is important, because at the end of the next Episode the Corinthian must join the Theban Shepherd in a mute background of grief and sympathy.

Now at last (1054) the two converging stories are one, and Oedipus and Iocasta face one another, eye to eye and mind to mind, for the first time in their married life. Each knows the truth, and knows that the other knows. This is their hidden bond, but it is not communication. They follow separate ways to the different ends they choose; Oedipus knows Iocasta's end and her reason; Iocasta does not know his. Her reason is human and simple: life has become for her unbearable and she must die. Oedipus' reason is dramatic and is also concerned with the art of living. He and his creator are one poet, and their design can be completed only by the appearance of the eye-witness whose presence has been hovering in the wings ever since Oedipus first asked about him in the Prologue (116). From Episode to Episode he has come steadily nearer, and he is now at the palace gate. Oedipus will play the king and defy the censorious Elders until, in the person of the aged Shepherd, *Dikē* herself takes over judgement from them, and assigns to them, for a while, the part of mourners. This stage of his pilgrimage Oedipus must tread alone; harsh words and a look of contempt must belie his love and grief for Iocasta, that no softness may weaken him. During the brief Third Stasimon he will remain on stage, both hearing and refusing to hear, and, I think, standing upright and motionless staring full at the audience and defying both their horror and their pity.

Iocasta has been on stage, silent, for seventy lines. A passage such as this is helpful in suggesting to the imagination how, when the face is covered by a mask, an actor can convey with a slight movement of hand or arm, an inclination or raising of the head, what the modern stage or screen tries to express realistically by the face. Iocasta's last two speeches were her reckless philosophy (979) and her false comfort (987). How much does she know? and in what sense does she know it? This question has already been raised in Chapter 4; and Sophocles has deliberately made the answer far less clear than in the case of Oedipus. Iocasta is the deuteragonist and her clarity of outline must not rival the hero's; also, she is not famous as a solver of riddles. She is a woman of some force and assurance; independent, embittered against oracles by her experience; devoted to Oedipus, and resolved to find comfort for him where there is none. All this is clear enough; it is clear also that during her seventy lines of listening she becomes fully alive to the truth. What, then, of her awareness in the Second Episode? Is there any reason why we should not be content to accept at its face-value her statement in 855–6, 'Yet that unhappy child of mine never killed Laius, but perished first itself'? Yes, there is reason. In the first place, this confident statement followed an exchange of evidence which convinced Oedipus that he killed Laius – with the reservation stated in 843–7, which the Chorus could hardly be expected to take seriously (see p. 197); it convinced the Chorus too; why should it not convince Iocasta? Secondly, she had then just spoken of the oracle which said that Laius would be killed by his son; and in reply Oedipus had told her that he was destined to kill his father. She despises oracles; but since in the present scene her prayer to Apollo suggests that her armour is not proof, can she entirely miss the coincidence of these two prophecies? The oracle given to Oedipus, moreover, included incest: has this bold-spirited woman simply refused to hear those words? or to recognise that Oedipus is the same age as her son would have been? But there is a third point, of a kind which belongs by dramatic tradition to an *anagnōrisis*.[1] When she handed over her son to be exposed she did not, as far as we are told, leave with him any tokens for recognition (cf. 'such signs' or 'clues', 1059), though the provision of such tokens is constantly referred to in stories of infant exposure. Iocasta, who did not believe in oracles, must have hoped for the child's survival as strongly as Laius, who did believe, hoped for his death; and the tokens – Sophocles makes her speak of them in 718, as if by compulsion of tender and bitter memory: the scars on his feet. If ever he returned to her, that was how she would know him. In the Second Episode she speaks these words to her husband knowing that he stands there on the deformed feet which have been familiar to her all these years. Could the poet have offered a clearer challenge to a reader to reflect on the deeply folded layers which the mind can hold of knowing and

[1] See, for example, Euripides' *Iphigenia in Tauris*, 808–26.

not-knowing, of self-scrutiny and self-deception? When a man is composing a play, how can he write a speech for Iocasta unless his mind sees clearly what her thoughts and feelings were at certain crucial moments in her past life which form the whole basis of the present drama? Those past thoughts are not 'in the play'; but until the dramatist knows what they were he cannot write the play. This is true of many plays, but pre-eminently true of *Oedipus Tyrannus*, because here almost the whole action is concerned with a reconstruction of the past. Then let us ask the question which no critic will allow us to ask: When Sophocles pictured Iocasta receiving the news of Laius' death, what thoughts did he give her? 'Laius has been killed; the oracle said my son would do it; if he has survived he is now a grown man – perhaps living as a bandit.' Some days later there stands before her a young stranger looking as Laius had looked at that age; but his feet are covered.

None of this is in the play; and all of it is relevant to our study of the myth which Sophocles studied in order to write the play; these images, half out of sight and half out of hearing, are pointed to by line after line that the poet has composed. They point to the great bond that unites Oedipus and Iocasta. Just as Oedipus, in marrying her, resolved to stake everything on the faint but undeniable possibility that all was well, and the glaring facts mere coincidence, so Iocasta's cruel *daimōn* offered her the possibility that in spite of all evidence she could claim her young husband with a clear conscience; even the scarred feet could be coincidence. So long as no further facts were investigated, so long as there was no communication, he and she could live in a precarious happiness under the protection of the goddess Chance. This was the great bond which both united them and kept them forever apart.

In Iocasta's last moments we should notice, first, her echo in 1061 ('sufficient is my own sickness') of Oedipus' words in 60–1, 'The sickness of none of you is equal to mine'; and secondly, the two wounding taunts that Oedipus finds to fling at her: that she with her royal descent is afraid she may find she has married a slave's son, and that, like a mother rather than a wife, she gives

him advice for his own good – and always has. These taunts both
spring from that side of Oedipus which in the Prologue was con-
trolled and concealed, but in the stress of excitement flares up:
the aggressiveness of the disinherited, the touchiness of the
younger man with the older woman, the insecurity of the newcomer with no background who stands only by his personal
achievements. There is a third point of significance, and it lies
in the verb 'speak to', *proseipein*, 1072: 'This is the only word I
can speak to you, and after this no other word, ever.' This sentence names the whole tragedy of Iocasta: Oedipus is her life, and
she cannot speak to him and never has been able to; guilt and the
flight from guilt have cut off communication. This too was the
essence of Oedipus' curse, as we see in lines 238, 352, 818. What,
in fact, has Iocasta succeeded in saying to Oedipus in her two
scenes? When he said to her, 'Creon hired a prophet to denounce
me', she answered nothing to the purpose; what she said does not
indicate that she gave his statement a moment's real consideration, or was aware of what it implied; she merely asserted, 'I
knew a prophecy once that was not fulfilled, therefore you may
assume that no prophet is worth heeding.' When Oedipus
questioned her about the manner of Laius' death, she could
supply certain factual answers; but after his long speech describing his encounter on the Delphi road and the fears which now
held him, she had not a single comment to make; and her total
inability to communicate was finally shown in 851: 'Even if he
should diverge somewhat from his earlier story . . .' is all she can
say. To 'diverge somewhat from his story' meant to 'admit that
Laius and his party were attacked by one man alone'; and this, as
Oedipus stated in 847, fixed the killing firmly on him and assured
his banishment. To this imminent fact Iocasta closed her mind
entirely, though it was vital to Oedipus whom she loved; she had
lost the power of either receiving or giving any effective communication by words. Similarly in the Third Episode, the only
thing she has to say to Oedipus is to attack an imaginary and
irrelevant fear – that of marrying his mother; for his real danger
she has no word of help or comfort, but seems indeed to be unaware of it. Her part in the play reflects the isolation that has been

her life ever since she married Oedipus. About the most real things she has never been able to speak a clear word to him; and now as she leaves him her word is 'Alas, alas, unhappy man!' The goddess Chance has betrayed them; now their one bond is grief and compassion.

During this scene the Chorus make only three remarks. The first is their answer to the question the Corinthian asked on entering: 'This is his house; he is indoors; and this wife is mother . . .' (927–8). Their second speech (1051–3) identifies Laius' travelling-attendant with the shepherd who carried the infant prince to Cithaeron, and concludes, 'Iocasta is the best person to tell you about that.' Their third interposition comes now after Iocasta's departure: 'Oedipus, why has the queen gone . . .? I fear that from what she has left unsaid evil may break forth.'[1] All three remarks of the Elders are to be interpreted in the light of their outspoken indictment in the preceding Ode; and this last one, 1073–5, has the same sinister undertone as the first two. The question does not ask for information; the Elders know what Iocasta has gone indoors to do, and it is the beginning of the answer to their prayer, 'May an evil fate destroy him'.

The famous speech which replies to the Elders and closes the scene again shows us Oedipus the dramatist. Since 1042 ('the child was exposed by a servant of Laius') what is to Iocasta clear enough to demand suicide is certainly clearer still to Oedipus. But his moment has not yet come; he has still to meet the man who saved his life. So, to sustain him a little longer, he has seized on the supposition that Laius was disposing of a child which some slave-girl had borne him. This pretence must serve until the final word is spoken by the old shepherd; and this motive runs through the speech. The man without background must live and claim recognition by his personal qualities alone,

---

[1] The Greek says, 'I fear that *from this silence of hers* evil may break forth.' But Iocasta has not been silent; in her last minutes she has spoken six times. 'This silence', then, or 'reticence', refers exactly to her last words, 'I have *no other word* to say to you henceforth for ever.' Her 'silence' is not only her refusal, or inability, to address him by the name she now recognises as his – 'My son'; it is a reticence which is about to become the silence of death.

and these are such as chance gave him. He will neither be dishonoured by his breeding (1081) nor feel ashamed of it (1085). The 'months which were born with me', *syngeneis mēnes,* are the whole span of time since he was born; but *syngeneis* also means 'kindred' or 'brothers', suggesting that the months too are children of Chance, i.e. that they bring varying and unpredictable fortune. Thus the whole speech is a pregnant and poetical utterance: 'Chance was my mother, Chance has guided my career; such is and always will be my nature.' It is partly a denial before the Elders of moral responsibility for the crimes of which they convict him, partly the assertion (whether justifed or not) of a courageous man's right to take the chances of life when they are offered, if there is a possibility, however slight, that they may be honourable chances. It is also a statement that, whatever mistakes he may have made, he will live their consequences through to the end. This last implication, however, eludes the Elders.

# 7

## The Catastrophe

The tone and import of the three short remarks given to the Chorus in the last scene have prepared us for a cautiously ironical utterance in the Third Stasimon. The Elders' words, 1086 ff., respond immediately to the king's last phrase, 'to learn the truth about my birth', and to the implications of his poetical claim to be 'the child of Chance'. They recall saying (499–501), 'It has yet to be proved that any mortal prophet can outdo me.' That was their argument then for believing in the innocence of Oedipus; it now reinforces their discovery of his guilt. What Sophocles is delineating is the self-centred assurance of ordinary men even in the face of tragedy.

'If I am a prophet or have any skill in judgement, I swear by Olympus that tomorrow's full moon shall not come without your knowing, Cithaeron, that it is you that Oedipus honours as belonging to his fatherland, as his nurse, and as his mother; and you shall be celebrated by us as the bringer of good gifts to our king. Phoebus, Healer, may all this be pleasing to you!'

Oedipus had boasted of his judgement, *gnōmē*, 398; by it he had triumphed; now the Elders triumph over him 'in judgement', *kata gnōmān*; and they support their assurance with an oath 'by Olympus' – the source and home of those eternal laws which are now to be vindicated by the destruction of the transgressor. Your mother, they say, was not Chance, but Cithaeron; the wild mountainside where the infant took his chance of hungry hyenas or compassionate shepherds; where Laius hoped for nine-nine chances out of a hundred, and Iocasta hoped for the one; Cithaeron fathered you, nursed you, mothered you – Oedipus, known by your feet. In the Second Stasimon the Elders had asked, 'If such deeds are held in honour, why should I celebrate any religious observance?' Since then the Corinthian's disclosures have made everything doubly plain, and the guilty king is on the verge of disgrace; so now Cithaeron 'will be celebrated by us with holy observance, as the bringer of good gifts to our king'. The words imply, 'His mother is not Chance, but Cithaeron, who gave him good gifts, first saving his life, and now revealing his royal parentage.' The whole tone is bitterly ironical. In the Second Stasimon the Elders had lamented that 'nowhere is Apollo conspicuous in honour' (909); now the prophecy has been proved valid, the pollution is about to be purged, and they pray that this unmasking of guilt 'may be pleasing to you, Phoebus, Healer!' They are confident that the god whose word Oedipus said was 'worth nothing' (972) will now confute his despiser.

The irony intensifies in the antistrophe. 'Who then was it, son, which of the long-lived nymphs was it, who lay with Pan of the mountains and then gave birth to you? Or perhaps your mother was one whom Loxias loved?[1] The highland pastures are all dear to him. Or perhaps Hermes of Cyllene, or perhaps the divine Bacchus who lives on the mountain-ridges, received you as an unexpected find from one of the nymphs of Helicon, with whom he often sports!' Oedipus' fanciful naming of Chance as his mother is thrown back at him with scorn: 'Your mother one of the long-lived ones?' The particle *ara* after *makraiōnōn*, 'long-lived', points the sarcasm; so does the suggestion of *four* possible fathers; so do the two conventional clauses in 1103 and 1109, explaining how very likely it is that such a thing might happen. The Elders' irony is not overt; here as in the previous Ode decorum is observed and the words can bear an innocent interpretation. Probably most of the original audience took this Ode at its face-value, as an expression of 'joyous excitement' (so Jebb puts it), 'delight in the prospect that Oedipus will prove to be a native of the land'. Certainly it was the poet's intention that they

[1] Loxias, another name for Apollo, was said to mean 'the speaker of crooked, i.e. deceptive, oracles'.

should be so satisfied. The less naïve, who followed the dawning of truth in the minds of the Chorus, will have found their attention diverted from the exulting Elders to the already defeated but indomitable king; who, now that swords are out, is fighting to the last stand, even mocking and defying them – as line 1110, 'If I too am to make a guess, who never met him before', mocks 1086, 'If I am a prophet and skilled in judgement'; who is resolved to give them all the evidence they can ask for, knowing that it is he himself who has told them all they have learnt, and that they, who condemn the surface of events, can never pursue him into the depth of knowing and seeing where he will be alone with his guilt and his courage. Oedipus' words as he sees the Shepherd approaching express this consciousness of the moment which he, the wielder of events, the 'equal of gods', is creating. 'I know the men who are bringing him as servants of mine' recalls 1042, the line which finally revealed the truth to Iocasta, 'He was said to be one of Laius' servants'; while the phrase following, 'But you know better than I do', recalls their last cruel word to the queen, 1053, 'Iocasta is best able to tell you that.'

By this time the audience has of course forgotten that when this man was first sent for it was as eye-witness to the killing of Laius. In that capacity he was not, as it turned out, necessary, for the fact was sufficiently established by other evidence; but the Chorus-Leader's recognition of him from thirty-five years ago reminds us that at least the oldest of the Elders may have possessed all along enough knowledge to see at once the significance of each detail that the course of the play has revealed; just as Oedipus' use (1113) of the words 'comparable' and 'tallies' reminds us that such calculation of time has been a feature of the plot all through the action, and is inevitable when we are asking questions about the past. Also, since the critical fact about this Shepherd is that he failed to carry out Laius' command in so important a matter (not to mention that he ran away when Laius was attacked, and then gave a false report to the authorities) the word 'trustworthy' in 1118 gives us yet another taste of the Leader's sarcastic mood.

The dialogue between Oedipus and the Shepherd hardly admits of comment. It is like the final entry of a fugue: it has been felt coming for a long time, and it is known by heart; yet its very certainty gives it an irresistible force. It is a ritual dance where every step is placed correctly and leads in clear smooth lines to the final tableau. The talk between king and shepherd is an inquiry; and the verb 'to inquire', *historein*, rings out four times like a refrain. So do the verbs 'know', *oida*, and 'come to know', *mathein*; the Corinthian, who knows a good deal, but not all, after being frustrated in the previous scene by Oedipus' apparent ignorance, can jog the Shepherd's memory without scruple – 'I know well that he knows', 1133–4; while the Shepherd in reply says that the Corinthian 'knows nothing' (1151). The king already knows everything; yet to know in the privacy of one's own mind is only a part of knowing. The formal questions and answers are not for Oedipus, but for the Elders and the audience. When they know the truth, and knowledge is shared openly, the king's private knowledge then, and only then, will receive its third dimension, will become complete, operative, blinding. A telling moment in the pattern comes just before the final blow falls in 1171. Oedipus abandons his four-times-repeated threat of violence, and in 1170 levels himself with the Shepherd; reluctant striker and resolute victim are at one in the instant of the stroke. The poetry of the whole dialogue presents a human experience which is rare, and is the proper material of drama: a situation where a group of individuals conscious of themselves, of each other, of time and of the unseen universe, open their eyes together and see the truth. Here all the concentric circles merge into one, to give a fleeting vision to those who are prepared to receive it. The moment lasts only as long as the four lines of Oedipus' last speech, 1182–5. The aim of a stage production must be that in these lines Oedipus, and the play, should rise in grandeur and universality of feeling above anything else that has yet transpired. For everyone on stage and in the auditorium, his words move aside the curtain of detachment and disbelief. The vindictive Elders forget their triumph and their bitterness, pitying the man they have cursed. The spectators stop appraising the art of poet and actor, to be appalled at the price of knowledge, the sublimity of human guilt. Oedipus, who has for so long known the facts with his mind, now sees reality with his heart and understands for the first time the life he has lived; and even this truth will only be complete when he has left the stage and seen the last sight of his life, Iocasta dead. That experience, or as much of it as can hope to be expressed, is in this speech:

> All true, all plain, fulfilled to the last word! O light
> Of day, now let me look on you for the last time!
> I am exposed – a blasphemy in being born,
> Guilty in her I married, cursed in him I killed!

A few details of the writing should be observed. When the Shepherd comes in, Oedipus tells him to 'look this way'. The old man, with every reason for apprehension, is avoiding the king's eye, trying to place the stranger, wondering whether the Elders are friendly or hostile; remembering that once before he attended a royal inquiry. As for the Corinthian, he is well-meaning and anxious to help; there is no need to ask how much he knows, for he is unimportant in the tragedy as well as fairly simple; but when he throws himself unprompted into the inquiry, he shows himself involved as deeply in the spatial as in the temporal aspect of the drama. He crowds four words about 'knowing' into two lines: 'Since he doesn't know, I'll make him remember; for I know well that he knows. . . .' His little speech, 1132–40, does something else: it sets this intense personal tragedy, this pattern of agony and sin, for a brief moment against the quiet eternal background symbolised by the world of flocks on a vast mountainside under the stars which mark the circle of seasons; a world of natural fertility, death and renewal, master and servant, the same now he is old as it was when he was young. Then 1146 brings to a head the pictorial contrast between two aged shepherds, the one relaxed and jolly, the other crushed by half a lifetime of conscious guilt and terror, moved to trembling by the word *kolastou*, 'a punisher'. Finally, in his last phrase the Shepherd bids Oedipus 'know . . .'. With this bidding Oedipus reaches the last stage of knowing but one; then enters the palace to achieve the last of all.

To many readers and lovers of this play it will inevitably seem that something is taken from the completeness of climax, the absoluteness of catharsis, which this scene of ritual revelation embodies, if Oedipus is in fact already aware of his guilt. I have little doubt that the poet too felt this (cf. p. 144.), and possibly felt moreover that the play which he offered to his popular audience was, in this respect, a better play than that which he designed for the more reflective. In any case, this is how he decided to write it; and if we judge that the traditional view is dramatically stronger, though we may be right in our judgement, it cannot alter any of the evidence for the existence of the 'hidden play' as an integral part of the work. Two further considerations are, I think, valid. First, if Oedipus is unwitting and blind, the predicament of which he becomes aware in this scene is one of a fascinating horror enhanced by the notions of purity and pollution which formed the religious climate of Sophocles' world; but his mental distress is bounded by what he says in 828–9: that these are disasters sent upon him by some cruel supernatural power, and he is not responsible for them. The moment thus shows a more sudden shock of revelation but a less profound disaster. If on the other hand he is aware, it is true that for Oedipus himself the shock of factual revelation is replaced by the ordeal of self-exposure; but it is equally true that the content of what is exposed opens a profundity of moral and psychological implication that carries with it an emotional shock even more disturbing, both to the hero and to the audience, than the simple disclosure of a predicament. This point will be pursued further when we come to the Messenger's speech (pp. 239–40). The second consideration is that the self-blinding as a result of the discovery was an unalterable part of the saga and Sophocles was bound to include it. To present it as an immediate result of an unforeseen revelation would have unquestionable dramatic power; but Sophocles has done more than this. The Messenger's narrative pictures for us the moment when Oedipus attains the final phase of true knowledge, which belongs not to the mind or to the memory, not even to the witness of sight, but to the communication between two persons in their bodily presence. Iocasta's death had demolished the barriers of seventeen years, and Oedipus knew at last what each was, and had been, to the other – the truth and the falsehood, the evil and the good. Kneeling beside her he knew that he had 'failed to recognise those whom he longed for'; and this reference to his longing for parental affection first illuminates his whole life's story, and then recalls, to an imaginative listener or reader, that earlier moment when he had knelt on a stony path beside another grey-haired corpse, and prayed that it might not be his father.

How are the Elders affected by this scene? and what will be their attitude for the remainder of the play? It is clear from the opening words of the Fourth Stasimon that their bitter condemnation has for the moment been forgotten in face of the picture of human life which they now have before their eyes. 'Alas, generations of men! When I number the years of man's life, they are as nothing.' This is a proper sense of the tragedy of mortality. Oedipus' life has ended while still in its prime; the Elders are nearer to death than the king was yesterday. Looking at his life as a parable (*paradeigma*, 1193),[1] they feel their own feebleness and insecurity in the world, and lament the unhappy state of man which they have shared with the king. But what do they think has happened or will happen in the palace? It is unfortunate that the last few lines of this Ode depend on defective manuscripts. In 1219–21 the most satisfactory reading is Jebb's conjecture, in which the key word, *iālemon*, 'dirge', suggests – what is surely more natural than anything else could be – that they are assuming Oedipus has killed himself. Even if Jebb's conjecture is not correct, the supposition that they think of Oedipus as dead makes dramatic sense of the last scene. It provides an extra element of surprise and shock in the Messenger's speech; and it accounts for the way in which, after the sympathy they have shown in the Ode, they then withdraw to the tone of cold condemnation. All

---

[1] Or 'demonstration'; see Knox, *OAT* 48–9. But Oedipus is a 'paradigm' because they think he is dead. When he insists on surviving, the lesson is not so clear to the Elders.

would have been so much easier if only Oedipus had done as they expected.

Meanwhile, however, they believe that they have heard Oedipus' voice for the last time; and the second stanza of their Ode, spoken in the name of all Thebans, turns from pity to admiration, gratitude and praise for his past exploits. By saying that Oedipus 'achieved a prosperity happy in all respects', they show that they have no inkling of his being aware of the truth before today, or, if they did think so, they have forgotten it. The phrase, 'You have been called our king', together with the word 'renowned', *kleinos*, in the following stanza, 1207, echoes line 8, 'called Oedipus the renowned'. Again the long span of the story is included within the drama, by reference to the crook-clawed Sphinx, the deaths she caused, and the victory of Oedipus by the bold arrows (1197) of his brain. The third stanza repeats the image of Oedipus as a sailor used by Teiresias in 420 ff., with reference to the husband who returned to the same 'harbour' whence he went forth as a son; and the other image of Oedipus as the farmer who ploughs his father's furrow. The last stanza refers three times to sight, recalling the very numerous uses of such words throughout the play, though of course the Elders have no notion how this theme is to be completed in the Exodus or final scene. Their closing words are about Thebes, and the difficulties and the grief which now face the city. 'I mourn like one who pours from his lips a funeral song. It is true to say that you, who once brought us back to life, now have laid our eyes to rest' – a phrase which echoes the words of the Priest of Zeus, 49–50. They are sure that he has paid his debt with suicide. They forget their resentment, and remember the qualities which won their love. Above all, they see themselves and Oedipus side by side as mortal men whose best years are gone before they have had time to learn wisdom, whose common inheritance is capacity for suffering, and weakness amidst the forces of Fate. Then comes the Messenger from inside the palace.

He stands alone before the Elders. There is a sense of emptiness in the stage: the once honoured king and queen are gone; Creon, so harshly repulsed, must wait his time to return; these citizens are all that is left to represent permanence ('always most honoured', 1223), and to them his story must be told. It is for the heroic spirits of royal houses to do and to endure; ordinary mortals show their nobility (*engenōs*) otherwise, by hearing, seeing and mourning (1224–5).

Horrors will soon come to light, he says, which were committed 'willingly, not unwillingly'. The Chorus used the same word in 1213, 'Time, that sees everything, has found you out, unwilling [though you were]'. In that line they meant that the inquiry undertaken by Oedipus had produced a result he did not intend. Here the Messenger alludes to the death of Iocasta and the blindness of Oedipus, both self-inflicted; and he adds, 'Of all griefs, those cause most pain which are seen to be self-chosen' (*authairetoi*).

This statement demands a digression. If the thesis of this book is valid, both passages, 1213 and 1230–1, have a dramatic irony of which the speakers are unconscious. Just as the Elders were wrong in thinking that the discovery of Oedipus' guilt was involuntary, so when the Messenger speaks of 'self-chosen griefs', his words suggest to us, as readers with time for reflection, not merely the hanging and the blinding, but the whole drama of the disclosure, self-chosen by Oedipus; and even beyond that, the parricide and the incest, from which the Delphic warning might have saved him. If this seems a fanciful idea, we have only to begin by examining the actual meaning of lines 1230–1 when taken at their face-value. They mean that the death of Iocasta, because it is self-inflicted, is a more piteous thing than the fact that unwittingly she married her son; and that Oedipus' blindness for the same reason causes greater pain to him and to the audience than the fact that he unwittingly killed his father. Now, such a statement may be felt by different readers to be more true or less true; and in any case it is a fairly banal comment on the story in its usual interpretation – and banal remarks from the Chorus are not infrequent in tragic plays, though I think there are none in this. It therefore seems reasonable to suppose that there is more in this sentence than its superficial meaning.

One of the problems that have taxed the resources of writers on this play is to explain how the story can be called truly a tragedy and not a mere sensational disaster. Knox, for example, in his opening chapter insists that the play is not to be described as a 'tragedy of Fate', because Oedipus himself chose to conduct the inquiry which led to his downfall and took the initiative in successive phases of the action. This argument, however, does not alter the fact that, on the usual view, the parricide and the incest were situations into which an unsuspecting man was lured by Fate; in fact, Knox's view comes near to suggesting that all would have been well if the truth had remained secret – and of this, the fact of the plague is a firm denial. In such a view, what more does the story offer than an extreme example of that undeserved suffering which Aristotle rejected as material for tragedy? Is any lesson implicit in the helpless and hopeless plight of such victims? Even if, as some writers contend, the poet is showing us how unfair life can actually be, does this provide a satisfying view of *Oedipus Tyrannus*, and are we to find here the sublimity of tragedy? Perhaps some of the answer lies in Sophocles' treatment of the oracle and its relation to human events, or in the significance of the plague as a symptom of pollution; but the pattern is hard to expound. If on the other hand the argument of this book is valid, if the crime of Oedipus can also be seen as in some degree 'self-chosen'; in particular, if the incestuous marriage was, ironically enough, 'self-chosen' by Oedipus in the very moment of his greatest courage, when he resolved to go and confront the Sphinx, knowing what the result of failure would be, and what the result of success would be; then this story embodies the richest elements of tragedy. Therefore when the Messenger, conscious only of the simple meaning, says (1230–1), 'Those sufferings cause most pain which are seen to be self-chosen', it is surely reasonable to think that in these words Sophocles is saying to those who will hear, 'The true tragedy, the cathartic pain, in which the power of the drama lies, is to be found in perceiving that every disaster here sprang from human choice.' Taken in this sense the remark is at least not banal; nor on the other hand does it expound too openly an idea which

Sophocles has preferred to leave only half revealed at so many points in the play; but it is a hint and a reminder of this idea, and tellingly placed before the Messenger's narrative.

'What news have you to tell us?' asks the Chorus-Leader. He has been mourning for Oedipus as dead; as he listens to the reply, the Messenger gives, for a line and a half, what is expected: 'This is the quickest account to speak and to hear: death has come to the godlike. . . .' In 1235 the name 'Oedipus' would fit the metre; instead comes the name 'Iocasta' – delayed, surely, so that the surprise of the Elders may be felt; and after the Leader's 'What caused her death?' the main narrative is launched. It begins with a quiet and powerful touch: instead of describing his own horror as an eye-witness he says, 'The worst pain is not for you, since you cannot see what happened.' In eleven lines he tells of Iocasta's last moments, and of her words which once again include within the drama the whole span of thirty-six years or more since, in that same bridal chamber, Oedipus was begotten. His description of Oedipus' frenzy gives a clear impression that he, at any rate, thought the king was asking for a sword to kill Iocasta (the word for 'find', *kichoi*, 1257, suggests this); whether this is so or not, the achieved effect is one of bewildered terror, culminating in the alliteration of 1262, *eklīne koĩla kleĩthra kampiptei stegēi*. The next two lines are still and breathless; then action begins again, to reach a second and more violent climax in 1270–6; here the repeated blows which Oedipus aims at his eyes are enforced by twenty-six words beginning with a vowel – a virtuoso passage for the performer. In summing up his report the Messenger says, 'Such are the evils which have burst forth . . .', using the verb Oedipus used in 1076, 'Burst forth what will!' The eloquence of the Messenger's last sentence is complete; but there is a phrase in 1283 which is puzzling. Why does he say *at this stage* that the former prosperity of Oedipus and Iocasta was 'prosperity in the true sense', *olbos dikaiōs*? Had it been so, the plague would not have come.

Why does Oedipus blind himself? This act is an important *datum* in the legend, which Sophocles could not change; in using it, the poet must invest it with 'thematic and symbolic importance of the first order'.[1] He has, as we should expect, made this act the climax of the play; but what motives does Sophocles mean us to assume in the mind of Oedipus? Here, I think, the traditional interpretation leads us in the right direction; while the hidden play, in which Oedipus is aware, adds one further 'turn of the screw'. It has usually been held that 'Oedipus put out his eyes because he was indeed all too blind'. 'The very heart of the play's symbolic action is Oedipus' insistence upon punishing himself. . . . In this gesture he recognises that he lived among illusions; hereafter, he will be like Teiresias – he will see with different senses, in a different world, in a deeper reality.' The 'illusions' referred to, the seventeen years of failure to see the obvious, are the result of a remarkable bluntness of perception; and it is dramatically right that the too-late recognition of such failure should drive Oedipus, who also has intelligence, to self-blinding. This is the proper interpretation of this act in the orthodox view of the play; how does it apply in the second play which lies, hidden and not hidden, just below the surface of the first? Very simply. The illusion which 'Oedipus aware' has cherished is that he can live his life on the basis of a belief which is almost certainly false, though just possibly true; that he can assert ignorance and innocence in face of multiple evidence. This is what, for the sake of a throne and a city, he has valiantly attempted to do. He might have succeeded – but the plague came. His sin was the corrupting of his own power of knowledge, the enthroning of a chosen illusion in the place of truth. His guilt was first presented to him in the sight of a city dying from plague; but this, however deeply he cared for his city, was external. The retribution did not reach his inner self until he saw Iocasta lying dead by her own hand. Then he perceived more of the truth than even the Theban Shepherd had shown him; he saw his fatal illusion – the pretence that he could live on pretence – for the sin that it was, a blindness of which he, the most perceptive of men, ought not to have been guilty; and the self-punishment that follows shows moral perception fully re-established.

[1] In this paragraph I am quoting several phrases from the letter of a careful and intelligent, but anonymous, critic.

When the narrative pauses at 1285 the Chorus, who are not inhuman, ask sympathetically if the king's agony has eased. In the Messenger's reply the entry of Oedipus is carefully prepared for. Since he is said (1287) to be shouting for someone to lead him out, and to be already groping at the door, his voice should surely be audible while the Messenger speaks – shattering groans of despair and pain. Then the door opens and Oedipus appears, and stands silent for eleven lines, while the Elders express their horror and pity.[1]

The first thing that Oedipus says gives the keynote for the whole of his scene with the Chorus, until Creon enters. 'Where [or How] does my voice fly about borne on the air?' When a blind man is talking he can tell by the sound of his own voice whether any person or object is near him. Oedipus has been indoors and is now outside, and notices immediately the different sound that his own voice makes, but still more he notices that he is alone on the stage, that the Chorus have withdrawn from him and are at some distance in the orchestra. The frigidity of the Leader's words in 1319–20 shows clearly that horror is proving stronger than pity; but Oedipus seizes on the Leader's voice and appeals to him: 'You are my steadfast friend, you do not shun the blind man's presence, I know you by your voice.' Surely with these words, Oedipus, his feet feeling the ground before him, descends from stage to orchestra and stretches out his hand towards his 'friend'. The Leader does not say, 'Here is my hand, Oedipus; though you are accursed, I pity you.' Instead he says, 'What a dreadful thing you have done! How had you the hardness to destroy your own eyes? What god led you to this act?' When Oedipus replies, 'What could I have pleasure in seeing?' the Leader agrees that there is nothing he could wish to see. When he appeals for a sympathetic word, and pleads, 'Lead me away, friends, lead me far away', the Leader answers, 'I wish I had never known you.' When Oedipus says, 'If only I had died as an infant!' the leader says, 'I too wish the same.' When Oedipus says, 'My suffering is immeasurable', the Leader replies,

[1] Euripides creates a similar effect with the first entry of Medea, after her cries and groans have been heard from inside.

'It was foolish to blind yourself; you would be better dead.' The quieter but passionate speech in which Oedipus replies to this shows in its opening lines that he feels the coldness which surrounds him; but as he enlarges on his fate he forgets again that those whom he calls 'friends' are no friends to him now, and in 1413–15 begs them all, not the Leader only, to come near and touch him, to break for a moment his awful isolation. Not one of the Elders says, 'Here is my hand.' Instead the Leader replies for them all: 'Fortunately, here comes Creon; he is the man to deal with your requests.' The Elders are not to be blamed; their concern, and their duty, is towards themselves – that is to say, it is for all the citizens of Thebes. Oedipus has ascended out of their reach onto the heroic plane of poetic tragedy; and this the ordinary man mistrusts.

Oedipus' long speech 1369–1415 presents a series of vivid pictorial images, and yet again includes within the scope of the drama the entire period of thirty-six years – and indeed begins by looking into the future, when the blind Oedipus will meet his parents in the shadows of Hades. The 'delight of the eye' in viewing noble streets, fortifications, statues; the 'pride of life' in being the noblest son of a famous city; the trackless pastures of Cithaeron, the palace in Corinth, the copse by the corner on the Delphi road; the marriage-chamber in the house of Cadmus – the blind Oedipus sees them all now in the pattern of his destiny. It is a speech of great beauty, but does not affect our interpretation of the play as a whole. Its final phrase, 'For my evils no mortal man except myself is able to bear' (like the earlier lines which it recalls, 60–4, '. . . There is not one of you whose sickness is equal to mine . . .') fits equally Oedipus aware or unaware.

The dialogue with Creon is straightforward. Knox has an interesting exposition (*OAT* 187–90) of the character of Oedipus as displayed in this last scene – a man who even in such a situation is still the commander of everyone who is in his presence, taking thought for Iocasta's burial, his own banishment, his sons' and his daughters' future. The most significant point, however, is that at the end of the play Oedipus is, as he was at the beginning, entirely alone at the centre of the dramatic pattern. The outer circle and the next within it merge together: the Elders now know as much as is known to the gods about everything that happened before the opening of the play. What they do not know is the self-awareness of Oedipus; the innermost circle remains intact around the nucleus which is Oedipus' self. Indeed, it may be questioned whether even the gods know this; for Teiresias apparently did not. Oedipus has something in common with Prometheus, whose mind was not known to Zeus; he is man independent, defiant, of the gods. Here, then, he is alone, and conscious of a situation which he can communicate to no one. In his agony he tells the Chorus (1329) that all has been brought upon him by Apollo – it is best for Thebes to continue to believe that;[1] he tells his daughters (1484) that when he became their father he saw nothing and made no inquiry – it is best for them still to believe that. Neither of these statements is true; but he does not forget, in his blindness, that they are necessary. To tell the truth would break his isolation; and that he cannot do. The truth is his burden and his alone. He tells the Elders (1414–15) that there is no man living who can bear his burden but himself; and that is true. Such is the triumphant skill with which Sophocles makes Oedipus express what seems by its nature to be inexpressible, and uses dialogue and the Attic stage to exhibit secrecy and solitariness.

When Creon enters, after a reassuring word to Oedipus he first reproaches the Elders for leaving the bloodstained head uncovered. (There is an interesting textual problem here, which is dealt with in a Note at the end of this chapter.) In doing so he speaks of 'the flame of our lord the Sun, which nourishes all things', and of 'earth, rain and holy light' as being affronted by 'such pollution'. The function of these phrases is to make it clear that the plague is forgotten, and the sources of life and growth are thought of as once again operating in their natural course. After so much impiety, Creon re-establishes (1431) the practice of piety. Then Oedipus, who has twice called himself 'evil' and 'most evil', repeats his urgent request to be 'cast out' and,

[1] Cf. Kitto, *FMD* 75, 'The god does nothing to bring about the catastrophe.'

according to the terms of his curse, 'not spoken to by anyone'. Humility and importunity alternate in his urgent pleading, most clearly seen in 1446, 'On you I lay this duty, and I beg of you . . .'; and urgency leads into the prophetic strain often associated either with the blind or with those near their end.[1] Oedipus speaks – though here his foresight is at fault – of Cithaeron as the chosen place of his death; and declares, 'This much I know, that neither sickness nor any other thing can destroy me; for I would never have been saved when I was dying, except for some strange [*or* terrible] evil.' This is a very vague statement. The 'strange evil' can evidently mean his present plight; but 'nothing can ever destroy me' must refer to the future. Certainly this cannot be a forecast of the apotheosis at Colonus, which was not 'an evil'; and the next line, 1458, specifically declines to make any prophecy. The point of the passage is to establish Oedipus, not as an unmasked criminal, nor as a wretch hated and destroyed by unjust gods, but as a man whose resolute decision to live self-directed, self-judged and self-sentenced has won for him already a unique position which even the gods will refrain from opposing, as they have refrained from entering, except as a remote background, into the human domain of this drama. It is indeed possible that in the figure of Oedipus Sophocles is embodying a conception which Aeschylus in *The Eumenides* seems to suggest; a conception of man, as represented (in *The Eumenides*) by the Athenian democracy, himself taking over from gods the moral government of the world, while assigning to them the place of a remote but revered final court of appeal.

Why did Sophocles bring the two children on stage? We should look for some other purpose than merely to pile agony on agony. We can find one purpose, I think, by noticing that the hopeless forecast of 1492–1502 is soon contradicted by the confident appeal to Creon which follows it. In any case those of the audience who had seen *Antigone* knew that Antigone was at least betrothed. The whole passage 1486–1502, then, may well be Oedipus' expiatory confession of the disastrous consequences

[1] Compare, for example, Polymestor in the last scene of Euripides' *Hecabe*.

for others of his two crimes – whether they were witting or un-witting. This confession was due to Iocasta, who cannot receive it; her daughters are to receive it in her place, and the subsequent appeal to Creon mitigates its harshness. A second purpose is, perhaps, to mitigate also the harshness of judgement which may be felt towards Oedipus by those who perceive that this sin was his own choice. In half a dozen passages already noted Sophocles has pictured the intense craving for family affection which marks the foundling; this at least is a good thing in itself. And the third value of this final passage is that it allows the audience, before the stage empties, to withdraw a little from the heroic and tragic plane into a calmer and more innocent atmosphere, according to the canon of Greek literary art. But the calm of the dialogue and the innocence of the children do not detract from either solem-nity or sternness; Oedipus' thrice-repeated request for banish-ment is still given an equivocal answer; and his last rebellion, 'No, don't take them from me!' is overruled.

As for the last seven lines, some editors call them spurious; for the reasons, I must refer readers to the various editions. Some say the Greek is poor; but Sophocles' Greek at times reads oddly to our deprived ear, and these lines are not much odder than some unquestioned passages. The matter of them is suitable, and if suitably translated satisfies an audience at the close of a good performance.

*Note on lines 1424–31, p. 92.* It has been suggested that these lines belong not to Creon but to Oedipus and that they should be transposed to come after 1415. Jebb mentions this suggestion, but does not give the pro's and con's. There are several points in favour of this alteration. First, it is strange that Creon should reproach his servants (1424) for 'not respecting the generations of mortals' by leaving Oedipus outside, since they have just come with him from the palace; while if his reproach is addressed to the Elders, as is reasonable, for not covering Oedipus' head (cf. Euripides, *Heracles*, 1159, 1198), he would hardly command them to take Oedipus into the palace, where they have no right to go. Oedipus himself, however, might well request to be taken into the palace, since he cannot see to whom he is speaking. Also, it is strange that Creon, who has given orders for Antigone and Ismene to be brought out of the house to Oedipus, should here so emphatically command Oedipus to be taken in, and then continue talking to him where he is. There are equally clear arguments against the proposed alteration. First, the Leader's phrase 'for your requests' fits lines 1410–12 better than line 1429. Secondly, it is strange that Oedipus in 1430–1 should envisage Creon as the most proper person 'to see and hear his troubles', and immediately after (1419) should be so agitated at the thought of meeting Creon. Moreover it is unlikely that Oedipus should ask in 1411 to be cast out, and ten lines later (1429) to be taken in, and fourteen lines after that (1436) to be cast out. On balance it seems better to accept the MS order of lines, and make the best of it by supposing that 1424–8 are addressed to the Elders, as a command to throw a cloak over Oedipus' head – which Oedipus certainly will refuse to accept; and that 1429 is a command to some attendants, which they do not immediately carry out (cf. the similar delay in *Antigone*, 885 ff., which lasts for fifty-eight lines) because Creon continues talking to Oedipus.

# Index of Lines Discussed

(Numbers preceding colons indicate lines in the play; numbers following colons indicate pages on which notes (pp. 2–98) or references (pp. 101–246) to these lines occur. In certain cases references to individual lines are subsumed under references to the group of lines in which they occur.)

# Index of Subjects Discussed

(Plays by Sophocles are entered under their titles; by other dramatists under their authors.)